HOT PURSUIT!

Brawner began hot pursuit. Via his shoulder-mounted radio, he notified dispatch of the foot race between him and the suspect. Across wet pasture and high grass, Brawner did the best he could to keep up with the faster, more agile suspect as Barbee hurriedly scampered down a thirty-five-foot embankment. Brawner watched as Barbee barreled through a barbed-wire fence, knocking down the metal post and momentarily becoming entangled in sharp barbs that ripped his clothing and pierced his skin.

After racing 100 to 150 yards, Barbee suddenly made a ninety-degree turn, crossed FM 2449 to Vintage Road, and ran into a thick wooded area.

During Brawner's pursuit of Barbee, his onboard video continued to run, later revealing the image of Ron Dodd's truck driving past the location where his friend had first been confronted by the law. But while Dodd was driving the roadways, Barbee was losing himself deeper in the woods.

"Send out a flare unit to the scene," Brawner told dispatch. The deputy would use the handheld thermal-imaging unit to pick up heat sources in the area and, hopefully, the unknown suspect.

LETHAL CHARMER

PATRICIA SPRINGER

PINNACLE BOOKS
Kensington Publishing Corp.
http://www.kensingtonbooks.com

Some names have been changed to protect the privacy of individuals connected to this story.

PINNACLE BOOKS are published by

Kensington Publishing Corp.
119 West 40th Street
New York, NY 10018

All Kensington Titles, Imprints, and Distributed Lines are available at special quantity discounts for bulk purchases for sales promotions, premiums, fund-raising, and educational or institutional use. Special book excerpts or customized printings can also be created to fit specific needs. For details, write or phone the office of the Kensington special sales manager: Kensington Publishing Corp., 119 West 40th Street, New York, NY 10018, attn: Special Sales Department, Phone: 1-800-221-2647.

Pinnacle and the P logo Reg. U.S. Pat. & TM Off.

ISBN-13: 978-0-7860-1735-5
ISBN-10: 0-7860-1735-X

First Printing: May 2010

10 9 8 7 6 5 4 3 2 1

Printed in the United States of America

*This book is dedicated to
Sheila Underwood and Jackie Barbee,
two mothers who love unconditionally.*

ACKNOWLEDGMENTS

There are many people who contributed to the writing of this book. First and foremost my sincere thanks to Sheila Underwood and Jackie Barbee. These women have endured great loss, and both were gracious and candid in helping me understand their perspectives. In addition, I thank Detective Mike Carroll, Assistant District Attorneys Kevin Rousseau and Dixie Bersano, Chief Deputy District Attorney Greg Miller, the Tarrant County Medical Examiner's Office, the office of the District Clerk of Tarrant County, Tina Church of TOVA, and Jan Blankenship LPC.

My special thanks and appreciation to editorial consultant LaRee Bryant, editor Michaela Hamilton, and editorial assistant Mike Shohl. Without these three this book would not have been possible.

INTRODUCTION

The expectation of a newborn child is generally a joyful occasion. Couples pick out cribs, purchase layettes, and attend birthing classes. Couples delight in their child's impending arrival—but there are exceptions.

Pregnancy is a life-changing event, not only for a woman but also for a man. There are expectant fathers who are thrilled with the prospect of sharing their lives with a newborn offspring; while others feel an imminent loss of power and control when their wife or girlfriend becomes pregnant. The birth of a child could mean the loss of the man's place as the woman's primary interest. He becomes jealous of his unborn child, and his jealousy festers into rage.

Financial responsibilities are also huge. Even if there is a divorce or a split in the relationship, the father's financial concerns remain. Child support could linger for as long as eighteen years, and in many cases the money drain continues throughout the child's college career. To many men it may appear as if it's never ending.

In some cases it is neither the emotional loss of the mother's attention nor the man's financial concerns, but his real or imagined belief that the baby isn't his own. He has no desire to raise a child that is not his biological offspring, and he may demand a DNA test to prove paternity. Entwined in his emotional struggle to accept paternity are often feelings of betrayal.

Regardless of the reason for a man's nonacceptance of the child, all these men have one thing in common: they are self-centered.

Abuse too often becomes a by-product of this selfishness, and if abuse is already in the picture, it often increases after conception, with as many as 324,000 women suffering intimate partner violence during pregnancy each year.

In what could only be described as desperation, some of these men go on to choose a permanent solution to what others would see as a temporary problem. Believing that if something was to happen to the mother and child, then those overwhelming responsibilities would disappear, these men choose murder.

Homicide has become the second leading cause of death of pregnant women, just behind motor accidents. In pregnant teens murder is the leading cause of death, and black women are three times more likely to be killed than whites. More than 50 percent of pregnant women who die at the hands of their husbands or lovers are shot; the others stabbed or strangled.

The most widely known case of its kind is that of Laci Peterson and her unborn son, Conner, murdered by Scott Peterson in Modesto, California. The notoriety of that case brought about "Laci and Conner's Law," establishing the murder of an unborn fetus as a federal capital offense.

A 2003 Texas law amended the definition of the word "individual" to include an unborn child at any stage of gestation from fertilization to birth.

At least thirty-six states have homicide laws now defining a fetus as a person, with most of those fetal homicide laws specifically exempting abortion.

Stephen Barbee, of Texas, was accused of such a murder.

It was a heinous crime, in which the life of Lisa Underwood was prematurely extinguished, along with that of her unborn child, mere weeks before the expected date of her birth. And what makes this case even more monstrous was the associated killing of Lisa's seven-year-old son, Jayden.

Lisa Underwood may be listed among those statistics of women who were murdered while pregnant, but Lisa Underwood was much more. She was a business partner, a friend, a daughter, and a mother. Lisa Underwood, her son, Jayden, and her unborn daughter, Marleigh, have left a void in the lives of those who knew them . . . a void that can never be filled.

1

Lisa Underwood rested her head on her hand as she read articles on her home computer from the Birthplan.com website. Lisa, seven-and-a-half months pregnant, checked the website regularly to keep up with changes in her body and the development of the baby growing inside her. Just after midnight she heard a knock, logged off the computer, and headed for the front door. Lisa rubbed her swollen belly as she walked through the living room of her north Fort Worth home. Pink gift bags rested on the hearth of the fireplace, just below photos of Lisa's seven-year-old son, Jayden. Although Lisa had been sick during the week, she looked forward to the baby shower being held in her honor the following day.

It was late. Jayden had been in bed for hours—like his mother, he was ill with a cold. They had both been on medication, and the effects of the winter illness had caused both mother and son to perform sluggishly during the week. Lisa had missed two days of work, and Jayden had been absent from school.

Lisa had no idea who had knocked at her door so late on a Friday night, but she padded across the floor, peeked through a small crack, and opened the white front door to her familiar, but unexpected, guest. The man stepped into the narrow entry; he faced a wall where a blond-wood coatrack hung, laden with jackets. As Lisa closed the door behind him, the wreath adorning the back of the door swayed gently, the decorative apples tapping lightly against the wood.

The visitor had been in the Underwood home before and recognized the layout. He gave a cursory glance around the comfortable, unpretentious living room. He was confident he and Lisa were alone, knowing that her son regularly spent weekends with his grandmother in nearby Dallas.

The man took a seat in a glider chair and began gently rocking back and forth.

"You need to pull the chair out," Lisa instructed. "It's hitting against the wall."

Her guest appeared nervous as he dragged the chair forward and again began a rhythmic motion. He began talking about Lisa, the baby, and the plans she was making.

The man's voice became louder, and just as unexpected as his arrival was the uninvited guest's sudden verbal assault against Lisa. He shouted at her, his fury rising with every syllable. Lisa, determined nothing would spoil her good mood and excitement over the upcoming baby shower, refused to enter into an argument. The man's confrontational demeanor quickly changed from verbal to physical when he reached forward with outstretched arms and shoved Lisa backward. Lisa stumbled to maintain her balance. Not the shy or withdrawing type, Lisa stood her ground and demanded the man leave her house. Lisa, however, was unaware of the man's determination not just to confront her, but to silence her. When he refused to leave, she angrily kicked him in the leg.

With the swiftness of a snake strike, the man hit Lisa

across her face, the blow jarring her off balance. As Lisa regained her footing, her temper flared and she struck back. The blow did no physical damage, but it infuriated the man and heightened his resolve to accomplish his mission.

The attacker balled his fist, drew back, and, with enraged power, slugged Lisa in the right eye. Lisa's highlighted, shoulder-length hair blew backward with the force of the blow. The tissue surrounding the eye immediately swelled. Discoloration began right away. The pain drove Lisa toward her attacker, screaming at him and physically retaliating, but his unrelenting assault continued.

She raised her arms in self-defense, while the man's strikes repeatedly found their mark on Lisa's slender limbs. Contusions began to appear on her right upper arm, her wrists, and her hands. One of the more forceful strikes snapped Lisa's lower right arm, about an inch above her wrist. Her right thumb also cracked. Lisa's counterattack was now driven not only by fury, but also by fear. Fear not only for herself, but for her children—one sleeping in the next room, the other still within her womb. Her fright, mixed with ferocity, kept her fighting through the pain.

The man, at least six inches taller than his victim's five-four frame, overpowered Lisa and thrust her to the floor, where he continued to beat her unmercifully. One harsh blow cracked Lisa's nose, causing blood to gush from the nostrils and make breathing difficult. Another strike pushed Lisa's teeth through her bottom lip. Her lips, as had her eye, quickly swelled to a misshapen mass. Red-tinged saliva dribbled from the corner of her bruised mouth.

Lisa's screams and the man's vile ranting awakened Jayden. The pajama-clad seven-year-old rushed into the room. Seeing his mother beaten and battered, he fearlessly began to defend her with the determination of a person three times his age. The youth slapped at his mother's attacker, yelling, "Stop! Stop hurting my mother!"

Lisa's panic switched from herself and the baby girl within her belly, whom she had planned to name Marleigh, to her cherished son. She clawed at the man and continued to fling her fists at his torso, but her attempts were futile. The man could not be deterred.

Pinned against the floor, Lisa attempted to twist her body, first to the left, then to the right, fighting against the pressure from the man to spin her onto her stomach. The thought of Marleigh was uppermost in Lisa's mind, but the man's strength was overwhelming. He successfully spun Lisa over and smashed her face into the carpet as he simultaneously warded off the ineffective attack of a mere child.

The man punched, socked, and slapped at Lisa's back, causing blood to rise to the surface, thus producing bruising. Lisa's screams were muffled when the attacker forcefully pressed his knee into her flesh, pushing his full weight into his victim.

Congested from the chronic bronchitis she had been treated for earlier in the week, and complicated by Marleigh's small body being pushed up toward her mother's chest, Lisa's breathing became more labored. She begged for her life, her baby's, and Jayden's as she gasped for air.

Over several minutes Lisa's wheezing diminished. The twitching of her body slowed, then stopped. Lisa Underwood was dead. But her killer's rage hadn't lessened; the beating didn't stop; the pressure on Lisa's face into the floor didn't ease. Even after death Lisa Underwood continued to be beaten.

Finally the man's attention turned from Lisa to Jayden. The boy hadn't been a target of the killer's intentions, but Jayden had seen his mother die: killed by a man he could identify. The boy had to be dealt with.

With the ease with which one carries a child to bed, the man tossed Jayden onto the green slipcovered sofa. Most of the fight in the boy had been spent, but the assailant continued his assault, pounding Jayden's small frame with dozens of blows, just as he had the boy's mother. He repeatedly struck Jayden's back, causing bruising and two-inch-long scratches in various directions. Jayden's arms suffered multiple abrasions as he weakly attempted to keep up the fight.

Incensed that he was forced to kill the child, the man pushed Jayden back onto the sofa, sat on him, and slapped his hand over the boy's mouth and nose. Like his mother, Jayden struggled to suck air into his lungs. The man, much stronger than the boy, held Jayden tightly against the soft cushions until the last quiver of his slim little body ceased.

The Underwood house in the 3700 block of Chaddybrook Lane was suddenly quiet. No sign of the laughter that had filled the three-bedroom home occupied by Lisa Underwood and her son existed. Neighbors slept peacefully. Only the faint sound of the patter of rain against the pavement could be heard on the deserted street.

Just as quietly as the killer had slipped into the neighborhood, he stole away, leaving behind the carnage of a destroyed family.

2

Stephen Barbee stood motionless in Lisa Underwood's living room. His mouth was dry from rapid breathing, and a thin row of sweat beads lined his furrowed brow. Barbee's brown eyes fixed on the bodies of the woman, with whom he had shared intimate moments, and her son, whom he had never formally met. The metallic odor of fresh blood assaulted his nostrils, and nausea gripped the pit of his stomach.

Lying on the floor up against the green slipcovered sofa, Lisa seemed to be staring at Barbee through the narrow slit of the one eye that wasn't swollen shut. Barbee cocked his head and leaned forward slightly. Covered in blood, with her face swollen out of shape, Lisa didn't look like herself, and for a moment Barbee wondered who it was that he was gawking at.

"Lisa!" Barbee screamed. "Lisa!" He waited for a response, then realized Lisa wouldn't be answering. He grasped the fact that Lisa was dead.

The room was silent, except for the rapid pounding of Barbee's own heart. He shook his head and ran a calloused hand through his thick brown hair as tears burned his dark eyes.

"What do I do?" Barbee shouted. "My God, what do I do now?"

Barbee ran from the house to escape the horror of the blood, the terror of Lisa's swollen, bulging eyes staring at him, and the sickening sight of the seven-year-old child's motionless body sprawled across the sofa. He tasted bile rising in his throat and leaned forward, certain he would vomit.

After several deep breaths of the cold February air, Barbee's eyes scanned the neighborhood. The quiet residential street was empty. No cars passed by the house; none were parked at the curb. Barbee was alone.

"Ron!" Barbee screamed into the night. "Where in the hell are you?"

Barbee pulled the cell phone that he always carried with him from the pocket of his black hooded sweatshirt and frantically hit speed dial for the number of Ron Dodd, Barbee's best friend and employee. .

No answer. Where had Ron gone after he watched Barbee enter Lisa's house? Why wasn't he waiting at the curb, as planned? Dodd knew Barbee didn't have a car. He knew he had no way to leave.

The realization that he was all alone swept over Barbee as a tidal wave of emotions sent him into full panic mode. His head reeled as he looked left and right, left again and right again, down Chaddybrook Lane. He could barely catch his breath. No one was there to help him decide what he should do. No one was there to help. Barbee ran back to the house, quickly closing the door on the normalcy of the world outside and locking inside the unspeakable malice of the murders of Lisa and Jayden.

Barbee again grabbed his cell phone and hit the programmed number of Dodd's cell phone. Barbee heard a number of rings before recognizing the familiar sound of his friend's voice.

"Shit!" Barbee swore as Dodd's voice mail again repeated instructions on how to leave him a message. "Where in the hell are you?" Barbee shouted into the small handheld device. "Why did you leave? What do I do now?"

With each question Barbee's voice took on a greater urgency and a louder tone as he paced the small living room.

Finally realizing he would have to handle the situation himself, Barbee took a moment to think. Lisa's car, it must be in the garage.

Making his way to the attached garage of Lisa Underwood's home, Barbee recognized Lisa's blue Dodge Durango SUV parked inside. He moved to the rear of the vehicle, lifted the back hatch, then surveyed the contents.

Like her home and business, Lisa's car reflected her neatness and cleanliness. The back of the SUV was virtually empty; only Jayden's black bike helmet was inside.

Moving quickly, Barbee reentered the house and went to the body of the woman with whom he had once had a relationship. Lisa would never have been considered fat, but now she had the added girth of the seven-month fetus inside her. Barbee had difficulty pulling her into the garage, maneuvering the body around the trash can on the right. A laundry basket on the left obstructed the space between the car and wall as well. After loading Lisa's corpse, Barbee paused momentarily to catch his breath. The beads of sweat that had lined his forehead now formed a smooth flow that rolled down his nose and dripped from the tip. Splashes of perspiration fell onto his sweatshirt.

Breathing more deeply, Barbee went back for Jayden. He carefully placed the boy next to his mother in the back of the Durango.

Slowly lowering the hatch, Barbee closed his eyes, leaned against the rear window, and wished to hell things hadn't gone this far.

What had happened? What had gone so terribly wrong? Barbee rubbed his temple, frowning, groping to understand. His head pounded with the force of a hundred horses' hoofs against barren earth. The pain was so intense that he was uncertain if he could continue, but he told himself he had to keep on.

Barbee returned to the living room after first exploring the kitchen for cleansing agents. He began liberally spraying at the crimson spots on the beige carpet, frantically scrubbing at the telltale signs of the struggle that had taken place less than an hour earlier.

The stubborn red splotches faded but refused to disappear. Desperation was setting in, and Barbee needed to get out of the house. He needed as soon as possible to get far away from Chaddybrook Lane.

Finding Lisa's vacuum cleaner, Barbee gave the carpet a quick once-over, then surveyed his work. *Hell,* Barbee thought, *it's still obvious a deadly struggle took place here.*

Barbee moved to the blond-toned coffee table, and lifting it easily, he set it down on top of the bloody stain. Anyone searching for Lisa might initially miss the discoloration of the carpet, but Barbee knew his attempt at covering up wouldn't be effective for long. Glancing around the living room one final time, Barbee decided there was nothing more he could do. He couldn't force the room to keep the secret of the deadly attack on Lisa and Jayden, and he couldn't bring them back to life.

Climbing behind the wheel of the Durango, Barbee backed out of Lisa's garage and headed down the deserted street. Barbee was uncertain where he would go, but he knew he had to get Lisa's and Jayden's bodies out of Fort Worth.

While Barbee traveled along the darkened roadway,

his phone rang. His body jerked, startled by the intrusive sound.

Checking the illuminated phone screen, Barbee recognized Ron Dodd's number.

"Ron! Where are you? You left me there. You left me alone with two dead bodies!" Barbee shouted at his employee on the other end of the phone. "I don't know what to do! Lisa's dead! And her son, he's dead too. Ron, I don't know what happened. Tell me what to do," Barbee said, his voice laced with the raspiness of fright.

"Calm down, Stephen. Drive out to Interstate 35 north, toward Denton, and take Exit 407, the Ponder exit. You can dump them out there," Dodd responded calmly, then hung up.

But Stephen wasn't sure if he should trust Dodd. After all, it was Dodd who had left him in the house alone with two bodies to take care of. What if Ron had set him up? What if there were people waiting for him at the Ponder exit? People ready to arrest him.

No, Barbee thought, *I'll find another place to hide them.* But Barbee didn't know the southern portion of Denton County the way Dodd did. He would have to drive around in order to find someplace safe.

Barbee's cell phone rang again.

"Stephen, I'm right behind you. Take the Ponder exit," Dodd instructed. "There's some open land out near Justin, not far from the 407 exit. I'll help you dump the bodies there and we can leave the car nearby. I have a friend who's interested in the engine and transmission of the Durango," Dodd said.

Looking through the rearview mirror at Dodd's truck close behind him, Barbee trembled as he guided the SUV north toward Denton County. His head throbbed.

Barbee traveled north on I-35W as Dodd had instructed, past Cabela's, one of the area's largest hunting and fishing stores, complete with a museumlike room containing stuffed native Texas wildlife set in displays of their natural habitats.

Just past Cabela's, Barbee spotted the exit for Haslet. His thoughts turned to Teresa, his ex-wife and business partner, living in the Haslet two-story house they had designed and built during one of the few happy times of their tumultuous seven-year marriage. Now it was Ron Dodd living in the house that his hard work had paid for, not Stephen. But Barbee wasn't bitter; in fact, he was happy Ron and Teresa were engaged to be married. Ron had become a good friend, as well as a trusted employee, and he only wished the best for Teresa. Barbee realized he and his ex-wife had been as compatible as oil and water, and regardless of the volatile and sometimes violent history they had, he was happy she had moved on, just as he had done.

Tears stung Barbee's eyes as he thought of Trish, his bride of two months. How would he explain the deaths of Lisa and Jayden Underwood? Lisa's pregnancy was a complication he hadn't expected or invited. He hadn't been able to tell Trish about it, but these two deaths were far worse than any unplanned, unwanted child would have ever been.

The tears in Barbee's eyes distorted the yellow, green, and red lights that illuminated the long runway at Alliance Airport to his left as he continued north.

Barbee drove past the Texas Motor Speedway, where four times each year NASCAR drivers, such as Jeff Gordon and Jimmie Johnson, sped around the banked oval track for one hundred thousand cheering fans. Finally, a few miles farther north, into Denton County—known as the tip of the Golden Triangle of Fort Worth, Denton, and Dallas—Barbee reached the Farm-to-Market Road 407 exit. He turned left at the frontage road stop sign and drove west toward the small town of Justin.

* * *

The area was desolate countryside. No streetlights illuminated the roadway, and no lights shone from the few scattered houses set back on the rough land.

Barbee looked back to make certain Dodd was still with him. Barbee felt lost as he drove along the narrow two-lane road bordered by stands of mesquite trees and tumbled brush. The bitter winter cold had stripped many of the native trees of their foliage, and the skeletal remains made an eerie sight.

Barbee felt easier as Dodd's voice on the other end of the cell phone instructed him where to pull the Durango off the roadway. He did as his friend directed and parked near a double row of barbed-wire fences, held in place by split cedar fence posts.

Barbee left the interior of the Durango to lift the hatch and expose his shocking cargo. Dodd moved beside him and helped Barbee lift Lisa's body from the SUV and drag it to the first of the parallel double fence rows. Struggling, the two men attempted to lift Lisa over the jagged barbed wire, but her weight was too much for them to handle. Barbee and Dodd dragged the body under the fence. Lisa's pants were pushed to her knees by the friction against the cold ground, and her shirt was shoved up over her swollen breasts.

Barbee stared down at the woman he had known for more than two years. Her inflated, protruding, bare belly bore evidence of yet another victim of the vicious attack she had suffered.

Barbee returned to the Durango, where Dodd was already pulling seven-year-old Jayden across the vehicle's carpeted interior. In one swift movement, Dodd tossed the boy's body over the fence and watched it land on the rough, unimproved land.

"Let's get the hell out of here," Dodd said.

"We gotta bury 'em, Ron," Barbee said.

"Let the animals eat 'em," Dodd responded, turning toward his truck.

"We can't do that," Barbee protested. "We gotta bury 'em. We can't just leave them out here."

Dodd reached into the bed of his pickup and pulled out a shovel, tossing it to Barbee.

"Do whatever the fuck you want," Dodd said with a sneer.

Barbee spread the wires of the crude fence apart; stepping through them, he moved near Lisa's body. Dried limbs hidden below the underbrush snapped beneath his weight. With choppy, quick strokes he raked the ground of loose limbs and dead brush, then began digging. Even though the night air was cold, sweat dampened Barbee's shirt as he labored to produce a makeshift tomb for Lisa and her son.

The grave was mere inches deep, but Barbee could not go on. His energy was spent. He pulled Lisa's body to the unearthed space, leaving her on her back. He then gently picked up Jayden and placed him on top of his mother, his right cheek resting on her shoulder.

Barbee tossed dirt onto the bodies, and in an effort to further conceal Lisa and Jayden from view, Barbee piled broken branches and other debris over them. He stood back and looked at the mound of rubble that concealed the horrors of a night he wished were only a nightmare, one from which he would awaken.

Barbee's head throbbed. He pressed the heels of his hands into his temples and made small circles in an effort to ease the pain. The headaches had been increasingly painful over the past few months; this one was nearly unbearable.

3

Stephen Barbee turned away from the makeshift grave to head back to the Durango, parked just beyond the fence line. He scanned the area, looking for Dodd, but the company-owned black truck his friend drove was nowhere in sight.

Where in the hell has Ron gone this time? Barbee thought.

As he had at the Underwood house, Barbee used cleaning solvent to erase any telltale signs of foul play from the rear of the SUV, then climbed back behind the wheel of the Durango. Barbee double-backed, crossed I-35W, and drove down Vintage Road.

Barbee passed the Vintage housing additions, with streets named Napa Valley, Vineyard, Sonoma, and such other wine-related names, to the end of the paved street. Barbee steered the Durango off road and drove down a grassy incline, keeping close to a fence line. He drove straight toward a low-level creek and ditched the SUV nose first in the shallow muddy water.

Barbee exited the vehicle, cold water rising to his knees and sending a shiver up and down his body. As a last-minute thought, Barbee tossed Lisa's tan Dooney & Bourke purse, a gift from her mother, toward the chilly water, along with the keys to her vehicle. The purse rested in a fallen tree limb that dipped into the creek, while the keys landed on the bottom of the creek bed.

Barbee sloshed out of the muck and glanced down the deserted road to see if the lights of Dodd's truck were approaching, but the night was as black as it was cold. Barbee turned again to his cell phone in an effort to reach Dodd, but there was no answer. He was freezing, his pants wet and muddy from the knees down, his shoes soaked with the frigid water and all his energy spent. Barbee just wanted the repulsive night to be over. He pulled the hood of his sweatshirt over his head and set out on foot through a light, cold mist, hoping Dodd would catch up with him and take him to the warmth and safety of his home.

Denton County sheriff's deputy David Brawner was on his regular deep shift patrol of western Denton County. The shift, 10:30 P.M. to 6:30 A.M., was usually quiet, with only a few trailer houses and isolated residences on mostly farm roads to watch over. About 90 percent of Brawner's district was composed of dirt roads and open pasture.

Brawner was one of only three deputies, and one supervisor, on duty at that time of night to cover the entire 959 square miles that comprise Denton County. Their responsibilities included the protection of the lives and property of those living within the county boundaries.

Aware that a big problem in his area of the county was burglaries, Brawner was on watch for any suspicious circumstances, pedestrians, or vehicles.

As Brawner exited Farm-to-Market Road 2449 and continued north, he noticed a white male walking in the same direction along the rain-soaked service road. The sighting was unusual in the sparsely populated region of fields and wooded areas, especially at three o'clock on a Saturday morning.

Brawner noticed no abandoned vehicle or any other individuals walking along the roadway as he pulled his cruiser behind the man and activated his emergency overhead lights. Simultaneously the in-car video camera system began to record.

"Checking a suspicious person on 2449," Brawner said into his car radio. "White male, dark-colored sweatshirt with hand warmer in front, light-colored jeans, and tennis shoes."

As Brawner exited his patrol car, *Denton County Sheriff* scripted on the side, he noted that the man had stopped cold in his tracks when the cruiser's overhead lights began to strobe. The man didn't turn to face the deputy as expected, but rather he appeared to freeze where he stood.

Only the light from Brawner's patrol car illuminated the overcast night. Not until the deputy was close to Barbee did he notice Barbee's jeans were covered with mud from the knees down, his sweatshirt wet and lightly marred with mud.

"Are you okay?" Brawner asked. "Do you have some identification?"

"No, I had an argument with a friend that lives in that housing addition up there," Barbee said, pointing in the direction he was walking. "I left my wallet at his house."

"What's your name?" Brawner asked.

"My name's David Weekley," Barbee lied.

"What's your date of birth?" Brawner inquired.

"3/16/67," Barbee responded.

"Do you know your driver's license number?" the deputy asked. "Or your Social Security number?"

"No, I don't know them. They're in my wallet," Barbee stated.

"Wait here," Brawner said, returning to his vehicle.

Barbee stood restless in the light of the patrol car's headlights as Brawner spoke into the radio to dispatch.

Brawner gave the name of David Weekley and the birth date of 3/16/67 as he watched the man closely through the windshield of the car. The man who identified himself as David Weekley appeared nervous, shifting his weight from one foot to the other, anxiously scraping his feet on the pavement.

Just a short time later, dispatch could be heard over the car radio.

"I was unable to find any type of information by the name and date of birth given," dispatch said. "No Social Security information, no driver's license number, no criminal history information. No information whatsoever."

Brawner's eyes narrowed as he stared at the man standing in front of him. Background information was readily available. The state of Texas kept good records on people, and it was easy to get that information. It was obvious this man wasn't David Weekley, a name familiar to most north Texans as a prominent home builder. Who was he, then?

As soon as the deputy opened the door to exit the vehicle to discuss the lack of information obtainable with the stranger, Barbee took off running in a southeasterly direction.

Brawner began hot pursuit. Via his shoulder-mounted radio, he notified dispatch of the foot race between him and the suspect. Across wet pasture and high grass, Brawner did the best he could to keep up with the faster, more agile suspect as Barbee hurriedly scampered down a thirty-five-foot embankment. Brawner watched as Barbee barreled through a barbed-wire fence, knocking down the metal post and momentarily becoming entangled in sharp barbs that ripped his clothing and pierced his skin.

After racing 100 to 150 yards, Barbee suddenly made a

ninety-degree turn, crossed FM 2449 to Vintage Road, and ran into a thick wooded area.

Brawner's breath was labored as he chased Barbee in uniform and full gear, but the young deputy had been able to keep up with Barbee until he disappeared into the woods. Meanwhile, dispatch had notified other deputies and local law enforcement agencies of the foot pursuit and requested assistance.

Deputy Gibbon, of the sheriff's department, was stationed on I-35, a quarter mile north of FM 2449; Denton Police Department (DPD) officers were instructed to respond to the housing addition on Vintage Road; the Argyle Police Department (APD) went to a second location, north of FM 2449; the Justin Police Department (JPD) joined Deputy Gibbon at I-35.

During Brawner's pursuit of Barbee, his onboard video continued to run, later revealing the image of Ron Dodd's truck driving past the location where his friend had first been confronted by the law. But while Dodd was driving the roadways, Barbee was losing himself deeper in the woods.

"Send out a flare unit to the scene," Brawner told dispatch. The deputy would use the handheld thermal-imaging unit to pick up heat sources in the area and, hopefully, the unknown suspect.

After two hours of searching for the unidentified suspect, by four different law enforcement agencies, the manhunt was abandoned.

Barbee's breath quickened and his heart beat rapidly as he crept to the corner of a metal building just off the interstate at the Bonnie Brae exit in Denton. Crouched down to make himself less visible, Barbee scanned the area around him. He jumped slightly when the phone in his pocket rang.

"Where are you?" Dodd asked.

"Where in the hell did you go, Ron?" Barbee shouted. "I've been dodging the cops. You were supposed to pick me up after I ditched the car."

"Where are you?" Dodd asked again.

"I'm at the end of Bonnie Brae Street," Barbee responded. "I'm sitting at the side of a building. I'll wait here."

"I'll be right there," Dodd said.

Within a few minutes relief flooded over Barbee as he saw Ron's familiar truck coming toward him.

Less than thirty minutes after Dodd picked up Barbee on the darkened rural road, Dodd steered his truck into the area right of Teresa Barbee's house in Haslet, where company vehicles were parked. Barbee changed out of his cold, wet clothing into dry jeans and a shirt he kept at the business shop.

"I'll get rid of them for you," Dodd said as he took Barbee's damp clothes.

Barbee got into his black Ford Explorer and drove home, all the way asking, over and over again, "How am I going to tell Trish what's happened?"

4

That same morning Stephen Barbee rose at about seven o'clock after only a few short hours of sleep. He had to get the dogs to their Saturday obedience class at 8:00 A.M. After making coffee and talking with Trish, Barbee learned the class had been changed to noon; he had an extra four hours. Barbee cooked pancakes for Trish's two kids, while his wife of two months slept in. Trish had had painful back surgery only weeks earlier, and Barbee had taken over most, if not all, of the household responsibilities.

Barbee smiled as he watched the kids devour the morning meal. It pleased him that they enjoyed his cooking. He loved stepdaughter Taylor and stepson Tanner like they were his own. He had always wanted kids, but it hadn't happened with his first wife. Barbee had fathered a child with a woman he had dated for a very short time, but she had only been interested in Barbee as a sperm donor. Neither she nor his daughter had stayed in his life. He hoped to have children with Trish. Even though Trish had a medical procedure to avoid any further pregnancies after her last childbirth, she promised Barbee she would have in vitro, which would allow her to carry his child. That's why Barbee hadn't told

Trish about Lisa's pregnancy. How could he, right after she had pledged to have his baby? Trish could have changed her mind, refused to give him a child, and then the perfect life he imagined would be gone.

"Anyone for more pancakes?" he asked, turning his attention back to the children.

After taking the dogs to obedience class, Barbee went by the mall, then took the kids to a movie. While Barbee laughed at the humorous antics on the movie screen, Sheila Underwood, Lisa's mother, and other family members and friends waited at Boopa's Bagel Deli, co-owned by Lisa and her friend Holly Pils, to celebrate the upcoming arrival of Lisa's baby.

At 4:05 P.M., Sheila Underwood paced the bagel shop floor, passing the racks of bagels with signs designating *sesame, cheese, onion,* and a variety of other golden buns. Sheila smoked cigarette after cigarette, returning time after time to the front window of the shop to see if Lisa was pulling into the reserved parking space designated for her at the front of the store. Staring through the glass front door emblazoned with *Boopa's,* Sheila occasionally glanced to her left toward Albertsons grocery store and across the parking lot of the shopping center to McDonald's, watching for Lisa. It was only a few minutes after the designated time of the baby shower, but Sheila knew instinctively something was wrong. She shivered, not from the cold, rainy weather outside the shop, but because Sheila felt impending doom.

Lisa had always been punctual, and Sheila was well aware that her daughter was counting the minutes until the time for the celebration. Lisa's enthusiasm was contagious. Sheila had bought dozens of pink clothes for the new baby. Lisa's best friend and business partner, Holly Pils, had been planning the party for weeks, always with Lisa's desires in mind, right down to the cake with specific flowers that Lisa had requested. Sheila knew her daughter would never be late to the shower. Something had to be wrong.

Like Sheila, Holly was troubled. Lisa and Jayden had been sick all week, with Lisa missing work at the shop the two previous days, and Jayden missing school at Riverside Elementary, where he was in the first grade. Holly had called her friend several times during the day on Friday to make sure she was okay and to ask if she needed anything.

"I'm feeling better," Lisa had told Holly. "I'll see you at the party."

Holly knew how eager Lisa was to have friends and out-of-town family share in her joy. Lisa hadn't had a shower when she was expecting Jayden, and she had been like a little kid anticipating a birthday celebration, complete with presents and cake.

The last conversation Holly had with Lisa had been the previous evening, about 7:45 P.M. Holly had been at Party Depot, picking up last-minute items for the baby shower, when she called Lisa with one final attempt at finding out the name of the expected baby. Lisa had been keeping the name a secret, and Holly had tried everything she could to find out. She hoped Lisa would announce the name of the baby at the party.

"I'm standing in front of the napkins," Holly had said while shopping at the party store. "If you'll just tell me the first initial, I'll be able to get napkins with her initials on them."

"Good try," Lisa had said, laughing, "but I'm not telling you."

That was the last time Holly had spoken to Lisa, instructing her to be at the bagel shop about five minutes before four. It was now past four o'clock. At first, Holly wasn't alarmed, knowing Lisa had a lot of things to do that day. Jayden was going to a birthday party at 10:00 A.M., and Lisa had other errands to run, but now Holly, like Sheila Underwood, was worried. All of the guests had arrived between 3:30 and 4:00 P.M., and most waited at the rear of the shop, where tables and chairs were placed for customer dining. Lisa was the only one missing. Holly picked up her cell phone and again tried to contact Lisa, but, yet again, the call went directly to her friend's voice mail.

At 4:15 P.M., Holly began to call area hospitals. After all, Lisa was pregnant, and perhaps Lisa wasn't able to contact them to let them know something was wrong. The calls netted no positive results.

Anxious and becoming more frantic, Sheila Underwood couldn't wait at the bagel shop any longer. Short in stature, but immense in strength of conviction, Sheila took a family member with her and headed to Lisa's house. They knocked on the door and rang the doorbell several times, but there was no answer.

Sheila jumped back as she felt a wet tongue against her leg. Johnny Jack, Jayden's dachshund puppy, was greeting her.

"What are you doing out, boy?" Sheila asked, her brow wrinkled in confusion. She took in a quick breath. *Why is the dog outside? And why is the house so eerily quiet?* Sheila wondered.

"Something's terribly wrong," Sheila stated.

Using a key she had to her daughter's home, Sheila unlocked the residence and stepped inside.

The worried mother noticed her grandson's only pair of tennis shoes on the mantel and the wrapped presents on the hearth. Sheila moved through the house to the garage. Seeing that Lisa's SUV was gone, Sheila left through the front door, locking it behind her.

"We have to get back to the bagel shop and call the police," Sheila told her sister.

Between 4:30 and 4:45 P.M., the Fort Worth police were dispatched to Boopa's Bagel Deli. Officers Paula Fredrick and C. C. Thomas, who were already in the area, were the first to respond. Holly and Sheila met with Fredrick and Thomas, explaining the unusual absence of Lisa Underwood and their concern for her safety, plus the well-being of her son and her unborn child.

"She's seven-and-a-half months pregnant," Sheila told the officer. "We're worried that something may have happened to her." Sheila told Fredrick that it was most unlike her daughter not to be prompt, especially to an event being held just for her. Holly stated that she had last talked to Lisa the night before, and Lisa had been excited about the party and looking forward to it.

The female officer took notes and agreed to go to Lisa's house and check it out. Sheila led the way to the tidy home on Chaddybrook Lane, with two of her relatives accompanying her, as the police patrol car followed. Sheila again used her key to unlock the door and let Officer Fredrick inside. Sheila and the others stepped just inside the house and waited.

Officer Fredrick checked the front door for forced entry, then went straight to the back door to do the same. There was no sign that anyone had pried open the doors, or forcibly pushed through them. Fredrick next inspected the windows. The screens had not been cut, and there was no sign of glass breakage. The four-year officer concluded that there had been no break-in at the Fort Worth house.

Officer Fredrick moved on to the garage and found it empty. No vehicle, no sign of a struggle. She went back inside the house to check out the interior.

Fredrick roamed through the house checking each of the three bedrooms and each bathroom to see if anyone was hiding, or if there was anyone in the house that was unable to respond. The little boy's bed was messy, as if it had been slept in, but Fredrick didn't know if the boy was required to make his bed each morning or if the messy state was ordinary. The room search netted no answers as to where Lisa and Jayden Underwood could be. As Fredrick walked back into the living room, where the others waited, her eyes fell on a stain near the coffee table.

"Does your daughter clean up spills as they happen, or does she leave them for later?" Fredrick asked, not knowing that Lisa was a fastidious housekeeper.

"Lisa keeps a clean house. She'd never leave a spill to stain her carpet," Sheila insisted.

Fredrick walked over to the coffee table and lifted it, revealing a much larger and darker stain than previously observed. The blotchy area was irregular in shape, but it measured approximately three feet by four feet. Fredrick's instant thought was *It's blood.* As she inspected the stain further, she gently laid the back of her hand on the splotch. It was wet. The area was saturated, with a crusty white film on top.

It looks as if someone went to a lot of trouble to clean up the area, leaving a soap film and vacuum tracks, Fredrick thought.

As the officer looked toward Lisa Underwood's waiting mother, she noticed a responding officer standing in the doorway. Fredrick pointed out the discoloration of the carpet to the officer and then called her supervisor for a Crime Scene Unit. Fredrick immediately began asking Sheila and the others to leave the house.

"What did you find?" Sheila asked anxiously.

"We want everyone to step back. This is now considered a crime scene," Fredrick announced.

Sheila's large eyes widened and she gasped. "Crime scene?" she asked breathlessly. "What do you mean?"

"No one's in there," the officer responded. "We've called in the Crime Scene Unit and they'll be arriving shortly. In the meantime no one can go back inside the house."

"What happened?" Sheila demanded to know. She had gone from concern to full-blown panic for her child and grandchild.

"We found some blood, that's all I can tell you at this point," the officer said, leading Sheila toward the door. "The Crime Scene Unit will be able to gather more information."

Sheila moved away from the officer to her family members, who engulfed her, lending their support.

Once Holly had gotten the remaining guests to leave the bagel shop and locked up, she drove directly to Lisa's house to join Sheila and the others. It was about 6:30 P.M. when she arrived. Holly could see black-and-white police cars parked at the curb, and Sheila and other family members mingling outside.

Unable to get inside the house, Holly only managed to catch a glimpse of the interior through the open doorway and, in particular, the fireplace.

"Jayden's shoes," Holly mumbled. She could see them on the fireplace hearth where Lisa normally placed them out of reach of the chewing puppy. They were Jayden's only pair of athletic shoes. He outgrew them so rapidly, Lisa only invested in one pair at a time. Holly knew that if Jayden's shoes were on the fireplace, and Jayden wasn't in the house, it meant wherever he was, he was barefoot. She also knew Lisa would never have allowed her son to be out in the cold, wet weather without footwear.

The atmosphere outside Lisa and Jayden's residence was as frosty and somber as the February night air. Friends and family shivered in the cold as neighbors began to join them in their vigil. Everyone shared the same emotion: fear. What had happened inside the quiet little house that no one seemed to have heard? Where were Lisa and Jayden? None of it made any sense.

Officer Paula Fredrick glanced at the growing group of family, friends, and neighbors congregating on the lawn of the Underwood house. She could see the concern in their faces, and their heightened anxiety as she began stringing the bright yellow crime-scene tape, which served as a barricade between them and the house.

Detectives Hadsell and Prioleau, of the Missing Persons squad, arrived on the scene and began questioning Lisa's family, friends, and neighbors. The thought of a pregnant woman and her young son missing was disturbing enough, but when the detectives saw the lightly blood-spattered walls and large carpet stain, they knew they faced a more serious situation than earlier reported. They immediately issued an AMBER Alert throughout north Texas for Lisa and Jayden Underwood.

"Did anyone see anything unusual? Did you see anyone go in or come out of the house?" Detective Hadsell asked persons who milled around, people who were obviously concerned with the absence of the Underwoods.

A neighbor said he had seen a black Corvette parked at the curb in front of the house, but no other vehicles were recalled.

"Do you know anyone who would want to harm Lisa?"

"Yes, Stephen Barbee," Holly responded.

"Who is Stephen Barbee, and why would Mr. Barbee want to hurt Lisa?" the detective asked.

"He's the father of her baby, but he refused to acknowledge it," Holly said. "He didn't want his name on the birth certificate and he didn't want to provide insurance for her. Lisa said she and Stephen argued about it a lot, and she was very upset about his reluctance to take responsibility."

The detective took notes, jotting down Barbee's name

as a possible suspect in the Underwoods' alleged disappearance.

At 8:00 P.M., Detective R. A. Gallaway's phone rang.

"Dick, Detectives Hadsell and Prioleau, of Missing Persons, have been at a house on Chaddybrook for a couple of hours. What they found seems to be more serious than what they normally handle," Sergeant Kemper, Gallaway's superior officer, stated. "An AMBER Alert has been issued for Lisa Underwood and her seven-year-old son, Jayden, but I'd like for you to go over to Chaddybrook and take on the role of lead investigator."

Detective R. A. Gallaway was a member of the Special Crimes Unit of the Fort Worth Police Department (FWPD). He often served as lead investigator on serious, life-threatening crimes.

By eight-thirty on Saturday night, February 19, Gallaway was driving down Chaddybrook Lane toward the house where it was reported Lisa and Jayden Underwood lived. Gallaway first noticed several police vehicles parked along the curb on both sides of the street. Gallaway rolled down the window of his unmarked vehicle.

"I want you to block each end of the street to prevent through traffic," Gallaway instructed two patrol officers standing by. Knowing the media would be swarming the scene as soon as they learned of the AMBER Alert, Gallaway then assigned another patrol officer to stage a media area at the end of the street, far enough away to keep them at bay, but near enough to give them access. Gallaway asked Captain Read to contact the police department's public information officer to come to the scene to brief reporters.

As Gallaway took in the scene, he made note that the Underwood house was located on the north side of the street, with the front door and double-car garage door facing south. Yellow crime-scene tape blocked the entrance to the front yard and residence. Gallaway observed that a six-foot wooden privacy fence surrounded the side and the back-yard. There was a closed wooden gate on the west side of the garage that opened toward the street, but it was blocked at the bottom with loose bricks.

Gallaway doubted that any possible perpetrator would have fled through the gate.

Gallaway crossed the street and approached four women standing near a vehicle in front of Lisa Underwood's residence.

Sheila Underwood, Lisa's aunt Marla Hess, family friend Kelly Madingly, and Holly Pils huddled together in shared concern as Gallaway moved toward them.

Sheila Underwood watched as the tall, handsome man, who looked to be in his early forties, drew near. Gallaway ran his fingers through his dark hair, pushing it straight back from his face.

"I'm Detective Gallaway," the detective stated. "I've been assigned as the lead investigator and I'd like to ask you some questions."

Nervously puffing on a cigarette, Sheila Underwood explained that Lisa, her daughter, hadn't arrived for her own baby shower at four that afternoon. She described how she had called Lisa's cell phone a number of times, but Lisa had never answered. Sheila told Gallaway that she then drove to Lisa's house, and when there was no answer at the door, Sheila had used her own key to unlock the front door and go inside.

"Lisa's Dodge Durango wasn't in the garage, but Jayden's only pair of tennis shoes were on the mantel. There were also two bagged presents on the hearth. I think they were for a birthday party Jayden was supposed to go to this morning at ten," Sheila explained.

Sheila informed Gallaway that she'd locked Lisa's house and driven back to Boopa's Bagel Deli, where she called 911.

Gallaway next spoke with Holly Pils, Lisa Underwood's business partner. Holly's face was marred with the fear she felt for her best friend, and her voice quavered from restrained tears.

"I last spoke to Lisa about seven-forty last night," Holly said. "I called her on her cell, the only phone she has. I could hear Jayden in the background."

Holly told the detective about Lisa's excitement over the baby shower, that Lisa had been sick on Wednesday and Thursday, and that she had last seen Lisa on Thursday night when she had gone by to check on her.

"It wasn't like Lisa not to tell me if she was going somewhere, especially if Jayden was with her," Holly added.

It was obvious to Gallaway that Holly and Lisa had been not only partners for six years but trusted friends. Holly explained that she lived just around the corner from Lisa and Jayden, and through the business she had paid Lisa's cell phone, credit cards, and car payment.

"What do you know about the father of her baby?" Gallaway asked.

"Lisa was ninety-nine percent certain the father was Stephen Barbee," Holly stated. "She had also dated a guy by the name of Ed Rogers, but I'm pretty sure she hadn't dated Ed for about a year."

Gallaway asked about Barbee, and if Holly knew if he and Lisa had plans for raising the child.

"Lisa's doctor was Dr. Armstrong, and she last saw him the first week of February. Lisa told me prior to that appointment that she had called Stephen Barbee and asked him for medical insurance information and to sign the birth certificate. Lisa said he had told her, 'Sure, that will be

fine,' but he didn't show up for the doctor's appointment—
nor did he call Lisa back after that conversation."

Gallaway's exchange with Holly ended when Officer
C. C. Thomas handed him a computer printout. The communication had been given to Thomas by the recipient of an
e-mail that had been sent by Lisa Underwood. The e-mail
message was brief, and only contained information concerning a birthday party Jayden was scheduled to attend on
Saturday at 10:00 A.M., but it had been sent by Lisa Underwood at 11:25 P.M. on Friday.

Gallaway mentally began to make a timeline of Lisa
Underwood's movements prior to the report of her disappearance.

Detective Hadsell had been assigned the task of contacting T-Mobile, the service provider of Lisa's cellular phone.
Hadsell advised Gallaway that the telephone was turned on,
but that the last call ended at 7:38 P.M. on Friday, February
18. The information corresponded with the call Holly told
Gallaway she had made to Lisa. Gallaway asked Hadsell to
maintain contact with T-Mobile for any updates.

The lead investigator then directed the police helicopter
to search a five-mile, then a ten-mile, radius for Lisa's missing Durango. He also instructed extra police personnel to
look for the vehicle.

Lisa's doctor was contacted to find out if she had been in
touch with him concerning any difficulties she may have
been experiencing, but Dr. Armstrong hadn't heard from Lisa.

Gallaway asked Detective Jamison and Sergeant Kemper
to locate and interview Stephen Barbee, and Detective
Loughman to speak to Ed Rogers. The St. Joseph, Missouri,
Police Department (PD) was asked to assist by interviewing Bradley Mejia, Jayden's biological father.

Gallaway was covering all bases, following all procedures. He lingered outside the Underwood house, imagining

the love and laughter that had once filled the modest home, as he waited for Detective Prioleau to complete a search warrant for the residence.

Once the warrant was signed by a local judge, Gallaway and the Crime Scene Search Unit would enter the house in hopes of finding some clue, or clues, that would lead them to Lisa and Jayden. Gallaway felt a gnawing in the pit of his stomach. He recognized the familiar sensation. The sense of doubt that came when he feared the missing person or persons they were searching for would not be found alive.

5

Stephen Barbee had lived in the Fort Worth, Texas, area all his life. Born March 30, 1967, at Glenview Hospital in Fort Worth, weighing seven pounds nine ounces, Stephen was the third child of Bill and Jackie Barbee. Five-year-old Kathy and three-and-a-half-year-old David were thrilled to have a baby brother. The Barbees and their three kids made their home in Azle, just northwest of downtown Fort Worth.

Azle, a small town in the shadow of a big city, had been established by German settlers who purchased the land from the state of Texas in 1856. The town was named for Dr. James Azle Stewart, a country doctor who rode mule-back to see his patients, and who had donated much of the land for the town's businesses, schools, and churches.

It was that spirit of a small country town that the Barbees had sought when selecting Azle to raise their children.

Jackie Barbee worked for the school district and Bill at Bell Helicopter, a major U.S. defense contractor. They were the average American family, but a family where tragedy would strike not once, but three times.

Known in his Azle elementary school as a class clown, Stephen was always making people laugh. He had a knack for putting smiles on the faces of others, and the fun-loving child had lots of friends. Stephen, however, remained closest to his older siblings. The three were inseparable.

As a junior high student, Stephen played football and sang in the boys' choir. The youngest Barbee seemed to have a bright future, when the first of many tragedies struck.

Stephen's older sister, Kathy, married Mike Cherry shortly after high school; eighteen months later she was expecting her first child. Stephen was thrilled to be an uncle and looked forward to holding his first niece.

Kathy, a lovely girl with long, blond hair, was studying to be a licensed vocational nurse at Weatherford College, less than twenty miles west of Azle. As she was pushing a patient down the corridors of Campbell Memorial Hospital, Kathy experienced immense pain. She bent over, clutched her cramping stomach, and was immediately whisked into the emergency room, where Kathy learned she was in premature labor. Doctors attempted to stop the contractions and delay delivery, but Jennifer was born two months early, weighing just over three pounds. Losing weight and down to two pounds, Jennifer was transferred to a neonatal unit in Fort Worth, where she gained strength and was able to go home two months later.

Jennifer was the image of her mother, with her fair skin and wisps of light blond hair. She was a wonderful addition to the Barbee family. It was a joyful time, although short-lived.

Even after Jennifer's birth Kathy's body remained swollen, and she seldom felt good. Kathy often complained to her mother that she was tired, and when flu-like symptoms befell her within five months of delivering Jennifer, Kathy was back in the hospital. Even though doctors had warned Kathy and her husband against having another child anytime soon, Kathy learned she was two months pregnant.

While doctors blamed Kathy's symptoms on her pregnancy, the young mother was certain that was not the cause of her discomfort, and she was right. Doctors discovered Kathy had a viral infection, but they were unable to pinpoint exactly what type of virus. Therefore, they were unable to determine an effective treatment.

"It's like a silver bullet," the doctor told Jackie Barbee. "It's attacking all her organs. Perhaps if she weren't pregnant, we could aggressively treat her, but it could endanger her unborn child."

Jackie Barbee wept. She could see her daughter slipping away, and there was nothing she could do but pray. Fifteen-year-old Stephen felt more helpless with each visit to the hospital. He soon lost his fun-loving spirit and became a quiet, solemn child.

On Christmas Eve the family was summoned to the hospital. Only two weeks earlier, Stephen had watched his angelic-looking sister, dressed as an angel, perform in the church's Christmas pageant. Now, the night before Stephen's favorite holiday, he stood by Kathy's bed staring at the tubes and needles that were helping to keep his sister alive. Kathy fought for life, but the virus was too strong and Kathy too weak. Kathy died the day after Christmas. She was only twenty years old.

After he left the hospital, Stephen returned to the Barbees' house. He stared at Kathy's unopened presents under the Christmas tree. Tears filled his eyes and anger filled his heart. Unable to cope with or understand his loss, Stephen Barbee became a disturbed troublemaker.

The young teen was a disruption at school. His mother

was able to bail him out of most of the scrapes. But Barbee soon turned from mischievous acts to stealing, and although he was caught each time he committed an offense, he didn't care. Then Barbee and some of his friends went to their Azle school and destroyed school property. To save her son from juvenile prosecution, Jackie Barbee paid restitution, but Stephen was expelled permanently from the school.

Jackie thought it best to put her youngest son in a Christian academy. She enrolled him in the Outreach of Love Christian School. Stephen had been raised in the church and Jackie felt they could help him through the rage of losing his sister and the acting out associated with the loss.

Stephen did well. He played baseball in the summer, joined the Boy Scouts, and spent much of his time with his brother, David, whom he considered to be his best friend. It appeared that Stephen Barbee was finally back on track and had returned to his easygoing self. Then heartbreak struck again.

David Barbee loved to cook. He volunteered to help with church suppers and often had dinner ready for his parents when they got home from work. It seemed natural that David would take a job as a cook, and Pizza Hut had been a good fit.

While working, David became friends with a cute, young female coworker. David arranged to take her home after work one night and requested to borrow Jackie's car for the evening. David drove the girl to her house, as planned, then spent about twenty minutes talking to the young lady's parents before heading home. No one knows exactly why David Barbee ran into the concrete culvert on the side of the road, but the car flipped. David was trapped by the seat belt and died of asphyxiation. David Barbee was twenty years old.

Jackie and Bill Barbee had spent most of that night looking for their oldest son, finally arriving at the office of the medical examiner (ME) on Montgomery Street, near downtown Fort Worth. They were told David wasn't there, but Jackie Barbee didn't believe them. Finally David's body was located in one of the coolers at the back of the building. In disbelief, Jackie stared at her son's lifeless body. He was still wearing the jacket he had left home in.

"We'll be performing an autopsy," the ME said.

"No!" Jackie Barbee said, wrapping her arms around her son. "Don't touch him. I'm not giving up on this one." She clung to David in an attempt to will him back to life.

Through the days and weeks that followed David's death, Jackie's sorrow could not be masked. She frequently cried uncontrollably. Bill, who had begun drinking after Kathy's death, retreated into his liquor bottles to numb the pain. Stephen was traumatized by the loss as well. His best friend, his only living sibling, was dead. Both Kathy and David had died at age twenty, and Stephen Barbee became convinced that he, too, would die in four years.

A burning desire to live life to the fullest led Stephen to decide he would return to public school to play football for Azle High School. But the school district refused to accept his credits from the Christian academy he had been attending. They informed him he would have to take the last two years of classes over again.

That didn't fit into Stephen Barbee's plan. He believed he only had four years of living to do and he intended to do it with wild abandonment. He drove fast and lived hard. He took chances, and Jackie Barbee feared she was destined to lose her last child prematurely as well.

On the day of Stephen's twentieth birthday, Jackie Barbee

woke her son with song. "Happy birthday to you," Jackie sang.

"This is the worst day of my life," Stephen told his mother, pulling the covers back over his head. "I'm going to die this year."

"Stephen, don't talk like that," Jackie urged, tears filling her eyes.

"I'm going to die, just like Kathy and David. Sometime this year I'm going to die," Stephen said with certainty.

Jackie's heart ached for her son. She understood his paranoia and she would do anything to help him through it.

"I've been saving some money," Jackie told Stephen. "On your twenty-first birthday it will be yours. You can use it for whatever you want."

But the offer of money did little to convince Stephen Barbee he would ever live to enjoy it. Certain he had but a short time to be in this world, Stephen continued to live life on the edge.

Then one day in early April 1987, while walking around the Fort Worth Boat Show, Stephen began dreaming of skimming along the surface of the water on nearby Eagle Mountain Lake. He would take his friends fishing, waterskiing, go for evening cruises, and enjoy what time he had left.

Stephen called his mother. "Mom, were you serious about saving money for me?"

"Yes, Stephen. I have put money aside for your twenty-first birthday," Jackie said, a curious wrinkle in her brow.

"Can I have it early?" Stephen asked.

"What for?" Jackie asked suspiciously.

"I went to the Fort Worth Boat Show and I want to buy a boat," Stephen told her.

"A boat?" Jackie questioned.

"Yes. I've always wanted a boat so I could go fishing. Can I still have the money?" Stephen asked again.

Jackie agreed, and Stephen Barbee became the owner of a sixteen-foot watercraft with an outboard motor. He loved soaring across the top of the water with the wind blowing his straight brown hair. He loved hauling in his catch of crappie and taking them home for his mom to fry up for dinner.

Jackie gradually saw a change in her son. He no longer dwelt on an imaginary impending death. Instead, he enjoyed life. When Stephen reached his twenty-first birthday, it was a festive occasion. Stephen's preoccupation with death was replaced with making plans for the future.

Always a hard worker, Stephen Barbee had begun a lawn-mowing business when he was just fourteen. He may not have been a scholar, failing the reading portion of his first GED test; however, with the aid of his parents' financial backing, he had built quite a business by age twenty-one. He eventually named it Four Seasons.

Stephen worked other jobs while simultaneously maintaining his lawn care company. He helped his uncle build houses and also worked for Cowboy Coring, a concrete-cutting company. He tried welding, completing 1,200 hours in trade school, only to find welding wasn't what he wanted to do. What Stephen wanted to do most was be a policeman. And it was while Stephen was employed for a pest control service that he realized his dream.

In order to get his foot in the door, Stephen became a reserve officer for the Blue Mound Police Department (BMPD), serving a small town of 2,300 people, located just eight miles outside Fort Worth. He had to commit to sixteen hours per month, at $6.75 an hour. The meager wages didn't matter to Stephen. He had all the authority and responsibilities of a full-time officer, and he loved it.

Stephen remained in north Fort Worth, but six months was the maximum time he spent in any one apartment. He moved often in an effort to find a place that would hire him for security in exchange for free rent. Still with the BMPD at the time, Stephen, like many certified officers, sought private security work to supplement his officer's salary. And, assigned only minimal hours at the police department, Stephen continued to work at the pest control company.

Many of his customers had carpenter ants caused by tree limbs resting on their houses. The customers were advised to have the limbs cut down, and Stephen regularly offered to perform the service at a nominal rate. Soon he was making $200 a weekend for cutting trees, and calls for his service were increasing.

At first, Stephen carried out the tasks alone, but eventually others were hired to help him at $7 per hour. Before Stephen knew it, his tree-trimming business had consumed most of his free time. After two and a half years, he left the police department's reserve unit, and, again with his parents' financial help to obtain a tree-trimming truck, Stephen Barbee expanded Four Seasons to include tree maintenance.

Four Seasons exploded. With the acquisition of state highway contracts and the hiring of additional laborers, Stephen had managed to build a successful, profitable business.

Stephen Barbee flourished financially and socially, and although there was never a shortage of women to date—many were drawn to him by his good looks and irrepressible spirit, as well as his sleek black Corvette—he was thinking of settling down. He wanted marriage. He wanted kids.

* * *

Stephen Barbee had fathered a child, a quick fling that had produced an offspring. His former lover informed him she only wanted a child, not a husband, and she took the child and left the area.

One evening, while sitting in the hot tub of his Euless, Texas, apartment complex, Barbee met a young flight attendant for American Airlines and her cousin. Teresa Sue Dawling wasn't impressed with Stephen. She thought he was a "runt," because he was less than six feet tall and remained slim from the physical labor demanded by Four Seasons.

Teresa's cousin, on the other hand, believed Stephen was cute; she blatantly flirted with him. But it was Teresa whom Stephen found to be funny, and he enjoyed her company. The two hung out casually until they lost contact when Stephen moved to another apartment complex in the area.

Months later, Stephen was thinking about the fun he had with Teresa, and although he hadn't been in contact with her for some time, he phoned her mother in an effort to get Teresa's number. It wasn't long before Teresa phoned, her mom having paged her after Stephen's call. The two reconnected, and they were together constantly from their first date.

On October 19, 1996, Teresa and Stephen had the wedding Teresa had always dreamed of. They were married in the Embassy Suites in Irving, Texas. Stephen's niece, Jennifer, played the flute, and her father, Mike Cherry, sang. Teresa walked down the aisle in a long white dress on the arm of her ponytailed father as Stephen, handsome in his black tux, beamed in admiration.

The couple enjoyed a sit-down dinner, toasted one another with champagne, and danced to tunes spun by a local DJ. The newlyweds honeymooned on a Caribbean cruise before returning to Texas. Stephen Barbee was happy. He looked forward to starting a family with his new bride.

The first few months of marriage were as blissful as Stephen had imagined. He and Teresa became children's church leaders, serving the spiritual needs of fifty to seventy-five kids each Sunday. Stephen's specialty was the puppets. He loved to make them come to life for the kids and use them to portray God's teachings.

In business he continued to work hard, developing Four Seasons while taking on additional jobs. He again worked for Cowboy Coring, and because of his work ethic and knowledge of the business, the owner offered to take him on as a partner. The offer was abruptly withdrawn when Teresa insisted on being included in the partnership, an addition to the business not relished by the owner. Rather than take two partners, the owner offered to sell the business to the Barbees: Cowboy Coring subsequently became Cowboy Cutters under the ownership of Stephen and Teresa Barbee.

Teresa became more and more involved in her husband's businesses while maintaining her flight attendant status with American Airlines. Teresa managed the office and prepared the job bids, while Stephen did the work and ran the crews. It didn't take long before Teresa began to run things not only at the office, but at home.

Stephen's family was concerned with the relationship of their son and his wife. They loved Teresa and had always treated her like a daughter, rather than just a daughter-in-law. However, they were increasingly concerned with Teresa's belittling of their son in front of others, and in front of his workers, in particular. Stephen had confided in his parents that Teresa told his employees not to talk to him because he was bipolar, although he had never been diagnosed with the disorder. The demeaning treatment affected the Barbees' marriage, and arguments became commonplace. Eventually the disagreements turned from verbal to physical, with each accusing the other of abuse.

Teresa desperately wanted a house, and Stephen felt it might be the thing that would patch the split in their marriage. He also hoped it would be the catalyst that convinced Teresa to have his baby.

The Barbees chose a plot of land in Haslet, north of Fort Worth, bordering on Saginaw to the south, and Azle to the west. They first erected metal buildings to house equipment used in Four Seasons and Cowboy Cutters, and they finished an apartment inside, where they lived while building their dream house.

By the time the house was completed, it was 4,800 square feet, and, along with the land and outbuildings, Stephen estimated the value at $850,000. Teresa later added a pool and pool house, at a cost of $65,000—$20,000 borrowed from her in-laws, which she never repaid.

But Stephen Barbee didn't enjoy the house for long. The problems between him and Teresa escalated. During one intense argument Teresa encouraged him to commit suicide, saying, "Why don't you just get in your car and go kill yourself."

After Stephen stormed out and didn't come home, Teresa called him on his cell phone and asked, "Where are you?"

"You want me to kill myself, I will," Stephen responded. But it was an idle threat—although he admittedly wanted out of the chaos of his life with Teresa, Stephen knew he could never take his own life, if for no other reason than the fact that he was his parents' sole surviving child.

Stephen returned home, took a large glass of whiskey with him to the backyard pool, and sat by the water's edge. He lay back on the cool deck, staring at the stars above.

Teresa saw her husband lying by the pool, so she frantically called 911, informing the operator that her husband was in the pool after attempting suicide.

Paramedics raced to the scene and transported Stephen Barbee to the hospital, where he was examined and released.

A year after moving into the house, Stephen Barbee moved out and into an apartment. All he wanted was to get on with his life. He left the house, contents, and most of his personal belongings to break away and begin again. The divorce documents cited "discord or conflict of personality" as the cause of their separation.

Lisa Underwood and her business partner, Holly Pils, owned Boopa's, a small bagel shop on the corner of Western Center Boulevard and North Beach Street. The two had been friends for years, ever since Holly, area manager of eight stores for a national bagel franchise called Bruegger's Bagels, hired Lisa to manage one of the shops for her. Lisa had extensive restaurant experience, and Holly believed she would be an asset to the company. Lisa first ran the Preston Road store in Dallas, then was transferred to the Camp Bowie location in Fort Worth.

In only a few months, Lisa and Holly had become good friends. Holly had also gotten to know Lisa's son, Jayden, just one and a half at the time.

On January 31, 1999, Holly received a fax from the corporate office of Bruegger's Bagels that would change her and Lisa's lives forever. The fax announced Bruegger's was closing all of the Dallas/Fort Worth stores and all employees were fired. Holly and Lisa put their heads together, and the next day they formed the corporation 2PW, standing for 2 Powerful Women. They never closed the two Fort Worth stores as directed; instead, they bought the equipment left by Bruegger's from the bankruptcy court, renamed the stores Boopa's (Jayden's nickname), and for the first time, each woman worked for herself. After a month and a half, the Camp Bowie store was closed, and both Holly and Lisa concentrated on making Boopa's, on Western Center Boulevard, a success.

Young Jayden grew up in the shop. Lisa took the boy with her at six each morning, laying him in the back room to continue sleeping while she readied the shop to open. Jayden would get up, dress for school, take time to visit with the customers, and by 8:00 A.M., Lisa had him on his way to school. Jayden loved being in the shop. He talked with the customers and took orders when his mother and Holly were busy.

Reared as an independent child, by the time he was six years old, Jayden would take $20 from the cash register and walk down the shopping strip to the hair salon for a haircut.

The salon's owner also took her little girl to work with her and she and Jayden often spoke.

"I'm the owner of this beauty shop," the little girl told Jayden proudly. And not to be outdone, Jayden replied smartly, "Well, I own the bagel shop," convinced that he did.

Jayden was an adorable boy, liked by all who knew him. He was often described as "looking just like the little boy in the movie *Jerry Maguire,*" and he did, with his sandy brown hair in a crew cut and glasses, which accented his bright, smiling eyes. Jayden also had a personality to match that of the small, precocious screen actor.

The young seven-year-old had just begun to play soccer and had recently joined the Cub Scouts. Jayden was popular with his classmates and was enjoyed by his teachers.

Although the boy was devoted to his mother, he was also

close to his father, whom he visited often at his home in St. Louis, Missouri.

Bradley Mejia and Lisa Underwood met when they worked together at a restaurant in St. Joseph. Lisa became pregnant with Mejia's son, but she moved to Texas prior to Jayden's birth.

Even though they lived far apart, Jayden's father had remained dedicated to his son. Mejia often visited Jayden in Texas, and Jayden had spent his seventh birthday in October 2005 celebrating with his father and extended Mejia family.

"We played basketball. We had birthday cake. I guess if you have to have memories, those are the ones you always want to remember," grandfather David Mejia later commented.

Next to his mother, Jayden was closest to his grandmother, whom he lovingly called "Tita," and whom he spent almost every weekend with in her home in nearby Dallas.

Sheila Underwood, who was only eighteen years old when she had given birth to Lisa, moved to Dallas when Lisa was a small child. Sheila left behind Lisa's father in Wichita Falls, a far north central Texas city divided from Oklahoma by the Red River, and known for little more than Midwestern State University, Wichita Falls State Mental Hospital, and the Oil Bowl, an annual high-school football rivalry between teams from Texas and Oklahoma.

The prairie city offered little for Sheila Underwood, who had higher dreams and aspirations. She had reached the top of the promotion ladder, as well as the pay scale, at her job, so Sheila moved on to pursue her career and to raise her only child alone in the upper-middle-class suburb of Lake Highlands.

The young mother and daughter grew up together along the way, and although both Sheila and Lisa were stubborn by nature, they both thrived in the new city.

There were tumultuous times when mother and daughter clashed, and times when Lisa would return to Wichita Falls to live with her aunt Marla. But Lisa was always keenly aware that her mother would always be there for her, just as she would be for Jayden.

Lisa Underwood thrived in school and was named to *Who's Who*. After graduation she went to the University of Mississippi to experience college life, but she left after being in Oxford, Mississippi, for only twenty minutes. The homesick teen was convinced by her mother to give higher education and Ole Miss a chance. Lisa returned to Oxford and remained a week and a half, but her heart was not there.

Most of Lisa's early work years were spent as a server in various restaurants in a number of cities. She knew the food business, liked it, and had found success. So when Lisa announced that she and Holly planned to begin 2PW and open Boopa's, Sheila became their biggest supporter.

Boopa's regular customers included employees of the Burlington Northern Railroad, who worked at the main office just down Western Center Boulevard in nearby Saginaw, others from nearby stores and offices, as well as Teresa Barbee, who often dropped into Boopa's to pick up bagels for the Four Seasons work crew before their day began.

After Stephen Barbee moved out of the house in Haslet, he began dropping by Boopa's himself on his way to the shop. That's where Barbee first met Lisa Underwood. They visited often at the shop, and Stephen found Lisa to be funny and easy to talk to. Wanting to see more of Lisa, he asked her out. Their first date took place in downtown Fort

Worth, where they sat under the stars and listened to the rhythmic sounds of a local band. Stephen Barbee enjoyed Lisa's company.

The two shared pizza at Lisa's apartment when Jayden was at his grandmother's house in Dallas, or they'd often be together at Stephen's apartment. Stephen helped Lisa out by cutting down a tree at her house and chopped it up for firewood. They laughed a lot, and they enjoyed their time together. But, even though they had become intimate, it was understood they didn't have an exclusive relationship. Lisa was seeing a local musician named Ed Rogers, and Stephen dated a number of women, on and off.

One day, as Stephen was driving down a Fort Worth street, he was surprised to see Trish Reinhardt standing on a corner. Trish's ex-husband had worked with Stephen at the pest control company; through him, Stephen had met Trish. Stephen had been instantly awed by Trish's good looks and bubbly personality. Seeing Trish again, he quickly rounded the block and pulled up next to the curb where Trish stood.

"Hey," Stephen said. "How are you doing?"

"Great. How are you?" Trish replied, brushing back her blond hair.

They talked and Trish accepted an invitation to go with him to Possum Kingdom Lake for the weekend to enjoy boat rides and fishing with her two children. Stephen instantly fell in love with the kids. Taylor and Tanner were just the kind of children Stephen had always dreamed of having.

Although Stephen had seen Jayden in Boopa's, Lisa had never allowed him to be around the boy. She explained that at one time she had been seeing someone who had gotten close to Jayden, and when he left, it had hurt the boy. Lisa was fearlessly protective of her son, vowing not to let anyone she dated meet Jayden unless that person was going to be a part of their life long-term.

Within weeks Stephen began seeing Trish more, and Lisa less. He was falling in love with Trish, and already loved her children as if they were his own. Lisa felt Stephen slipping away and she tried to hold on. His calls became less frequent, and when Lisa would go to his apartment and he didn't answer, she would leave notes on his car, asking why he no longer called.

Convinced of his love for Trish, Stephen decided he would ask her to marry him. He would have an instant family, and, hopefully, they would have more kids. But Barbee was devastated when Trish said no to his proposal and informed him she wanted no more children. Trish had been cheated on before, and she trusted no man.

Stephen turned to Lisa, his former lover and good friend, and told her of his disappointment at Trish's refusal. Still caring for Stephen, Lisa said she would marry him. She would bear his children. But it was Trish whom Stephen loved. It was Trish he wanted. But as much as Stephen wanted Trish, he had told her he would never propose again.

"Why don't you just move in?" Trish asked.

"I won't just live with you," Stephen said. "Marry me, or I won't live with you."

While Trish continued to see Stephen, Lisa continued to pursue him. Stephen worried that Trish might see Lisa as a threat. Then, on July 4, 2004, Stephen, Trish, Tanner, and Taylor were having a picnic when Trish produced a box. Opening the lid, she took out four Barbie dolls: a brown-haired male, a blond female, a redheaded boy, and a brown-haired girl. The dolls represented Stephen, Trish, Tanner, and Taylor. The brown-haired male and the blond-haired female were dressed in wedding attire. Trish looked at Stephen and said, "Will you marry us?"

Stephen nearly burst with joy. He loved Trish, and although he was certain she didn't love him with the same intensity, he felt she would, in time.

Stephen began making plans. In just a little over a year after they first began to date, he and Trish would fly to Las Vegas and marry. They would make their home in Fort Worth and they would start a family. Stephen busily began packing up his apartment in anticipation of his new life.

While in the midst of the debris of packing paper and boxes, Lisa dropped by unexpectedly.

"What are you doing?" Lisa asked.

"Trish proposed," Stephen replied, a broad grin covering his face.

But Lisa wasn't smiling. She was hurt and disappointed by the news. Lisa made it clear to Stephen that the affair was over. He and Lisa would no longer be lovers, and Stephen was uncertain they could ever be friends.

Several weeks after Lisa and Stephen had their parting conversation at his apartment, and six months prior to her death, Lisa telephoned Stephen. He stared at the phone receiver, stunned at the news Lisa had given him. Lisa was pregnant, and she believed he was the father. His mind was swirling. Stephen immediately had his doubts—after all, they didn't have a monogamous relationship. He knew she had simultaneously been seeing a local musician while he had been seeing Trish.

After the initial shock at hearing he might be a father, Stephen was consumed with fear: *What if Trish finds out? I'd be sure to lose her. Lose the kids.*

Unlike Stephen, Lisa was certain he was the father of her unborn child. She and her best friend, Holly, had calculated the last time Lisa had been intimate with Stephen and the gestation of her pregnancy. The calculations matched, and Lisa wanted Stephen Barbee to acknowledge his unborn child.

Lisa was excited to be a mother for a second time, but she wanted Jayden to feel he was just as special as ever. She began redecorating his room in an African theme. While Sheila kept Jayden at her home in Dallas, Lisa was busy painting the walls ocean blue with pictures of Africa, complete with elephants and tigers. Once the room was finished and Sheila took her grandson home, he walked into his room and asked in delighted surprise, "What happened in here?" He loved the changes.

Stephen pondered the chances that the child Lisa was carrying was his. Lisa continued to wear her snug-fitting jeans whenever he saw her, not showing any sign of pregnancy. He considered that her announcement might just be a way of attempting to get back together with him. He decided he had to know for sure and would tell her the next time they spoke.

While working in Abilene, Texas, with his crew, 192 miles west of Fort Worth, Stephen got a message from Lisa. She wanted him to call. His cell phone didn't work in certain areas of the open land near Abilene, so he drove fifteen minutes toward town in order to get a signal that worked without breaking up.

"Stephen, I want your name on the baby's birth certificate. It's your baby, and you need to admit it," Lisa said firmly.

"First, I want a blood test," he responded.

"What?" Lisa screamed.

"I just want to know for sure," Stephen stated, but there was no reasoning with Lisa. She was angry—angry that he was with Trish, and angry that he doubted the paternity of the child.

* * *

Stephen Barbee wanted to be certain he was the father of the baby before telling Trish. Stephen had been the subject of a paternity suit by a Granbury, Texas, woman in 1993, and, as then, he wanted to be certain he was the father before telling Trish that Lisa Underwood was having his baby. It was going to ruin everything. Trish, who was unable to have a baby due to a prior medical procedure, had agreed to go through in vitro fertilization in order to give him a child. How could he tell her that "Lisa's having my baby" after she had promised to give him the one thing his ex-wife, Teresa, never would?

Stephen also wanted to keep the news from Teresa. He feared Trish would leave him, but he was certain Teresa would laugh at him. He didn't want any further humiliation from his former wife.

Confused and anxious, Stephen confided in his best friend, Ron Dodd.

"I don't know what to do," Stephen said, raking his hands through his short brown hair. "If Trish finds out, she'll leave me."

Stephen paced the shop floor, wringing his hands and begging Ron for an answer to his problem.

"I can help you find a hit man," Dodd stated calmly.

"What?" Stephen asked, looking at Dodd in disbelief.

"Yeah, I can find you a hit man. That would solve your problem," Dodd replied.

Stephen stared at Dodd. "No, there's got to be another way."

6

Saturday night, February 19, 2005, Stephen and Trish, along with Trish's two children, arrived home about ten-thirty. It had been a long day for Stephen Barbee after an arduous, horrific night. Barbee was spent, both physically and emotionally.

Before tucking the kids into bed, Stephen Barbee went to the phone to hear any messages that may have been left while they were out. Barbee grew pale as he listened to the voice of a Fort Worth detective asking him to call.

Barbee went to Tanner's room, and as he pulled the covers up to the boy's shoulders and kissed him on the forehead, his mind raced. *Why do the police want to talk to me? How could they possibly know I have anything to do with Lisa and Jayden's disappearance?*

As Barbee considered what he would say to the police, the phone rang.

"Mr. Barbee, this is Detective Jamison. We'd like to drop by and talk with you," the detective said.

"It's kind of late," Barbee replied, hoping to gain more time to think.

"It won't take long," the detective responded.

Barbee placed the phone in the cradle, closed his eyes,

and took in a deep breath. Within moments he heard the doorbell ring.

Barbee was stunned to see two Fort Worth police officers standing at the threshold. *How did they have time to get here so fast? They must have been calling from their car.*

"Mr. Barbee, I'm Sergeant Jamison and this is Detective Kemper. We'd like to ask you a few questions."

Barbee opened the door, stepping back to allow the officers to enter. He took a deep breath to steady himself.

"Mr. Barbee, your name came up in an investigation into the disappearance of Lisa and Jayden Underwood," Brian Jamison stated.

"I know Lisa," Barbee admitted.

"Did you know she and her son are missing?" Kemper asked.

"Yeah," Barbee responded, "I heard the AMBER Alert."

"No one seems to know where Lisa and Jayden are, and since you once dated Lisa, we thought you might have an idea of where she might be. Do you know anything?"

"No, I don't. I haven't seen Lisa in some time," Barbee replied.

"Where were you last night, Mr. Barbee?"

"I was at Ron Dodd's home last night," Barbee said. "Ron works for me and he lives with my ex-wife. My shop is out by their house," Barbee explained.

"What time did you get home?"

"I'm not sure. It was kinda late. My wife was already asleep," Barbee responded.

"Mr. Barbee, one of the neighbors reported seeing a black Corvette at Lisa's house. I understand you own a black Corvette—is that right?" Jamison asked.

"Yeah," Barbee stated.

"We'd like your permission to spray your car with luminol," Sergeant Gary Kemper said. "Do you have a problem with that?"

"No, I have no problem with that," Barbee responded, knowing his car was free of any trace of Lisa and Jayden.

"Someone will be over to run the test. We're through for the moment," Kemper told Barbee, "but if we have some more questions for you, will you be in town?"

"I'll be around tomorrow, but I have to be in Tyler, Monday, on a job," Barbee responded.

Barbee closed the door behind the two detectives and leaned against it to steady himself. He breathed a sigh of relief that they were gone. He tried to steady himself before joining Trish in bed.

Barbee's explanation to his wife for the police interest in him was simple, as Trish knew he had dated Lisa Underwood for a while. Naturally, the police were interested in talking to him, just as they were probably interested in anyone who knew her.

Later that night the Crime Scene Unit arrived and ran the test on both of Barbee's vehicles. Not only was Barbee's black Corvette tested with the blood-seeking chemical luminol, but his black Ford Explorer as well. And just as Barbee had silently predicted, the results netted no positive findings for blood in either vehicle.

As Stephen Barbee slept with Trish in his arms—his wife of two months, blissfully unaware of her husband's deadly secret—Detective Dick Gallaway instructed Jamison and Kemper to locate and interview Ron Dodd and Teresa. Gallaway didn't feel comfortable with Barbee's explanation of his recent whereabouts. He wanted Stephen Barbee's story verified as soon as possible.

In the meantime the search warrant had been signed, and Gallaway and Crime Scene Search Unit officer Gass entered the Underwood residence for the first time.

"There appears to be no forced entry," Gass stated as they crossed the threshold of the house, "but there seems to be blood on the inside dead bolt."

Gallaway's eyes scanned the room. "Looks like a bloody stain on the carpet, near the coffee table," Gallaway pointed out, "and a smaller red stain between the two large ones." Gallaway drew in a deep breath. "Smells like ammonia," Gallaway said, "or some other cleaning product." Noticing small wheel tracks across the carpet, Gallaway added, "And it appears someone attempted to brush or vacuum the red stains on the living-room carpet."

Gallaway recalled Holly Pils saying she had given Lisa a vacuum cleaner recently, but there was no vacuum in sight.

"I'll check out what appears to be a possible blood transfer on the couch slipcover," Gass stated, "and a few more red stains on the entertainment center and baseboard."

As Gallaway and Gass proceeded through the remainder of the house, they found no other signs of a struggle.

Gallaway asked that Lisa Underwood's computer from her bedroom be removed and a forensic examination of the hard drive be completed. The analysis later revealed that the 11:25 e-mail concerning a birthday party Jayden would attend had been the last activity logged on Lisa Underwood's computer.

The remainder of the night, and all the next day, the search for Lisa Underwood's vehicle continued, while background checks were conducted on Lisa's acquaintances.

The AMBER Alert issued for Jayden and Lisa Underwood was broadened from Texas to include the neighboring states of New Mexico, Oklahoma, Louisiana, and Arkansas. Every effort was being made to find the missing mother and son, hopefully alive, but police were beginning to fear the worst.

* * *

On Sunday, two days after the murders, Stephen Barbee drove to Haslet to prepare for a job set to begin on Monday, February 21, in Tyler, Texas. Teresa Barbee and Ron Dodd weren't there, as Barbee had expected, so he decided to head to a gas station and have the oil changed in the company truck. While at the station Barbee happened to meet Detective Jamison, one of the officers who had been at his house the previous evening and who had questioned him about his relationship with Lisa Underwood. The two men spoke briefly before Stephen Barbee headed back to the shop.

Teresa and Dodd were still not home. Barbee attempted to open the shop door, but the loud shrill of an alarm blared throughout the neighborhood. Barbee fumbled with the alarm keypad, but his mind refused to bring up the code. Frustration flooding him, he finally gave up trying to remember the preset numbers and their sequence and called Teresa from his cell for the code.

Teresa and Ron Dodd asked him to join them for dinner, but Barbee refused. All he wanted to do was get set for work the next day and hurry back to Trish and the kids.

Barbee sharpened the tools, gassed up three of the company vehicles, then drove home.

Gallaway had slept little since catching the Underwood disappearance case on Saturday night. But at nine-fifteen, Monday morning, February 21, he stood in front of Stephen Barbee's residence, along with crime scene officers, collecting Barbee's curbside trash. They hoped to find some lead that would help them nail down the suspicion that Stephen Barbee had something to do with the strange vanishing of Lisa and Jayden Underwood.

Stephen Barbee had left for Tyler, as planned, early

that morning, unaware that the police would be at his home minutes later to search his refuse for leads in the case.

While they collected Barbee's curbside trash, Gallaway's phone rang.

"Where?" Gallaway asked. Closing his cell phone, Gallaway told the others, "Lisa Underwood's Dodge Durango has been found. It's off Exit 82, on I-35W, in Denton County. I'm headed up there."

When Gallaway drove north of Vintage Road in Denton, as directed, he spotted Lisa Underwood's Durango nose down in a creek bed, with a small amount of creek water running through it. The rear hatch of the vehicle was open, and Gallaway could clearly see that there was no one inside.

Gallaway's eyes scanned the low-hanging tree limbs that swept downward toward the receded water level and the sparse winter-brown vegetation on the banks.

Lisa and Jayden aren't here, Gallaway thought, *but where are they?* The sick feeling in the pit of his stomach returned.

"Conduct as much of a search as possible," Gallaway instructed the crime scene officers. "Then secure the vehicle in a security bay at the PD auto pound."

"Detective," one of the crime scene officers shouted as he raised his arm in the air, "we found the keys to the Durango in the water."

News helicopters and media vans quickly swarmed the area. The discovery of the Underwood vehicle was big news, and every radio and television station in the Dallas/Fort Worth metroplex sent reporters out to cover the story.

Regular programming was interrupted for the breaking news of the discovery of Lisa Underwood's SUV, and the failure to locate either Lisa or her son, Jayden. The sighting was also the lead story of every regularly slated newscast in the Dallas/Fort Worth area.

* * *

Deputy Brawner was sitting in his Denton County home and watching the news when the discovery of the Underwood vehicle, south of Vintage Road, caught his attention. He recalled the night he had stopped a man walking near that area, and that the man had taken off when the deputy called dispatch to check his identity. Brawner immediately drove to the scene on Vintage Road to talk with investigators.

Locating the lead detective Gallaway, Brawner approached the Fort Worth lawman to relate the story of his encounter with the unknown suspect two days earlier.

"I stopped a white male covered in mud on Saturday, February twentieth, at about oh three hundred hours," Brawner told Gallaway. "The white male was on the shoulder of I-35W service road."

Brawner informed Gallaway he had spoken briefly with the man who had given a false identity before he ran from him and escaped. The description the deputy gave Gallaway matched that of Stephen Barbee.

"I have a videotape recording of the encounter in the squad car," Brawner informed the investigator. "I'll get it for you."

On the video Gallaway could plainly see Stephen Barbee talking with the deputy and then minutes later running from the officer.

Gallaway's belief that Stephen Barbee had something to do with the disappearance of Lisa and Jayden Underwood was growing in strength. Then, as if to confirm his suspicions, an anonymous caller contacted the Fort Worth Police Department.

"I have information about the Underwood murders," a male voice stated. "Stephen Barbee killed them."

7

Stephen and Trish Barbee, along with the two kids, arrived in Tyler, Texas, Monday morning. Trish and her children wanted to spend time with Stephen, especially Tanner, who looked forward to watching his stepfather trim trees along the highway. The four of them planned to stay in the Four Seasons company recreational vehicle (RV) during their time in Tyler.

Tanner looked up through the foliage of a tree as his stepfather stepped onto a large limb. The boy was enthralled as he watched Stephen climb tall branches, cut limbs, and follow the huge boughs as they tumbled to the ground.

With the help of Ron Dodd, Stephen Barbee went about his work without the knowledge of the tip given to the Fort Worth police by the unidentified caller, or that Detective Dick Gallaway had identified him as the man running from the Denton County deputy in the wee hours of the morning following Lisa and Jayden's disappearance. For Barbee, it was work as usual, until late that afternoon.

About 4:00 P.M., Barbee was contacted by Detective Mike Carroll on his cell phone. The detective asked if he and Ron Dodd would meet him in the parking lot of the Tyler

Wal-Mart. Carroll explained he needed a written statement from Barbee concerning his relationship with Lisa. Barbee readily agreed to meet at the designated location.

Barbee took Trish and the kids with him when he went to meet the detective, planning on some impromptu shopping at the superstore after speaking with Carroll. Ron Dodd arrived in a second company vehicle.

Detectives Carroll and McCaskill drove to Tyler, and after picking up Detective Brian Jamison, who had flown in by helicopter, they appeared around 6:00 P.M. at the pre-arranged location. John McCaskill spoke with Ron Dodd, and Jamison with Barbee, while Detective Carroll interviewed Trish Barbee in the city-owned brown vehicle that they had driven to Tyler.

Nearly an hour later, both Barbee and Dodd were asked to follow the detectives to the Tyler Police Department (TPD), where their statements would be taken, and where Trish and the kids could wait.

Barbee followed directly behind the Fort Worth officers, while Dodd trailed Barbee. Unfamiliar with Tyler, the detectives had difficulty finding the police department. Finally a frustrated McCaskill phoned a friend who was a Tyler cop and asked for directions.

Stephen Barbee's anxiety grew as he steered his truck through the downtown Tyler streets. He glanced from the tall majestic pine trees, which lined many of the streets, to Trish, sitting beside him. She was so beautiful, and he had been so happy during their short time together. Barbee breathed deeply as he looked in the rearview mirror at the children who meant the world to him.

Barbee rounded the corner onto Ferguson Street, then wheeled into the Tyler PD parking lot. He cut the engine and, with the calloused hands of a working man, gripped the steering wheel tightly.

Slowly Barbee turned to look into the eyes of his wife. "Trish, I love you. Always remember, I love you," Barbee said. He tried to keep his voice from shaking and he turned his head to look at the children in the backseat so that Trish wouldn't see the tears forming in his eyes.

Trish Barbee and her children walked up the front steps of the Tyler PD and through the double glass front doors, hand in hand, with Stephen. They faced a wall with a bank of two large glass windows that held information personnel who were protected from any possible intruders. Stephen glanced around the foyer, looking for Carroll or any of the other Fort Worth detectives he had agreed to meet.

At approximately 7:30 P.M., Detective Carroll joined Stephen in the lobby, then escorted him through double doors to the right of the information windows. They passed through a metal detector, down a long hall, turning left into a shorter passageway, and finally into one of three small interview rooms. Barbee sat at a table and was told someone would be in to take his statement.

While Stephen Barbee waited in the inner sanctum of the police department, Trish, Tanner, and Taylor sat waiting for his return in three straight-back chairs that lined the large windows of the station lobby. In a short time Ron Dodd was led through a back door and placed in the first interview room next to the video equipment area, two doors down from his friend and employer.

Barbee looked up as Detective Jamison walked in and asked him, "Do you want something to drink?"

"No, I'm okay," Barbee replied.

"I'll be back in a few minutes," Jamison said as he left the room.

Barbee looked around the eight-by-eight cubicle devoid of any decoration and leaned back as he waited for Jamison's return.

Just down the hall the Fort Worth detectives watched as Tyler officer Richard Cashell set up Tyler PD's video-digital recording equipment. From inside the small video room, the technician would be able to see and hear what was going on in any of the interview rooms on a small television receiver and then record the interviews on a digital disc. The setup took Cashell ten to fifteen minutes.

In the lobby Trish's children periodically got up to get a drink of water from one of the two wall-mounted fountains, or use one of the restrooms on either side of the bank of drinking stations. Tanner passed the time playing games on his mother's cell phone, while Taylor stretched across two chairs, her head resting in her mother's lap. Trish intermittently glanced at her watch, wondering why it was taking so long for police to take her husband's statement.

Detective Mike Carroll, his milk chocolate skin shiny under the bright fluorescent lights, entered the room where Stephen Barbee sat across the table from Detective Jamison.

"Stephen, I need to read you the Miranda warning," Carroll explained as he sat next to his fellow detective.

Both officers were casually dressed in slacks and sports shirts, while Barbee remained in his work attire of jeans and a white T-shirt.

"I understand," Barbee responded.

At that point the recording in the room down the hall began, as well as recording on a small, handheld black recorder placed on the table by Mike Carroll. Carroll excused himself, leaving Jamison and Barbee alone while he checked on Ron Dodd, who was with Detective McCaskill two doors down.

Barbee had an air of easiness about him, not showing any sign of internal nervousness. He leaned forward in the straight-back blue upholstered chair, resting his forearms on the table as he and the detective talked in an informal way about the night of February 19, only two days earlier.

"I went to Ron's because my truck wasn't working well. I'm not a mechanic, and I thought Ron could fix it," Barbee stated, explaining his whereabouts on the night in question. "Ron said it might be some bad gas and to take it and blow it out [on the highway].

"When I got home, Trish was asleep. The kids were asleep on the couch, so I laid down with them so as not to wake up Trish. She had surgery last week."

Jamison sat expressionless, letting Barbee go on with his story.

"I got up at seven and took a bath. I woke Trish up at seven and she was aggravated because it was so early. Then I got the kids up at ten till eight and we went to the dog place," Barbee stated, not explaining that the dog had been enrolled in a scheduled obedience class.

Barbee sat back in his chair, waiting for Jamison to make a comment, or to ask a question.

"You went out with Lisa Underwood, didn't you?" Jamison asked, getting right to Barbee's relationship with Lisa.

"Yeah, we had a couple of dates, just hung out," Barbee replied in a relaxed tone.

"When was the last time you had a date with Lisa?" Jamison asked.

"Several months ago," Barbee stated, moving slightly in his chair.

Jamison broached the subject of Lisa's baby and the possibility of who the child's father could be, if not Barbee himself.

"Did she say the child could be anybody else's?" Jamison inquired.

"Yeah, a guitar player in a rock band," Barbee stated.

The detective wanted to find out more about the women in Barbee's life and asked who else he had dated.

"I went out with a girl named Jennifer that lived across the hall, and Denise in Austin, a friend. I knew it would never work out with her. She's way down there," Barbee explained.

The detective returned to the subject of Lisa Underwood, trying to get Barbee to open up more about the extent of their relationship.

"I never stayed a night with Lisa. She was adamant about never meeting her son," Barbee said, informing the detective that Lisa had told him that Jayden had been hurt when a previous boyfriend had left her, and she didn't want another such episode. "I saw the boy at the bagel shop. I went in there, maybe six times. He was there waiting for school."

"How frequently did you communicate with Lisa?" Jamison inquired.

"Once a month, or once every other month, she'd call me," Barbee stated as he folded his arms, tucked his hands into his armpits, and leaned back in the chair. "I was in the process of getting with Trish. I was leaning more toward Trish than anybody."

Barbee smiled as he began to tell Jamison about a time when three of the women he was seeing all arrived at his apartment.

"Trish was there, Jennifer had brought over soup, and Lisa was beating on the door. I joked and called it 'my buffet line.' I was dating so many girls at once." Barbee laughed.

"When was the last time you saw Lisa in person?" Jamison asked.

"Several months ago, August 2005. I was traveling a

lot. We were cutting two hundred sixty-four miles of trees in Abilene," Barbee responded.

Jamison began to move the conversation to more immediate concerns. "Ever drive Lisa's car?" the detective asked.

"No, I think I rode in it once," Barbee stated.

"What were you wearing?" Jamison inquired.

"Jeans, shirt, boots," Barbee replied.

"What were you wearing when you went over to Ron's house that night?"

"Jeans, shirt, boots."

"Did you wear a jacket? It was cool that night."

Barbee thought momentarily. "Probably had a jacket."

"What kind?"

"Black," Barbee said, shrugging.

"Any logos?"

"Cowboy Cutters," Barbee replied, indicating the name of one of his companies that appeared on his and his employees' clothing.

Mike Carroll, who had quietly reentered the room while Jamison had been questioning Barbee, stated, "I see some scratch marks on your arms."

Barbee glanced at his forearms. He was unconcerned about the abrasions. It was one of the hazards of his business. His arms often showed signs of tree limbs scraping across his skin.

"We're going to take a picture of those, if you don't mind," Carroll said.

"No," Barbee answered as he watched Carroll again leave the small interview room and return moments later to sit by Jamison.

Carroll asked, "Steve, you were stopped in Denton County about three or three-thirty in the morning of the twentieth. How'd you get up there?"

"I was driving my truck," Barbee said, moving forward

in his chair slightly. "It was spitting and sputtering, so I called Ron and told him what it was doing. He told me to get it back on the highway and blow it out."

"What kind of truck was it?" Jamison asked.

"A Ford three-fifty."

Mike Carroll spoke up, referring to the rights read Barbee prior to the interview. "Steve, the Miranda warning is still on tape. How did you come in contact with the officer?"

"I was walking," Barbee said.

"Were you intoxicated?"

"No."

"What were you doing out there walking?" Carroll asked.

"I was mad," Barbee said, indicating frustration with his poorly running vehicle.

"Did you give the officer a name?" Carroll asked.

"David Weekley," Barbee said.

"Why?"

"I was mad and thought he was harassing me," Barbee replied, signs of stress beginning to show in his face.

Carroll continued his questioning concerning Barbee's contact with the Denton County deputy, with Barbee admitting that when the officer went to his vehicle, he took off running.

"Did you get back to the truck?" Carroll asked.

"No. Yeah. No," Barbee stammered.

"Did you get back to the truck?" Carroll repeated.

"No," Barbee replied, explaining the truck wouldn't start, so he called Ron Dodd to pick him up. Barbee told the detectives he returned to the truck the following day with a mechanic, who changed out the filters and managed to get the vehicle running.

"I didn't say anything about the police, 'cause I knew I'd get in trouble," Barbee stated, explaining why he hadn't mentioned the Denton County deputy in his earlier discussions with Jamison and Carroll.

"In trouble for murder," Carroll said accusingly.

"No!" Barbee said loudly as he rose, placing his hands flat on the desk and leaning into Jamison's space. "I didn't do this."

"Steve, there are lots of ways to explain this," Carroll said in a calm voice as he got to his feet.

"We'll stop tape and talk to Ron in the next room," Carroll stated.

Sitting in a room identical to the one his friend Stephen Barbee occupied just down the hall, Ron Dodd freely gave detectives his version of the events of February 19, implicating Stephen Barbee as the Underwoods' killer. According to Dodd, he dropped Barbee off at the home of Lisa Underwood and left to meet Teresa Barbee for dinner. Dodd continued by saying that later that evening Barbee called, stating he needed help and asking him to come to his aid in southern Denton County. When Dodd asked Barbee how he had gotten from Lisa's house to Denton County, Dodd said, Barbee told him he had driven Lisa's car.

Dodd expressed his shock and repugnance when he arrived and saw the lifeless bodies of Lisa and Jayden Underwood in the rear of Lisa's 2000 Dodge Durango. When asked if he was so repulsed by the senseless deaths, why he didn't call authorities, Dodd emphasized his close relationship with Barbee as both his friend and his employer. But Dodd denied he helped dig the shallow grave or cover the corpses.

Dodd was asked, "Where did y'all leave the bodies?"

"Out near Justin, off Highway 407, off of I-35 West," Dodd replied.

"Why would Stephen Barbee kill Lisa and Jayden?" Carroll asked.

"Because she was pregnant and threatening to tell Steve's new wife," Dodd stated flatly.

After further discussion of Barbee's relationship with Underwood, and events of the night Lisa and her son disappeared, Mike Carroll left Ron Dodd in the interview room and called Denton County authorities, giving them Dodd's vague directions of where to find the bodies of Lisa and Jayden. As that search began, Carroll returned to the room where Stephen Barbee was waiting.

Asked if he needed to use the restroom, Barbee said he did and was led down the hall, past the double doors he entered when he first arrived at the Tyler police station. Through the narrow windows of the heavy wooden doors, Barbee saw Trish surrounded by the children asleep on chairs beside her. Tears filled his eyes.

Barbee used one of the two wall-mounted urinals, washed his hands at one of the two sinks that stretched across the opposite wall, and dried them on paper towels from the metal dispenser. Carroll talked with Barbee in the restroom for close to an hour as the suspect began to reveal details of the night Lisa and Jayden died. Not anticipating the impromptu discussion, Carroll hadn't taken his handheld recorder with him. Barbee and Carroll then returned to the interview room, where Carroll's interrogation continued on tape.

"Can I talk to Trish?" Barbee asked, tears beginning to flow from his eyes.

"No, I don't want her to get all emotional and stuff, so let's get this done," Carroll responded.

Barbee grabbed a tissue from the box to his right, wiped the tears from his cheeks, and blew his nose.

"Let's get this done," Carroll stated.

Barbee snagged another tissue and again blew his nose as Carroll leaned in close. "You aren't going to get into that stuff with Ron, are you?" Carroll said in a low tone.

"No," Barbee replied, his head down.

As Carroll sat in the chair opposite his suspect, he said, "We've gone over your rights and you don't want an attorney, right?"

"I'd like one," Barbee stated with no conviction in his voice.

"You want one now?" Carroll asked, his voice elevated.

"Is that bad?" Barbee asked meekly.

Detective Carroll explained if Barbee *didn't* want an attorney, they could continue to talk, but if he *did,* their conversation would have to stop.

Barbee's weeping persisted as he pulled the last tissue from the box.

Failing to make a definitive request for an attorney, Barbee announced, "I want you to stop the tape and make a deal."

"What kind of deal do you want to make?" Carroll asked.

"I want to talk to the family."

"Whose family?" Carroll inquired.

"Lisa's. I've lost relatives myself, and I know how it feels," Barbee said through tears.

The detective indicated he would have to talk to the Underwood family to see if they would agree to speak to Barbee. He could make no promises. Then, returning to the focus of his interrogation, Carroll asked, "Ron took you to her house that night. What time?"

"Maybe around ten o'clock," Barbee replied.

"Did you have a key?" Carroll asked.

"No."

"She let you in?"

"Yes."

"What did she tell you about Trish? She wanted you to leave her?" Carroll continued.

"Yes," Barbee said softly, picking up one of the used tissues, which he had laid on the table, to wipe his nose again.

"You killed her," Carroll stated.

In a soft tone, barely audible, Barbee said, "Yes." He nodded his head and repeated his answer in a louder timbre, "Yes."

Barbee's soft weeping turned to sobs. His right hand was on his forehead and his face was turned downward. Barbee's body rose and fell with each moan.

"You said you buried the bodies and prayed for her," Carroll said.

"Yes," Barbee acknowledged.

"She let you in?"

"Yes."

"You sat down and talked to her. What happened?" Carroll pried.

"She kept throwing up everything about it. She'd tell Trish," Barbee said.

"What would she tell Trish?" Carroll asked.

"I don't know," Barbee said, his voice an octave higher as he talked through his whimpers.

"What happened?" Carroll prodded.

"I wanted to leave. She got mad and kicked me. That's what the bruises are from," Barbee said, rubbing his right leg.

"What did you do?" Carroll asked calmly.

"I bopped her in the nose. We were fistfighting," Barbee said, his head down, speaking between sobs. "Then I wrapped my arms around her, holding her down. I knew I did something wrong."

Barbee covered his face with both hands, his voice barely capable of being heard.

"The boy came out, screaming. I put them together, 'cause they needed to be together," Barbee explained.

"You put them in the back of the car?" Carroll prompted, eager to have Barbee tell them the location of the bodies.

"Yes."

"Did you take the 407 exit, off I-35?"

"Yes. Ron brought me a shovel," Barbee stated.

"That's when he saw the bodies?" Carroll asked.

"Yes."

"Then what?" Carroll asked, encouraging Barbee to continue with the story.

"I dug a little hole and I prayed," Barbee said.

"Did you put both of them in the same place?" Carroll asked.

"Yes."

"Did you put stuff over the bodies, or is it pretty obvious?" Carroll asked, attempting to get more detailed information for his fellow officers who were searching for the remains of Lisa and Jayden Underwood.

"Pretty obvious," Barbee replied.

"Did you get back on I-35?" Carroll asked.

"No."

"Where'd you take the car?"

"Down a muddy trail," Barbee said.

"Sitting there, straight up, or in the water?"

"Sitting there, not in the water," Barbee clarified.

"Where are the keys?" Carroll inquired.

"I left them in there," Barbee answered.

"Was the hatch up or down?" Carroll asked.

"Down. I was boxed in. There was a fence there," Barbee explained.

"Did you climb the fence?"

"No, it was open."

"Was the fence on the right or the left?" Carroll asked.

"On the right," Barbee said.

"Were there trees?"

"Yeah, trees all around. I called Ron to come get me. The police came up on me and I ran from them," Barbee stated.

"Where did you run? Into the woods?"

"Yeah," Barbee replied.

"Is that where you got scratched?" Carroll asked.

"No, from the tree work," Barbee stated, reiterating his earlier explanation of the scratches on his arms.

"Did you cut your pants?" Carroll inquired.

"Yeah, running through the briars," Barbee said.

"You told me you tried to clean up the blood," Carroll affirmed.

"Yeah."

"Hers?"

"Yeah."

"What about the boy?" Carroll asked.

Barbee sat for a moment without speaking, his head down, as he picked at his hands.

"No blood from him," Barbee stated. "I didn't hurt him. I just closed his mouth."

"Where was the blood?" Carroll asked.

"All around her. We were fighting and she was hitting me. I was trying to hold her down. I got on top of her and she quit moving, and I knew I'd made a mistake. I didn't mean to kill her. I was just trying to save my family, 'cause I love them very much. I didn't want them to find out, and she was going to tell them, no matter what." Barbee took a deep breath before continuing. "She kicked me, and I was trying to keep her from hitting me," Barbee said, moving his arms up and down in exasperated movements.

"Did you get a key and lock up her place?" Carroll asked.

"No. I went out the garage door," Barbee said.

Barbee sat silent for a moment, breathing deeply as the tears continued to stain his cheeks.

"I want to talk to them in court. I want to apologize in court," Barbee said, referring to the Underwood family, as he hung his head.

"I don't know," Carroll responded, shaking his head.

Mike Carroll had spoken to Sheila Underwood personally as his investigation began, and he understood the anger and the hurt she was feeling. He doubted the mother/grandmother of the victims would want to hear anything their killer had to say.

"I want to, 'cause I know they're hurting," Barbee persisted.

Winding down his interrogation, Carroll needed Barbee on tape stating he had been allowed to use the restroom and hadn't threatened him in any way. The statement on tape would ensure Carroll's integrity during the interview in the event Barbee later accused him of mistreatment. With Barbee answering yes, and no, respectively, Carroll told Barbee that he would let the Underwood family know of his request. Then, as he stood to leave the room, he asked if there was anything Barbee needed.

"I want some more Kleenex," Barbee said.

Barbee was alone in the small room, a scattering of used Kleenex across the table before him. He was left by himself to ponder the statements he had just made to the police.

Barbee stuffed each of the used tissues back into the empty box, then rested his head in his right hand as he took a drink from a paper cup. He cried, wiping his nose with his hand and then on his jeans.

Head down, Barbee ran his hands through his thick hair. His shoulders rose as he inhaled deeply, then fell sharply as he yelled out, "God Almighty, what have I done?"

8

As her husband was being questioned by Fort Worth detectives, Trish Barbee's phone rang at about 11:00 P.M.

"Hello," Trish answered.

"Trish, why haven't you answered my calls? I've been trying to reach you for hours," Teresa Barbee practically yelled into the phone.

"Tanner was playing games on the phone," Trish said. "What's going on?"

"Where are you?" Teresa asked.

"I'm at the Tyler police station with Stephen," Trish responded. "Why?"

"Trish, listen," Teresa said, "Stephen is the father of Lisa Underwood's baby. That's why the cops are talking to him."

Trish Barbee's face lost all color. Her breathing became labored.

"What?" Trish asked. "There must be some mistake."

"No. Lisa was pregnant by Stephen," Teresa said.

Trish sank into a seat next to her children. "No," she said. "No. He couldn't be."

* * *

Mike Carroll took a box of tissues to Stephen Barbee, as he'd requested, and asked, "Do you want to see Trish?"

"Yes," Barbee sniffled.

For several minutes Barbee sat alone, mumbling to himself.

Nearly two hours after Trish received Teresa's phone call, Detective Mike Carroll went to the police department lobby and asked if she'd like to see her husband.

"Is it true?" Trish asked. "Is Stephen really the father of that woman's baby?"

"Yes," Mike Carroll answered. "Trish, Stephen confessed to killing Lisa Underwood."

"No!" Trish screamed. "No! He couldn't. He wouldn't."

"He wants to talk to you," Carroll said.

Trish Barbee wasn't sure she wanted to talk to her husband, except she had to know the truth. She had to ask Stephen why.

Trish approached the interview room with anger mixed with confusion. She opened the door and entered the room, where her husband sat alone, crying.

Slamming a box of Kleenex down on the desk, Trish sat down hard in the chair once occupied by Mike Carroll, opposite her husband.

"I'm sorry. My life's over," Barbee said through tears.

"What did you do? What did you do? *What did you do?*" Trish asked, her voice louder with each question.

"I don't know," Barbee whined.

"You killed her!" Trish yelled.

Trish rested her head on her left arm, which lay across the desk beside her. She sobbed loudly, her upper body rising and falling with each breath.

"I didn't mean to," Barbee said between moans. "She threatened me. She started kickin' me, and I held her."

Trish rose from her seat, went to her husband, and straddled him as she sat in his lap facing him. She buried her face against his shoulder. The couple clung tightly to one another, with Barbee's face pressed against the front of his wife's long white T-shirt and his hands on the back of her blue jean shorts. The couple spoke muffled words. Each cried uncontrollably. The entire tragic scene was caught on tape in the video room just down the hall.

After several minutes Barbee lifted Trish and transferred her weight to his right leg.

"She started fightin' me. I didn't mean to," Barbee whimpered.

"I know," Trish consoled her husband as she stroked his head.

"I don't know what to do. They're going to kill me," Barbee said.

The words brought on deeper sobs from both Trish and Barbee. They tightened their holds on each other, with Barbee knotting the back of Trish's T-shirt in his fists. The crying lasted several minutes before Trish asked, "What are we going to do?"

"I don't know," her husband said.

Trish held Barbee's head to her chest, rocking back and forth as she cried. She turned, took a Kleenex from the box, blew her nose, and tossed the tissue to the floor.

"God, Steve. Oh, God," Trish moaned, her breaths quick and deep as if she were about to hyperventilate.

Barbee's arms encircled his wife's waist as she again rubbed his head and they gently swayed. Barbee spoke to Trish, but the words could not be made out later when the tape was reviewed by police.

"Please forgive me. *Pleeeeeeease.* Please don't leave me. Please don't leave me," Barbee begged.

"Why did you cheat on me?" Trish asked between sobs.

"I didn't, sweetie," Barbee said.

"She was eight months pregnant. You were with me eight

months ago. How could you do that?" Trish asked, hurt in her voice.

Stephen Barbee failed to give his wife an answer. There would be time to talk later; time to tell Trish he didn't think the baby was his; time to explain that he had chosen her over Lisa.

The Barbees remained tightly joined as Mike Carroll entered the room.

"What's going to happen to me?" Stephen Barbee asked.

"We have to put you in jail and you'll be arraigned. I'll tell the DA you were very cooperative. If you can make bond, you can get out. Otherwise, you'll sit in county jail until you go to trial. It's not like you see on TV. The new jail in Tarrant County has single cells and no bars," Carroll explained.

Although he had never been arrested before, Barbee was acquainted with the facility. Cowboy Cutters, his concrete-cutting company, was a subcontractor currently working a job at the jail facility. Ironically, Barbee had a photo ID allowing him access to the downtown jail, adjacent to the Justice Center next door.

Mike Carroll's phone rang, and he left the Barbees alone as he took the call.

"What am I going to tell your mom and dad?" Trish asked. "What am I supposed to do, Steve? They're going to take you from me. I can't sleep at night without you there."

"I'm so sorry," Barbee said in an effort to console his wife. "I'm sorry."

Trish kissed his forehead gently. "The kids love you so much," she said.

The Barbees sat silently for a few moments; then Trish moaned. "I can't go home, Steve. I can't go home."

Barbee wailed loudly as if an animal in pain.

"Oh, my God!" Trish said, gasping.

Once Barbee regained composure, he told Trish, "I need to talk to them people. I didn't mean to do it."

The two sat quietly with Barbee's head buried against his wife's chest until Detective Carroll again entered the room. He looked at Trish, who shrugged her shoulders. She had nothing to say to Detective Carroll.

"Steve, you need to come with me. If you want to stay here, you can," he said, looking to Trish.

"No, I want to go. Do you have the truck keys?" Trish asked her husband.

Trish stood as Barbee rose. He shoved his right hand into the pocket of his jeans. He pulled out a set of keys and handed them to Trish.

Trish picked up the box of tissues and left the room without another word. Stephen Barbee remained, his head in his hands, sobbing.

During the hours Stephen Barbee had been trimming trees along the highways of Smith and Rusk Counties, and being questioned by the Fort Worth detectives, other Fort Worth officers had been busy searching the residences of both Barbee and Ron Dodd. They confiscated a shovel and other items deemed to be of evidentiary value.

Once the raids on both houses were complete, an arrest warrant was prepared by Detective Dick Gallaway, then signed by a Tarrant County judge for execution.

The initials RAG, representing Richard Gallaway, appeared at the bottom of the third page of the arrest warrant.

With the document prepared and signed by a Tarrant County judge, it was ready to be executed. In addition to authorizing the warrant, the judge set bail at $2 million.

This was a sum that would be impossible for the Barbees to raise.

Detectives Carroll, Jamison, and McCaskill were notified of the signed arrest warrant and instructed to take Stephen Barbee into custody in Tyler for the murders of Lisa and Jayden Underwood.

9

After leaving the interview room, Trish Barbee spoke to Mike Carroll in the hallway.

"Trish, would you like for us to put you and the kids in a motel room for the night? Your family can come pick you up tomorrow," Carroll offered.

Trish's mind was whirling from the shock of learning her husband had not only impregnated Lisa Underwood, but had also killed her. The newlywed still couldn't bring herself to accept that her husband, who had been so gentle and loving to her and her children, had taken the life of a mother.

Tired and emotionally spent, Trish agreed to go to a motel for the night.

In the meantime Stephen Barbee was officially taken into custody and transported to the Smith County Jail.

The jail, only a few blocks from the police department, was just off the main street of downtown Tyler. A uniformed Tyler patrolman was enlisted to escort Barbee. The officer steered his patrol car through the jail's secure sally port. He

then led Barbee into the small entrance hall of the county
jail through a secure side entrance. At 3:15 A.M., Barbee
was fingerprinted, booked, and led to a holding cell, just
steps from the book-in area. Barbee would remain there
until later that morning, when he would be taken back to
Fort Worth.

Ron Dodd was arrested for violating his parole from a
1997 aggravated assault conviction. Dodd, like Barbee,
would be transferred to the Tarrant County Jail. But Ron
Dodd would be held without bond.

Once Mike Carroll knew Trish Barbee and her children
were comfortably settled at a local motel, and Stephen
Barbee was secure in a Smith County cell, he settled down
in the Tyler Police Department bunk room. The bed was
small and generally uncomfortable, but it had been a long
and exhausting day. Within minutes Carroll was sound
asleep.

As Barbee stressed in jail over decisions he had made and
actions taken the year leading up to his arrest for murder,
Denton County authorities began hunting for the grave site
described by both Barbee and Dodd. During one of the
breaks in Barbee's interrogation, Mike Carroll had phoned
his supervisor and notified him that a search should begin
off Exit 407 and Interstate 35W toward Justin.

Officers on horseback and others using bloodhounds concentrated on probing the area described by Carroll. If it was
located, the Denton County authorities would secure the scene
and wait to turn over the excavation to Fort Worth police. After
all, it was the FWPD's case, and they wouldn't infringe

on their jurisdiction or later be accused of mishandling a crime scene.

About three hours after falling asleep, at 6:00 A.M., Carroll was awakened by a Tarrant County fugitive retrieval officer. Carroll had ridden to Tyler with Detective Mc-Caskill, but since McCaskill had returned to Fort Worth earlier in the evening, Carroll had been left stranded. The fugitive officer, already in the area, agreed to transport both Carroll and Barbee back to Tarrant County.

It was two hours later before the detective and his suspect were on their way. Barbee first had to be arraigned by a Smith County judge, since he had been booked into their local jail.

At the same time that Barbee stood in front of the Tyler judge, educators at North Riverside Elementary School prepared to answer tough questions from Jayden's classmates as they returned to school.

Barbee climbed into the rear seat of Officer Mark Thornhill's police department truck, with Carroll taking the front passenger seat next to Thornhill.

"How was the food at the jail?" Carroll asked. "Do you want something to eat?"

"No," Barbee replied.

As Thornhill drove the truck down Interstate 20, Barbee and Carroll made small talk for a long while, with Barbee talking mostly about Trish and his family. Then he began to express concerns about going to the grave site, as he had agreed to do the night before.

"I don't want to see the bodies," Barbee said. "And I don't want to be seen by the media," he added.

"You won't have to see the bodies, and I'll make sure

the media isn't present when we arrive at the scene," Carroll promised.

As Thornhill entered southeast Tarrant County, he turned off Interstate 20 onto Highway 287, traveling north past downtown Fort Worth.

Carroll knew there were officers on the scene, and he suspected that the media was already in the area as well. He texted his sergeant to let him know they were close by. The plan was for the sergeant to get the media out of there so that Barbee wouldn't be seen.

As the truck approached Interstate 35, their planned route, Barbee said, "No, take this street," pointing to another roadway that would take them a back way to the location.

Directed by Barbee, Thornhill guided his truck through a gate.

"To your left will be two barbed-wire fences," Barbee directed. "Over the second barbed-wire fence will be a fresh dug grave, with a mound of shrubbery on top."

They drove a little to the left, as Barbee instructed; then Carroll noticed a mound of limbs and twigs, and a little farther down was a second stack.

At first, Barbee indicated it was the first pile of shrubbery, but then he shouted, "Wait! Wait! Go farther down."

Reaching the second mass of dried debris, Barbee decided it was the first and instructed Thornhill to back up. At that point Carroll exited the truck, climbed over the barbed-wire fence, and began to walk the area.

Officer Thornhill stood near the truck, relaying instructions to Carroll from Barbee, who remained inside the truck.

"Walk farther to your left," Barbee shouted, with Thornhill repeating the direction for Carroll to walk back toward the first of the two mounds.

Carroll surveyed the stack of twigs, limbs, and dried

brush to determine if it was indeed the grave site Barbee had described.

Small limbs, twigs, and underbrush covered the spot, but one telltale sign peeped through the dried vegetation suggesting that the pile held a deadly secret: a speck of red that appeared to be out of place amongst the brown foliage. Upon closer examination it was discovered the red spot was the polished nail of a person's big toe.

Hearing the hum of a helicopter approaching, Carroll knew the media would be there soon.

"I want you to drive him to the Mansfield Jail," Carroll told Thornhill.

By the time the helicopter was overhead, Thornhill and Barbee were well on their way to Mansfield.

With Dick Gallaway in charge, the unearthing of the grave began. A number of officers stood by as the layers of brush were painstakingly removed, and a thin coating of dirt covering the corpses of two bodies eventually exposed: one large frame, one small. A crime scene investigator, with blue latex gloves protecting her hands, as well as the crime scene, carefully brushed away dirt with a blue-handled brush, exposing the left side of the head of Jayden Underwood.

Just as Stephen Barbee had indicated, Jayden Underwood lay atop his mother, his head resting on her shoulder. The sight of the two bodies was an emotional knife that pierced the hearts of the seasoned policemen who gathered around the makeshift grave.

With news helicopters hovering overhead, Lisa's and Jayden's bodies were carefully removed from the site and transported to the Tarrant County Medical Examiner's Office on Feliks Gwozdz Place in Fort Worth. There, positive identifications would be made and the exact cause of death determined.

With the discovery of the bodies of Lisa and Jayden

Underwood, the AMBER Alert was canceled, and the detectives set about the work of putting together a case that would be presented to the Tarrant County district attorney (DA) for prosecution.

That night, about two hundred people gathered for a candlelight vigil outside Boopa's Bagel Deli. Dozens of flower bouquets, balloons, and cards, along with photos of Lisa and Jayden, filled the sidewalk and rested against the threshold of the store. The mood was somber. The crowd quiet. The hopes they had held for finding their friends and loved ones alive had been shattered.

"It's devastating. Lisa never did anything to hurt anybody," one mourner said, sobbing.

The murders of Lisa and Jayden Underwood had made national news. On Nancy Grace's cable-TV program, she interviewed Lieutenant Gene Jones, the Fort Worth Police Department spokesman.

"We were personally invested in this case. We were motivated by these two individuals. That's what drove us," Jones said.

Nancy Grace showed the scene at Boopa's Bagel Deli and the makeshift memorial that mourners had made. Then Grace changed to a shot of the place where the bodies were found.

"Can you imagine that? That's where those two people were laid to rest—a mother and son," Grace reported.

A discussion ensued between Grace and Ed Lavadera, a CNN correspondent, concerning Ron Dodd and his role in the Underwoods' homicides.

"What had generated all the buzz around Ron Dodd today is that, according to reports, Dodd would have known about the murders Friday or Saturday morning and never called authorities," Lavadera said.

"I just can't believe it. Somebody opens a trunk of a car

and there's a dead pregnant woman and a little boy. And this guy goes, 'Sure, I'll get you something [to bury them],'" Grace said with her familiar sarcasm.

As Nancy Grace went to break before switching to a discussion of Michael Jackson's molestation trial, the camera again revealed the soggy, shallow grave where Lisa and Jayden were buried, then switched to the makeshift memorial.

Grace signed off, saying, "That's what's left of Lisa and Jayden."

10

While Barbee waited in the jail in Mansfield to learn what would happen next, the bodies of Lisa and Jayden Underwood were taken to the Tarrant County Medical Examiner's District Morgue in the southern section of Fort Worth.

The injuries of both victims would be documented by written reports and photographs. The highly respected medical examiner's office would present their findings as to the exact cause of death to Detective Gallaway, who, in turn, would notify the Tarrant County District Attorney's Office, in preparation for a possible trial.

Lisa Underwood was the first to be laid on the ME's autopsy table, at 6:00 P.M., February 22, 2005. Under the bright lights of the examination room, the thirty-four-year-old white female showed visible signs of an immense struggle for her life.

Dr. Marc Krouse, the chief deputy medical examiner, recorded the body as being clothed in a partially displaced T-shirt, stained with blood. Her white underpants were found around her knees, and gray-colored sleep pants were beneath her body. A pair of eyeglasses, missing a left lens, was entangled in her hair.

Dr. Krouse had first seen Lisa Underwood three hours earlier, when it was determined that initial rigor mortis was fading and bruising over the posterior body surfaces was uniformly purple.

As the victim's body was cleaned and examined more closely by the veteran ME, it was noted that Lisa had a heart tattooed on her right breast, a flower tattoo on her left lower abdomen, a cartoon dove on her left shoulder, and a pink-colored triangle on the lower left calf. Her long, straight brown hair was dyed blond. She also had two healed piercings in each ear.

Dried blood was observed in Lisa's nose and mouth, as well as superficial lacerations to her mouth. Lisa's gray eyes were closed, but when opened by Dr. Krouse, he noted that the left cornea was cloudy, while the right was clear.

Bruises and abrasions covered Lisa's five-four frame and revealed multiple blunt-force traumatic injuries to the head, face, back, and extremities. She also showed hemorrhaging of the soft tissue of the neck. At the time of her death, Lisa Underwood weighed 174 pounds and appeared to be approximately eight months pregnant.

Lisa had undergone a severe beating, but she had not been sexually assaulted. It was obvious that rape had not been a motive in the death of the young woman.

Dr. Krouse noted a one-half-inch contusion on Lisa's lower lip that ran downward at an angle. There were also multiple lacerations of the mouth, more prominent on the left side of her face than the right. An abrasion, measuring three-fourths of an inch by one-fourth of an inch, ran vertically on the right side of her face. Lisa's left eye was severely swollen, and a dark bruise covered the entire upper lid, as well as a significant portion under her eye. A general hemorrhage, or reddening of the skin, appeared on her left cheek with more hemorrhaging on the right. The beating experienced by Lisa Underwood had obviously been painful and intense.

As the medical examiner continued his assessment, he observed a bruise, three inches by three inches, on Lisa's upper right arm, and another, half that size, just above the elbow. Multiple contusions covered her wrists, and the right wrist itself was broken, along with her right thumb. Lisa Underwood had put up a fight.

In addition to the wounds Lisa suffered prior to her death, postmortem injuries were also present. The majority of those after-death injuries were more than likely sustained when her body was dragged through the rough ground to the makeshift grave. Numerous postmortem abrasions appeared on the nose, neck, upper arms, and wrists. Additional abrasions were scattered across her back, over the shoulders, buttocks, thighs, right knee, left calf and ankle, and both feet. There were even signs of scraping under the elastic waistband of Lisa's underpants.

Dr. Krouse found no abnormalities of Lisa Underwood's cardiovascular, pulmonary, central nervous, or gastrointestinal systems, nor the kidneys or thyroid. Lisa's brain revealed only mild swelling. Lisa Underwood appeared to be in perfect health at the time of her death.

Next, gently and with respect, Dr. Krouse removed Lisa's baby from her uterine cavity. Gestation was estimated at seven and a half months. Baby Marleigh weighed only three pounds and six ounces, and was just eleven inches long. She was a tiny, perfectly formed bundle in the large hands of Dr. Krouse. Brown hair topped the baby's flawlessly shaped head, and she had all ten fingers and ten toes. There was no external evidence of fetal injury. Marleigh was beautiful and, like her mother, was healthy at the time of her death.

Marleigh was cleaned, and both palm prints and footprints were taken. Tissue samples were reserved, along with two blood cards. At a later date DNA testing would be done.

Dr. Krouse secured blood samples from Lisa Underwood for toxicology testing, which would later come back negative for alcohol and all drugs—except an analgesic, such as aspirin.

Also collected for evidence from Lisa were scalp hair, nail cuttings, a sexual assault kit (swabs), her larynx and hyoid, fingerprints, and her clothing. These items would be held for authorities, along with Dr. Krouse's report that stated the cause of Lisa Underwood's death was traumatic asphyxiation. The manner of death was homicide.

Dr. Krouse returned to the county morgue the next morning to autopsy Jayden Underwood. At 10:40 A.M., on February 23, 2005, Dr. Krouse began his examination of the seven-year-old boy who lay on the stainless-steel table of the morgue.

The medical examiner began by noting that Jayden's clothing had been removed by trace evidence technicians during the course of processing the body.

The boy's nude body was weighed, measured, and scanned for initial findings. Dr. Krouse later wrote that Jayden was a normally nourished and developed white boy, forty-seven inches in height and weighing sixty-seven pounds. The boy appeared to be age seven, as had been previously stated to the ME.

Jayden's body showed signs of early decomposition, with red-purple and blue-purple discoloration on his skin. The corneas of his eyes were clouded. Jayden's straight brown hair was four inches long. The boy had two stainless-steel crowns on two right upper molars, and the remaining teeth were in good condition. Clearly, the mother had made certain her child had regular dental care.

Curiously, there was moisture wrinkling of the skin of both hands and feet.

As Dr. Krouse began to examine the boy's injuries, he observed red-purple contusions on the upper left back, as well as one on the upper right back, just below the top of the shoulder. Scratches, no more than two inches in length, were scattered in various directions over the back of the right arm and forearm. Several abrasions were located on the child's lower back, and a few scattered scratches were in multiple directions over his right buttocks, and one was on the back of his right calf.

Jayden's right eye was dark red-purple and blue-purple, with the bruise extending to his left forehead and into the scalp. A small amount of blood had seeped from beneath his lower eyelid.

In addition to Jayden's other facial injuries, there was a bruise three-and-a-half inches by four inches in the right temporal region. He also had suffered contusions of both lips, with a small amount of blood present in his mouth. Like his mother, the boy had suffered quite a beating.

As with Lisa Underwood, Dr. Krouse found no abnormalities within Jayden Underwood's body. He was healthy, except for some congestion, at the time of his death.

Dr. Krouse took blood, urine, and tissue samples for further examination, but they revealed no irregularities.

Jayden Underwood also died from asphyxia by smothering, and the manner of death was homicide.

News of the arrest of Stephen Barbee stormed through Dallas/Fort Worth newsrooms. Every reporter rushed to get the first interviews with Barbee's family, friends, neighbors—

anyone who might be able to give them information concerning Stephen Barbee and some inkling as to why he would kill a mother and child.

Reporters also made attempts to contact Sheila Underwood, but like Barbee's mother, Lisa's mother also avoided the press. Sheila had no desire to grieve in public, and no intention of talking to the media about her daughter and grandson, or the monster she believed killed them. She remained in close contact with detectives, but she never spoke publicly about the murders.

Jackie Barbee, bombarded by the media, finally refused to answer her door and only reluctantly took phone calls, hoping it would be Stephen phoning from the county jail. Barbee called his mother as much as he could, three to four times a day, whenever he could secure the phone he shared with other inmates. But as stressful as the persistence of the media was, Jackie was more concerned about her husband, Bill. Bill hadn't been feeling good for some time; he was losing weight and had no energy.

On the day of Lisa and Jayden's murders, Bill had been diagnosed with cancer. Jackie had called Stephen to give him the disturbing news, but it was Trish who had answered the phone. When Jackie was told her son wasn't at home, she informed her new daughter-in-law of Bill's condition.

"Please don't tell Stephen," Jackie urged Trish. "I want to tell him myself."

But Trish hadn't heeded her mother-in-law's request, telling Stephen later that day of his father's ill health.

As expected, Stephen was devastated by the news. His family was dying before his eyes—first his brother and sister; now his father. Stephen also knew his mother was in poor health, suffering from diabetes. He clung more tightly to Trish, Tanner, and Taylor, hoping not to lose them as well, fearing the news of Lisa's baby would destroy what family he had left.

Sitting in her home office in Indiana, Tina Church answered a phone call from a friend in Texas. Church, a private investigator and founder of The Other Victims Advocacy (TOVA), was known to many death row families. The friend who called had gotten close to Church when Church intervened on behalf of her son. Church had managed to secure him a stay of execution, based on a claim of mental retardation.

As she had done with so many families of defendants, Church called Jackie Barbee. Church knew it was imperative for the Barbees to get help for their son as soon as possible. But Jackie Barbee, having been flooded with phone calls from the media, refused to talk to Church.

Refusals of cooperation seldom deterred Church from her goal. Church had founded TOVA in the belief that the families of those accused were victims themselves. She was sincere in her belief that they were not to blame for the acts of others, yet often experienced undue persecution. Church was well aware that families seldom, if ever, knew how the justice system worked and, therefore, could not be effective in the defense. She was also a strong opponent of the death penalty.

It was Church's goal to help the Barbees from the time Stephen Barbee had been arrested, through the time of his execution, if that was his fate. Along the way Church would work on looking for glitches in the investigation, request further DNA testing, if the need presented itself, speak with experts on aspects of the case, or perhaps find some other legal relief for the defendant.

Undeterred by Jackie Barbee's refusal to speak, Church immediately phoned John Niland, of the Texas Defender Service, to solicit help for Stephen Barbee.

Jackie Barbee began to hear of efforts made by Church on behalf of her son when a call came in from Pam Davis, of Fort Worth.

"I know Tina Church very well," Pam told Jackie. "She pulled my son off the gurney."

It was enough to convince Jackie to talk to the Indiana advocate.

The next time Church contacted the Barbees, Jackie was willing to listen. Church began to educate Jackie about the system and what actions should be taken.

The number one thing the Barbees wanted was Stephen released from jail. They yearned to have him home, where they could care for him and shield him from the unpleasantness of the jail noises, which persisted twenty-four hours a day, the unpalatable food, and the taunting of fellow prisoners. But wishing for his release wasn't going to bring Stephen to their Azle home. It would take $200,000, 10 percent of the $2 million bond set by the Tyler judge.

There was no way the modest Barbee family could possibly raise that kind of money. Stephen had given up any claim to the Haslet house to his ex-wife and the businesses were in both names. Jackie and Bill Barbee had to resign themselves to the fact that their son would be condemned to the Tarrant County Jail until his trial, at which time they were certain he would be exonerated.

11

Thirty-nine-year-old Trish Barbee was having a difficult time accepting the arrest of her husband, and an even tougher time believing he had killed not just Lisa, but also Jayden Underwood. Trish saw her life, the life she believed she was building with Stephen, rapidly unraveling.

In an interview just three days after Stephen's arrest, Trish spoke with local media, declaring her love and support for her husband.

"No matter what Stephen has been accused of, I still love him," Trish told reporters, tears glistening in her eyes.

"Stephen is a gentle man who only wanted to make me and my two children happy. He often told friends I was the love of his life. He wouldn't give me up for anything. He's a wonderful man. An angel," Trish said, choking back sobs.

Wiping tears from her face, Trish added, "I don't think he did this. He's the sweetest thing in the world."

When asked about her husband's relationship with Ms. Underwood, Trish Barbee stated, "My husband dated Ms. Underwood a long time ago. Stephen doesn't believe he is the father of Ms. Underwood's unborn child.

"She wouldn't go away. He kept telling her to go away and she wouldn't go away," Trish attempted to explain.

Trish privately recalled the night at the Tyler PD when Stephen cried in her arms and asked for forgiveness. She wasn't emotionally strong, and she felt lonely and abandoned. Waiting for her husband's trial would be a test of her loyalty and affection.

While Trish Barbee pined publicly over the absence of her husband and his arrest for murder, Sheila Underwood was grieving privately.

Detective Carroll kept her advised of any new developments in the case and had called on Thursday to let her know Lisa's purse had been found by divers in a creek, near where Lisa and Jayden had been found.

Sheila had given Lisa the tannish brown Dooney & Bourke purse as a gift. Sheila loved handbags, had collected dozens, and often presented her daughter with one of her recent "finds." The notice of the purse being found only brought back more memories for Sheila, and more grief.

Sheila was surrounded by family and friends, but nothing could console the grieving mother and grandmother. She had the daunting task of planning a funeral for her child and grandchild, something no one ever anticipates having to face. True to herself, Sheila chose a private service, announced by a spokeswoman, and continued to elude the press and persisted in mourning in private.

Knowing there were many friends and customers of Boopa's that would want to say good-bye, Sheila and Holly decided on a public reception at the business for all those close to Lisa and Jayden.

* * *

In Mansfield, Texas, a city in southeast Tarrant County, which, in the last one hundred years, had transformed from a rural community to a thriving suburb of fifty thousand, Barbee was held in a small detention center. He would later be transferred to the main county jail in downtown Fort Worth. It was in Mansfield that Barbee had the first opportunity to visit with his mother and father, to see their tormented faces, and to experience their pain firsthand.

From behind her glasses, tears streamed from Jackie Barbee's eyes when she saw her son. It was heartbreaking for Jackie to see Stephen, dressed in dingy jail garb, behind the secure glass window. It was unimaginable that he had been charged with the murders of a pregnant woman and child.

"Stephen, I love you," Jackie cried.

"Mom, I love you too. It's not like it seems, Mom. I didn't do what they said," Stephen exclaimed.

"But, Stephen," Jackie sobbed, "the police said you told them you killed those people."

Standing beside Jackie, Stephen's father looked frail and sorrowful. He listened closely to his son's response.

"They told me if I said it was an accident, I'd be able to go home," Stephen moaned. "I just wanted to go home."

"Stephen, what happened?" his mother begged to know.

"It was Ron. Ron did it," Barbee told his parents. "I made a big mistake. I should have called the police," Stephen whimpered.

Jackie Barbee couldn't stop the flow of tears that poured from her eyes. Stephen was her only living child. She couldn't endure losing him.

Barbee hated seeing his mother in such pain and he would do anything to spare her the heartache he saw in her loving face.

Barbee's mother wasn't the only one to whom he told it was Ron Dodd who had taken the lives of Lisa and Jayden.

He also told his ex-wife when she visited him in Mansfield, insisting, over and over, that it was Ron Dodd, Teresa's fiancé, who had killed the Underwoods.

Barbee didn't know if Teresa believed him, or if she ever suspected her live-in boyfriend, but it appeared she was more interested in taking over the businesses they had run together than in supporting either of them.

During the few days that Barbee was held in Mansfield, Teresa went to him, asking him to sign over to her all interests in the businesses they owned.

"Stephen, people will be suing us. We'll lose our state contracts. You have to sign the businesses over to me," Teresa insisted.

Teresa's long, dark hair fell around her face as she learned forward to take papers from a case. She had prepared documents for Barbee to sign that would give her full control of both Cowboy Cutters and Four Seasons.

Confused, scared, and suffering from frequent migraines that impaired his thinking, Barbee did as his first wife asked.

Three days later, Chris Edmondson, a spokesman for Teresa Barbee, announced to reporters, "Cowboy Cutters LLC and Teresa Barbee would like to express their shock, sadness, and dismay at the disgusting and despicable events that took place."

Edmondson stated that Teresa Barbee had been running the daily operations of the business, which had been divided between the two during their 2003 divorce, and that Stephen Barbee hadn't been active in the company recently.

"He'd come by every once in a while and pick up a paycheck," Jeanne Crowell, construction coordinator for the firm, added.

The statements pierced the heart of Stephen Barbee. He had been an intricate part of building the business. After all, it was he who had worked for the company before buying it, and he who had been on the Tarrant County Jail job, as well as the Dallas Water Treatment Plant job only a month earlier.

It was while Barbee had been on the Dallas Water Treatment job that he had been struck in the head with a twenty-foot-long, four-hundred-pound steel beam. Barbee had instructed Dodd to pull the guidelines tight to secure the plank while he directed it into place. But Dodd had released the line, sending the beam crashing into Barbee's head, shattering his hard hat, and causing him severe pain. Barbee had been suffering from acute headaches since the event. Now, as he sat in a lonely jail cell, Barbee wondered if the incident had truly been an accident, or had his friend and employee deliberately let go of the line? Had Dodd actually tried to kill him? And was Teresa a part of the plan so she could take over the businesses and have Ron take his place?

Stephen Barbee's whole world was falling apart. In desperation he sent word to Detective Carroll that he had to talk to him.

Barbee sought to tell Carroll that he didn't want to plead guilty. He wanted to tell Carroll that it was Ron Dodd who had committed the murders. But Carroll never returned to Mansfield to give Barbee a chance to recant his initial statements.

Within days, Stephen Barbee was transferred from Mansfield to the jail in Fort Worth, where he would wait until trial. He was placed in a single cell for his own protection. During those first days of his incarceration, Stephen Barbee requested a court-appointed attorney to represent him. The court believed he was not indigent and not eligible for provided counsel. After all, Barbee was co-owner of two seemingly successful businesses, drove a Ford Explorer and a Chevrolet Corvette. Judge Robert Gill denied his request.

It was more than a week before it was learned that Stephen Barbee, who had signed full ownership of his businesses to Teresa, had no access to any funds to help with his defense. At that time Bill Ray was appointed to represent Barbee. Since Barbee had been charged with capital murder, with multiple victims, Texas law provided that two attorneys represent him. Tim Moore was assigned to assist.

William "Bill" H. Ray served as president of the Tarrant County Criminal Defense Lawyers Association and had worked as a special prosecutor for the Tarrant County District Attorney's Office in the past.

Born in Waco, Texas, in 1950, Moore was a member of the Fort Worth law firm of Evans, Daniel, Moore, and Evans. He had graduated from the University of Texas in 1974 and the South Texas College of Law in 1985. Moore had served with the Tarrant County District Attorney's Office from 1985 to 1988 before entering private practice, where he specialized in criminal law.

On the other side of the aisle, Tarrant County deputy chief assistant district attorney Greg Miller had reviewed the list of assistant prosecutors under his tutelage and selected Kevin Rousseau to head the prosecution of Stephen Barbee. Rousseau, like Miller, had obtained his undergraduate degree from the University of Texas at Arlington. Rousseau, like Moore, had then gone on to secure a law degree from South Texas College of Law in Houston. He had spent fourteen years with the Tarrant County District Attorney's Office.

Miller considered Rousseau his best court chief, and knew he could always count on him to prepare thoroughly and to present the case effectively.

Rousseau, a tall, lean man, was known for his tenacity and, by his own admission, a "smart-ass" attitude in the courtroom. Rousseau often boasted that sarcasm was his weapon of choice. When given the word by Miller that he would be heading the court case against Barbee, he relished the opportunity to present the case to a jury.

Miller and Rousseau discussed who would be Rousseau's trial partner. Miller believed there should be a female prosecutor on the case, and Rousseau selected Dixie Bersano. Bersano was an attractive blonde with unique law experience. She was a tough assistant district attorney (ADA) who was, at the time, working in the Crimes Against Children division of the DA's office.

Bersano had begun her career at the Arlington Police Department (Arlington PD). After seventeen years, she left as the sergeant over homicide to attend Baylor University School of Law in Waco, Texas. Miller had sat in on Bersano's interview at the DA's office, and was so impressed with her that he went to see Tim Curry, Tarrant County district attorney, and told him he needed to hire Bersano before some other DA's office snapped her up.

Miller was pleased with the team of Rousseau and Bersano. He was certain they would be formidable, as well as compassionate, during the prosecution of Stephen Barbee.

Once appointed to represent Stephen Barbee, Bill Ray and Tim Moore immediately began to file motions with the court on behalf of their client. Their first acts were to file a constitutional motion for a speedy trial, a motion for discovery, including expert witnesses to be called by the prosecution, and a motion for appointment of an investigator for the defense. Ray was taking initial steps to secure the fundamentals needed to defend Barbee. Later, Ray would file a motion to allow him to review the grand jury transcript, and another to examine the physical evidence gathered against his client.

Stephen Barbee, however, was dissatisfied with his attorneys' performances.

When either or both Bill Ray and Tim Moore would visit Barbee at the county jail, Barbee felt intimidated by the attorneys. He sensed they were not committed to defending him against the charges of capital murder. And when he questioned their tactics, Barbee felt they became hostile toward him. They didn't believe him when he denied the killings and accused Ron Dodd. Barbee lost all confidence in his attorneys' abilities, or desires, to fight for him in court.

On July 7, 2005, four and a half months after Barbee's arrest, Judge Robert Gill received a letter from Stephen Barbee, where Barbee expressed great reservations about his court-appointed attorneys, Bill Ray and Tim Moore. He claimed that Ray and Moore made it impossible for him to contribute to his defense. He thought that the attorneys were rude and belligerent toward him, and he speculated that their heavy caseloads would prevent them from spending an adequate amount of time on his defense.

Barbee sent copies of his letter to the criminal court of appeals, the Texas State Bar Association, attorney Bill Ray, and attorney Tim Moore. In addition, Barbee sent letters to Bill Ray, asking that he utilize the services of a Denver, Colorado, law firm and John Niland, with the Texas Defender Service, in his defense, as Tina Church had suggested.

Receiving no response from either the court or his attorneys, but feeling that the hostility from his lawyers had increased, Barbee again wrote Judge Gill, on September 19, 2005, asking that his attorneys be dismissed. He cited a breakdown in communications as cause for his request.

Apparently angered by his client's letters to the judge, Bill Ray arrived at the Tarrant County Jail, requested that his client be escorted to Judge Robert Gill's courtroom, and stood beside Barbee in front of the judge's bench.

Barbee looked up in silence at the brown-haired judge, with the neatly trimmed short mustache. Just to his right stood Bill Ray, the attorney he had complained to the judge about, and the man who made Barbee fear for his life.

Judge Gill asked Barbee if he still desired a change of representation, as stated in his previous two correspondences.

Barbee cut his eyes over to Ray; trembling slightly, in a soft voice, he said, "No, they're okay."

Judge Gill announced that both Ray and Moore would continue to represent Stephen Barbee and carry on preparations for the capital case.

Thus, Ray and Moore persisted in filing motions to the court on behalf of their client. Those motions included requiring the state to reveal any agreements entered into between the state and their witnesses. Had Ron Dodd been offered any type of "deal" in exchange for his testimony? It would be learned later that Dodd had not been offered any reduction in sentence for his testimony.

The defense counsel also asked that criminal records of all state witnesses be released to them. They knew that Dodd had previously been convicted and sent to prison for aggravated assault, but did he have any other convictions not known to the defense? They needed the information if he would be testifying against their client. Did any other witnesses have criminal records? Did the state intend to bring in a jailhouse snitch to testify against their client? The motion was a fishing expedition to see who would be facing them in court.

Among the numerous other motions filed by Ray and Moore was one that would allow Stephen Barbee to appear in court wearing civilian clothing, rather than his county-issued jail suit. The attorneys knew that if their client appeared in court dressed in the bright orange attire of a county inmate, and shuffled in wearing his jail shower shoes, that it could instantly prejudice the jury against him. They also asked that funds be made available to pay for the clothing.

In addition, the defense requested that they be placed at the table nearest the jury. Although Barbee doubted their commitment to his case, Ray and Moore were doing all they could for their client prior to trial. The maneuvering and gamesmanship of trial had begun.

12

Performing as a team during trial preparation, Kevin Rousseau and Dixie Bersano each worked on various aspects of·the Barbee case. One of the first assignments Bersano accepted was to obtain DNA results from test samples taken from both Stephen Barbee and Ed Rogers, the other man Lisa Underwood had been dating during the time she became pregnant. On May 12, 2005, Detective John McCaskill took those samples, along with the blood card of Lisa Underwood and the fetal blood card of her unborn child, to the University of North Texas (UNT) Health Science Center in Fort Worth. The center would determine the paternity of Lisa's child.

At the end of June, Dixie Bersano sat in her office on the sixth floor of the Tarrant County Justice Center. Surrounded by stacks of three-ring binders, sheaths of paper, and her law school diploma hanging on the wall, Bersano held a sealed envelope from UNT Health Science Center in her hands. She turned the envelope over and tore open the sealed flap.

The first of the five-page forensic DNA report listed the items received by UNT for testing. The second revealed the results of thirteen genetic loci (the position in a chromosome of a particular gene) for Lisa Underwood, Baby Underwood, and Stephen Barbee. Two columns of numbers appeared under each name, giving Bersano no idea if Stephen Barbee had been determined to be the father or not.

The third page of the statement was similar to the second, with the exception that Ed Rogers's name appeared where Stephen Barbee's had previously been listed. Once more, Dixie Bersano couldn't tell the identity of the father of Lisa's unborn child. But the first line of the fourth page of the report made it unmistakably clear who had fathered the baby.

Bersano rested her left elbow on the desk, her fingers threaded through her blond hair as she studied the DNA conclusions. After a few minutes she walked to the office of Kevin Rousseau.

"The DNA results came in," Bersano announced, handing Rousseau the report.

"Well?" Rousseau asked.

"Barbee wasn't the father," Bersano stated.

"You're kidding?" Rousseau asked, not expecting an answer.

The prosecutors had determined the motive for Lisa Underwood's murder had been the paternity of Lisa's unborn child. But even though the child had been fathered by Rogers, rather than Barbee as they had thought, it wouldn't change their case preparation. Still, the results were a surprise. They believed Stephen Barbee had killed a woman he thought was carrying his child, had murdered her son, and had taken the life of an unborn baby just so his wife wouldn't find out about the other woman and the child whom he thought was his. Suddenly the senseless acts took on an even more meaningless quality.

Dixie Bersano returned to her office and again read the DNA report:

CONCLUSIONS:

The alleged father, Stephen Barbee, is excluded as the biological father of the child, Baby Underwood.

Based on the DNA analysis conducted, the alleged father lacks the genetic markers that must be contributed to the child by the true biological father at 6 of the 13 loci examined.

The alleged father, Ed Rogers, cannot be excluded as the biological father of the child, Baby Underwood.

The probability of paternity is 99.9993% as compared to an untested, randomly chosen person of the Caucasian population.

When informed of the DNA outcome by Kevin Rousseau, Sheila Underwood was stunned. Sheila and her daughter had talked about what Lisa had believed to be the baby's date of conception, and Lisa had been certain the father was Stephen Barbee. Sheila knew Lisa had also been seeing another man, but Lisa had been so certain that Barbee was the father.

No reason could ever be accepted for such a vicious, pointless act, but knowing Barbee wasn't even the father of her unborn grandchild turned Sheila's anger to rage. A simple blood test could have saved her family, but Barbee had chosen a permanent solution to a temporary problem. She hoped Stephen Barbee would die on the gurney in a Texas death chamber.

Meanwhile, Stephen Barbee continued to tell his attorneys, his wife, and his parents that he was innocent of the killings. He claimed his and Dodd's roles in the episode had actually been reversed—with Dodd committing the murders and he assisting in disposal of the bodies. Barbee also informed Bill Ray and Tim Moore that he had never confessed to killing Lisa and Jayden.

"But they have you on tape," his attorneys reminded Barbee.

"Detective Carroll lied to me during that interview," Barbee told his attorneys. "He told me, if I explained that it was an accident, I could go home. Carroll also intimidated me by banging on the desk, yelling, and telling me I'd die if I didn't tell him I killed them. I didn't want to die. I just wanted to go home."

But other than his family and Tina Church, no one would listen to Barbee's disclosures.

While Stephen Barbee was secluded in the Tarrant County Jail, Ron Dodd was free to go about his business.

Fort Worth detectives had no evidence that Ron Dodd had helped with the murders of the Underwoods in Tarrant County. Detectives, along with Sheila Underwood, believed Dodd had a much larger role in the murders other than just helping to dispose of the bodies. However, there was no proof to take to a grand jury. Denton County, where the bodies had been buried, had jurisdiction over Dodd.

Dodd, eventually freed on a $10,000 bond insured by Burgess Bail-Bonds of Denton, was back in Haslet with Teresa Barbee. But the stress of Barbee's arrest, Teresa's fear of losing the businesses, and Dodd's pending charge of tampering with evidence were straining their relationship.

Before Barbee went to trial, Sheila Underwood decided she had to talk with Kevin Rousseau. She called Rousseau's office and requested a face-to-face meeting.

Rousseau had been cordial, showed compassion, and

promised Sheila he would do his best to secure a Barbee conviction. The seasoned prosecutor had never met anyone like Sheila Underwood. She was highly intelligent and had a bulldog spirit that Rousseau related to and admired. Sheila Underwood had suffered a complete loss, and Rousseau had never known anyone who suffered more. Her entire reason for being had been snuffed out in one senseless act by a selfish killer.

Sheila was confident in the assistant prosecutor's ability and sincerity, but she needed continued reassurance, calling Rousseau occasionally to request other meetings.

Sheila always found Kevin Rousseau willing to give her his time and patiently listen to her concerns. He walked her through the upcoming court proceedings so she would be prepared for each step along the way. He had even said he would tell her at what point in the proceedings she should leave the courtroom to avoid the most unpleasant aspects of the court case.

"Do you think I'm crazy?" Sheila asked Rousseau during one of their meetings.

"I think you're crazed by a situation you can't control," Rousseau responded kindly.

Sheila knew he was right. She had no control over the trial, she had to trust in Kevin Rousseau and Dixie Bersano to secure a conviction for the accused killer of her daughter and grandson. She was encouraged by their determination.

As the trial grew nearer, Sheila Underwood was overwhelmed by the love and support she had, not only from her relatives and close friends, but from her family of coworkers. As the director of admissions at Huguley Hospital in south Fort Worth, Sheila knew nearly everyone on staff.

At the time of Lisa and Jayden Underwood's deaths,

hospital officials were discussing creating a prayer garden where patients, relatives, and employees could meditate, reflect, and pray. It was a unanimous decision that the prayer garden should bear the names of Lisa, Jayden, and Marleigh, Lisa's unborn daughter.

On a cold day in January 2006, just two days before Lisa Underwood would have celebrated her thirty-fifth birthday, dozens of Underwood loved ones stood three deep around the newly erected prayer garden in front of Huguly Hospital. The crowd consisted of family, friends, hospital staff, and customers of Boopa's Bagel Deli. Little boys, dressed in the traditional blue shirts dotted with patches of the Cub Scouts, participated in a flag ceremony as they mourned the loss of one of their own. They would sorely miss the bright-eyed, always smiling Jayden Underwood.

The hospital chaplain spoke of the importance of memorials and led the crowd in a prayer.

Pete Weber, the hospital's president, stood in front of the garden, which was adorned with an angel fountain, benches, flowers, and a plaque baring a photo of Lisa and Jayden. Weber looked toward Sheila Underwood and, with sorrow in his voice, said, "During these times I think it is important for us, as an employee family, to support the ones we love. Sheila, today we want to tell you we love you."

As attendees placed rocks on which they had written messages to loved ones in the garden, eight-year-old Cub Scout Ryan Conover slowly walked forward and laid his stone among the others. It read, *Jayden was my best friend.*

As tears fell from the eyes of mourners, a bevy of butterflies, released by the Scouts, rose in the sky, carrying a message of love up to Lisa and Jayden.

13

For all of her rhetoric that she believed in her husband's innocence, less than a year after Stephen Barbee's arrest, Trish Barbee filed for divorce. Trish had visited Stephen in jail and talked with him by phone, but the visits and calls dwindled until Barbee's wife finally decided she had to move on without him.

Barbee's attorneys had encouraged Trish to stay the course, believing their client would benefit in trial by a supportive wife. Trish tried to remain strong for Stephen, but she could no longer give her moral support to a man she eventually felt she never really knew. Just weeks before Stephen Barbee's trial began, the divorce was final.

News of the divorce devastated Barbee. He had hoped Trish would stand by him, that he would be found not guilty, and that they would go back to the family life he had loved. Learning that Trish had abandoned him was difficult for Barbee to take. Then Barbee learned that Trish had sold his deceased brother's gun and kept the money. She also retained nearly $75,000, which the couple held in savings, a tax refund check, and other resources, but she didn't offer one cent toward his defense. Barbee was crushed by feelings of betrayal and resentment.

On February 3, 2006, nearing the one-year anniversary of Stephen Barbee's arrest for the murders of Lisa and Jayden Underwood, Barbee was in court with his attorneys on a motion to suppress the recorded interviews of him at the Tyler Police Department after he had asked for an attorney. Judge Robert Gill would hear the motion. No jury would be present.

Attorneys Bill Ray and Tim Moore knew that if the taped interviews were seen by the jury, these videos would be prejudicial to their case. They hoped to keep them out of trial by claiming Stephen Barbee was under custodial interrogation at the time of the so-called interview by Detective Carroll and that Barbee was not free to leave. Their argument was based on Barbee's statement more than two hours into the interview when he stated, "I think I would like a lawyer."

Moore planned to argue that as soon as Barbee made that declaration, the interview, or interrogation, as he characterized it, should have ceased. Because it had not, Barbee's Fifth Amendment right was violated. The defense was requesting the court suppress anything that happened after Barbee made his utterance concerning an attorney.

Assistant District Attorney Kevin Rousseau, on the other hand, planned to argue that Barbee didn't specifically request a lawyer, but rather he had asked Detective Carroll if he should get one. Rousseau would support Detective Carroll's response that he couldn't advise the defendant, that it was wholly his decision. And since Barbee continued to speak freely with the detective, and did not ask for representation specifically, the detective was well within the rules of protocol to continue talking with Barbee.

Judge Robert Gill would hear the evidence impartially and make his ruling. The judge called court to order and asked if the attorneys for both sides were ready to begin.

Sitting on long benches outside the courtroom doors, Jackie and Bill Barbee waited with hope in their hearts. They didn't have much faith in Ray and Moore, believing they acted more like prosecutors toward their son than defense attorneys, but the attorneys seemed to be confident they could obtain suppression of the tapes.

Lisa Underwood's mother, Sheila, elected not to attend the suppression hearing. Kevin Rousseau had notified her of what would be taking place, and Rousseau felt confident that however Judge Gill ruled, it would not deter them from a successful prosecution of Stephen Barbee.

Sheila was also aware that Mike Carroll would be testifying. Carroll, like Rousseau, had assured her that even if the judge disallowed the tapes to be presented at trial, he would be able to get Barbee's confession before a jury. Sheila refrained from attending the hearing because she had confidence in Rousseau's ability and faith in both Rousseau and Carroll to let her know the outcome.

Outside the courtroom doors Ray, a large, round-faced man, approached Bill and Jackie Barbee.

"I've changed my mind. You can't come in," Ray told Bill and Jackie, who were waiting for Ray to call them into the suppression hearing.

Bill was angry.

"Good God, I'm going to the truck," Bill said, leaving the courtroom, and eventually the Justice Center.

Jackie sat alone on one of the long wooden benches. She watched Teresa and Ron Dodd with interest as they talked with one another. Ron was dressed in what Jackie thought was a preppy look, appearing to be in his twenties, rather

than his actual midthirties. Jackie was certain Teresa had
picked out his clothes.

Ray exited the courtroom doors and approached Jackie.

"You can come in now," Ray told Jackie.

Teresa jumped to her feet.

"I'll go get PaPa," Teresa volunteered, referring to her
former father-in-law.

Within minutes Bill and Jackie were back in the courtroom, sitting in the back as instructed by Ray. He had warned
them, as well as their son, not to make any visual or audible
reactions to the testimony.

Rousseau rose from his chair beside Dixie Bersano and
called Detective Mike Carroll, the state's first witness.

Stephen Barbee clenched his fist and blew air from his
mouth. He hated Mike Carroll. The defendant believed the
detective had tricked him into telling about the night Lisa
and Jayden had been killed. He believed Carroll had lied
to him. Barbee glared at the tall, dark-skinned detective
as he approached the witness chair, but he didn't look him
directly in the eyes.

Barbee had complained to his attorneys about Carroll's
tactics during his Tyler interview, but he had received no support for his position. Both Ray and Moore knew that lying to
a suspect was not against the law and was a common tech-
nique used by police while attempting to secure a confession.
Nonetheless, Barbee believed he had been wronged—and
that Carroll was responsible for his pending prosecution.

Barbee rubbed his arms to warm them. He had been held
in the suicide watch cell at the county jail with only a paper
sheet for warmth. The holding cell behind the judge's bench
was cold, as well as the large courtroom. His attorneys had
provided him with only short-sleeved shirts and no jacket.

Barbee shivered, if not from the cold air, then from the anticipation of Carroll's testimony.

Six-foot-four Rousseau was a towering figure in the courtroom. As the ADA approached Carroll, he asked that the detective begin his testimony by explaining how he had arrived at the Tyler Wal-Mart, along with Detectives Mc-Caskill and Jamison, for a prearranged meeting with Stephen Barbee.

Barbee sat at the defense table, listening intently as the homicide detective spoke. Scrutinizing every word, he avoided the detective's stares.

Carroll first explained that he, along with Detectives Mc-Caskill and Jamison, had arranged to meet Trish and Stephen Barbee and Ron Dodd at the Tyler Wal-Mart store. Carroll stated he had recorded his conversation with Trish Barbee using a digital recorder while sitting with her in the Barbees' vehicle outside the superstore. The detective declared that simultaneously McCaskill interviewed Ron Dodd and Jamison spoke with Stephen Barbee. He admitted that neither of those interviews had been recorded.

Carroll continued his account of how the detectives, the Barbees, and Ron Dodd drove to the Tyler police station so that Barbee could be interviewed extensively while being recorded.

"The Tyler detectives had a way of recording, kind of a video-digital set up to record, so they walked us through the process, even though I had a digital recorder," Carroll explained.

"Who from the Tyler Police Department was in charge of running the equipment?" Rousseau asked.

"Richard Cashell," Carroll said.

"Did Detective Cashell take part in any of the interviews that night?" Rousseau inquired.

"No, sir."

* * *

With the help of Carroll, Rousseau pointed out that at the beginning of the recording, Barbee was read the Miranda warning and was also provided a written copy. The ADA emphasized that Barbee had waived his right to an attorney and agreed to speak to the detectives.

Rousseau strolled to the prosecution table, picked up two DVDs, and placed them into evidence. Rousseau stated to the judge that DVD number one contained the portion of the interview when Barbee actually made admissions that amounted to a confession. There was no objection from the defense, and both tapes were placed into evidence.

"Did you have with you a handheld recording device that only records sound?" Rousseau asked Carroll.

"Yes, sir."

"And did you make a backup recording with that?" Rousseau asked.

"Yes, sir."

Carroll, an experienced courtroom witness, continued his testimony by telling the court that, at that point in the interview, he stopped the tape and left the room to get a camera to photograph Barbee's body. During that break the detective also explained he spoke with Barbee about a white male being stopped in Denton County by a deputy sheriff.

"I told him I believed he was the person on the tape, that the deputy was coming to view the videotape, and if he was the person on the videotape, he would have a problem."

Carroll smugly admitted he had lied to Barbee. The deputy was not en route to Tyler, but had already viewed the tape before the Fort Worth detectives ever arrived in Tyler. The bluff had worked. Barbee admitted he had been stopped by the officer and had subsequently run.

"He made a comment that he was worried about running

from the police being a bad thing, and I emphasized to him that he's about to be in trouble for murder, and that was more serious than running from the police," Carroll said.

Carroll explained he then left Barbee in the interview room while he went to find out what Dodd had to say. Carroll had expected Detective Jamison to be behind him, but he had hung back to talk with Barbee himself. Before Carroll reached the video control room, only a few feet from where Barbee was left, Detective Cashell stopped him.

"Detective Jamison is making your boy mad," Cashell told Carroll.

At that time Carroll turned back around and reentered Barbee's room, instructed Jamison to leave, and Barbee was left alone for about thirty minutes, while Carroll listened to and watched a portion of Dodd's interview.

Carroll reported to the court that he returned to Barbee's room, opened the door slightly, and asked Barbee, "Does Farm Market 407 sound familiar?" Without waiting for a response, Carroll closed the door and returned to the video room.

"I wanted to plant a seed in his head that we may have more information against him than he might think we have. I wanted him to think about that for a while," Carroll explained.

Carroll continued, stating that while he was in the control room, he realized Barbee was walking out of the interview room. Carroll met Barbee in the hall and asked, "What do you want?"

"I need to use the bathroom," Barbee replied.

Detective Carroll stated he escorted Barbee down a maze of corridors to a restroom located just inside the double doors off the lobby. He followed Barbee into the area of the bathroom where urinals hung on the wall, and stood by the door as Barbee relieved himself.

Under the oath he had taken before beginning his testimony, Carroll stated, "I continued to talk to him while he used the facility. I pointed out to him that he'd already admitted to running from the police and that the area he ran from was very close to where the victims' vehicle was found. Also that Ron Dodd had already admitted that he had seen him with the bodies in the victims' car and that he wanted shovels to bury the victims.

"So I pointed out to him that it's looking more like he's a killer and Dodd's going to testify. I also told him that the Underwood family needs closure and I don't think he's a bad guy. At that point he starts making comments that he was going to be in jail the rest of his life and started to confess to the murder."

Bill Ray and Tim Moore exchanged quick glances. This was the first the defense attorneys had heard of any bathroom confession. Each attorney began to make quick notes on the legal pads in front of them.

Barbee bristled. His body stiffened and tenseness showed in his brown eyes. Barbee turned to his attorneys to object to Carroll's testimony, but he was shushed into silence as their attention remained on the witness and questions they would ask when they cross-examined Carroll.

"You and Mr. Barbee are in the restroom and you fed him these facts that you know. Did it eventually have an effect on him?" Kevin Rousseau asked.

"First he said he was going to go to jail for the rest of his life," Carroll repeated. "I asked him, 'What do you mean by that?' He went on to say that he didn't mean to, but he killed Lisa. From there, he went on to talk in detail about what happened."

"What detail do you recall him giving you at that point?" Rousseau asked.

"He talked about why he went to Lisa's house. He said she

was trying to break up his marriage with Trish. He loved his wife very much and he didn't want to lose their relationship. He also talked about a plan to kill Lisa that he and Ron had discussed," Carroll stated. "They had gone to the house to carry out the plan, but he couldn't do it. He called Ron Dodd and said, 'I can't do it,' so Ron picked him up."

Carroll further explained that the plan was to meet at Dodd's house. Barbee would leave his car there, and Dodd would take him to Lisa's house. When Barbee got to Lisa's, he couldn't go through with the murder, so he left and called Dodd. Dodd picked Barbee up and they returned to his house where they discussed the plan further. At that point Dodd made the comment, "Should we hire a hit man?" and Barbee said, "No. I can do it." Dodd then took Barbee back to Lisa Underwood's house.

Carroll stated that evidently the plan was for Barbee to provoke an argument, a fight with Lisa, but he couldn't get her mad. Thus, Barbee couldn't get mad enough to kill his former lover.

"I don't think he could go through with it unless he could get upset or mad at her," Carroll speculated.

"The second time around he went back and they got into a fight. Barbee said Lisa let him in, they got into an argument. She kicked him in the leg and he punched her in the nose. Then they began to fight. He held her down on the carpet for quite some time. He told me he thought he held her down too long and she stopped breathing. At that point in the struggle, seven-year-old Jayden walks in and he's crying. So he approaches Jayden, put his hand over Jayden's mouth and nose, and suffocates him."

Toward the back of the courtroom, soft whimpering could be heard from Jackie Barbee. She believed in her son's innocence, but she felt for the mother and child, as described by Carroll, who lay dead on their living-room floor.

"Did he tell you anything more about the crime while you were there in the bathroom?" Rousseau asked.

"He did talk about trying to clean up the crime scene, straighten up the place. He left the house through the garage, because he didn't have a key and the house would appear to be locked. He put both bodies in the back of Lisa's vehicle and left," Carroll stated.

"Did he make other comments about things he did or things he felt during this time period?" Rousseau inquired.

"Yes," Carroll replied. "He told me that he had lost a loved one and he felt he understood what Lisa's family would be going through. He said he buried both victims together and said a prayer for them. He also wanted closure for Lisa's family and he asked if he could speak with them."

"Did Barbee say anything else while you talked to him in the restroom? Did he say anything about Ron Dodd?" Rousseau asked.

"Yes, he did," Carroll said. "He said he didn't want to talk about Dodd wanting to hire a hit man."

"Did he say why?"

"No."

Stephen Barbee looked toward his parents. He had told them that the reason he didn't talk to Detective Carroll about Dodd's offer to hire a hit man was because Dodd had threatened to hurt them if he talked. He wanted to protect his parents, with whom he now exchanged sorrowful looks.

Carroll testified that his conversation with Barbee in the Tyler PD restroom lasted forty-five minutes to an hour, and that no one else came in to use the facility while he and Barbee talked. The conversation had actually taken place at 11:00 P.M. when most of the Tyler detectives had long since gone home, and patrol officers generally gathered in the locker room provided them at the rear of the building.

As Stephen Barbee listened to Carroll's rendition of

the "bathroom confession," as it would come to be known, he shook his head. Following his indictment for capital murder, he had asserted to his attorneys, his parents, and his family's newfound advocate and advisor, Tina Church, that he had spent no more than five minutes in the restroom with Carroll—and never confessed to killing Lisa and Jayden. For all the tape recording that had gone on that night— Carroll's conversation with Trish, his own video interview, as well as Dodd's—Carroll now claimed he didn't have a recorder with him at that crucial time.

"Did you say anything to Mr. Barbee about putting what he told you in writing or on videotape?" Rousseau asked.

"Yes. I said, 'We need to go back and document all this if you're being sincere and you do want closure. We need to go back and put this on tape or continue our conversation on tape,'" Carroll stated.

Carroll explained that he didn't take Barbee directly back to the interview room but rerouted him to Detective Cashell's office in an attempt to extract an exact location of where the bodies were buried. Cashell pulled up a map from MapQuest of the general locale where Carroll thought the burial site might be, based on information provided by Dodd. Carroll stated that Barbee "kind of" pointed out where the bodies might be found and provided a description of the site. It would be that location and description Carroll would pass on to Fort Worth officers in order for them to begin the search for the bodies of Lisa and Jayden Underwood immediately.

"When you get him back in the interview room, you mention something about him not wanting to talk about Ron Dodd, correct?" Rousseau asked.

"Correct."

"You reference that he wants to talk to somebody. Who is he wanting to talk to?"

"He wants to talk to Lisa's family, and he wants to talk to his wife, Trish."

"In a couple of minutes, he asked you to turn off the recorder," Rousseau stated.

"We were talking about what he wanted," Carroll responded. "He wanted some kind of a deal and he wanted a meeting with Lisa's family. He didn't want to meet them in a courtroom setting. He wanted a face-to-face. That's what he wanted to talk about, the deal he wanted us to make."

"Did you make him that promise?"

"No, sir."

"Did you threaten him in any way?"

"No, sir."

"You go back on tape and you reference the Miranda warnings, but you didn't actually read them again, right?" Rousseau asked.

"That's correct."

Rousseau began to address the issue of Barbee's lack of legal representation by pointing out that Barbee agreed to talk to Carroll without an attorney present. But at one point in the conversation, Barbee said, "I'd like to get one," meaning a lawyer.

Carroll stated that Barbee asked if getting an attorney would be bad, and he informed Barbee he couldn't advise him, and that Barbee continued to talk of his own accord—*without* benefit of counsel.

"Did he then voluntarily go ahead and answer questions regarding what happened in the deaths of Lisa and Jayden Underwood?" Rousseau asked.

"Yes, he did," Carroll responded.

"The recording speaks for itself for what he says, and we'll rely on that," Rousseau stated as he spoke directly to Judge Gill.

Carroll gave details about Trish's visit with Barbee at the

Tyler police station, sending Barbee to jail, and spending the night himself in the police station bunk room. Directed by Rousseau, Carroll then turned his attention to the trip from Tyler to the area north of Fort Worth and into Denton County, where Lisa and Jayden were put in a shallow grave.

"He asked you some questions," Rousseau said. "What were they?"

"He wanted to take us to the bodies, but he didn't want to see the bodies. He also didn't want to be seen by the media," Carroll stated. "Those were his two concerns."

"What did you tell him?"

"I said he wouldn't have to see the bodies and I'd make sure the media wasn't present when we arrived at the scene," Carroll explained.

Carroll stated that when they got close to the area he texted his sergeant to clear the media so that Barbee wouldn't be seen.

He then described climbing over a barbed-wire fence and getting specific directions from Barbee, who remained by the truck, until he found the freshly dug grave with loose shrubbery on top.

"What is the next thing that happened?" Rousseau questioned.

"I had Officer Thornhill take Stephen Barbee on to jail. I stayed at the scene," Carroll answered.

Stephen Barbee took a deep breath as Rousseau announced he had no further questions for Detective Carroll. It was Tim Moore's turn to question the detective.

Moore stood and walked toward the witness. Being of average height and a bit on the heavy side, his body type was a stark contrast to Rousseau's tall, lean frame. Moore's curly red hair also differed greatly from the prosecutor's dark, straight mane. Both attorneys were exceptional litigators.

Moore immediately challenged Carroll's role in the investigation and his recordkeeping of the events. Carroll admitted he was not the lead investigator on the case. His involvement was limited to February 21 and 22, 2005, and the only written record of his interview with Barbee was made just a few weeks before the scheduled start of trial while reviewing the videotapes. Carroll had thrown away any other notes he had taken on the case.

Moore went through much of the same questioning pursued by Rousseau. In addition, he asked Detective Carroll about "a big old whopper" of a story the defendant told about Barbee, Ron Dodd, and a truck that wasn't running right. Carroll acknowledged that Barbee had told him such a story prior to the detective's going into Dodd's interview with Detective McCaskill.

"That's when you learned Ron Dodd had said he had seen Barbee with the bodies of Lisa and Jayden before he buried them, right?" Moore asked.

"Correct," Carroll responded.

"Then Dodd tells McCaskill that the bodies were buried near FM 407, and that's when you walk in and drop the hint about FM 407 and walk out," Moore commented.

"Yes."

"Then that's when Barbee had to go to the bathroom."

"Yes."

"At that point in time, he couldn't have just walked out and said, 'I'm through. I'm going to walk out that door and go home.' He couldn't do that, could he?" Moore asked.

"Well, with the new law, he did run from the police and he had admitted to that—so, no, we could detain him at that point," Carroll explained.

"You and Steve Barbee are the only two people in the bathroom?" Moore asked.

"That's correct."

"You don't have a tape recorder with you?" Moore continued.

"No."

"You don't have your video camera with you?"

"No video camera in the bathroom," Carroll stated.

"There's no way to memorialize this conversation other than your word, correct?" Moore asked with a slight smirk on his face.

"Correct."

"And that's when Steve Barbee makes his heart-wrenching confession to you, correct?" Moore asked sarcastically.

"Correct," Carroll responded with a lack of any emotion.

"But that's not in writing anywhere, and not on audiotape anywhere," Moore stated.

"Correct."

"Then you go back to a computer room and he shows you where he buried the bodies. Right?" Moore asked.

"Yes."

"Now, it's almost two hours and forty minutes after y'all went to the bathroom, correct?" Moore asked.

"Roughly."

"This is confession time, right?" Moore asked.

"Yes."

"So you go back on tape and Barbee's upset, crying pretty hard. Right?" Moore asked.

"Yeah."

"Y'all sit down and you say something to the effect, 'Now we are not going to talk about this Ron Dodd stuff,' correct?"

Stephen Barbee was beginning to get irritated. Never having been in a courtroom before, he didn't understand the repetitiveness of questioning, or the continued use of the word "correct." He found the questioning and the responses tedious.

Moore then brought out the fact that Carroll reminded Barbee he had agreed to talk without benefit of a lawyer, but at that point Barbee said, "I'd like to get one."

"There was no doubt in your mind he was talking about a lawyer at that time, was there?" Moore asked.

"Yeah. He wasn't asking for an attorney, if that's what you're asking me. No, he wasn't asking for a lawyer," Carroll insisted.

"So when you said, 'We talked about talking without a lawyer,' and he said, 'I'd like to get one,' what do you think he was talking about?" Moore said sharply.

"That at some point in the future when it goes to trial, he'd like to have an attorney. My thinking was actually that there would be a time, I thought, when this went to trial. When he was brought back to Fort Worth, he would like to have an attorney, but not then," Carroll responded.

"You just assumed that, Detective Carroll, didn't you?" Moore continued.

"That's true," Carroll admitted.

"He didn't say that, did he?"

"No."

"And you didn't stop the interview at that time, did you?" Moore pushed his point.

"Only because he asked me not to stop it," Carroll responded.

"Well, that's up to Judge Gill to look at the video and see if that indeed is true," Moore challenged. "But the question is you did not stop the interview when he said, 'I think I'd like one,' did you?"

"No," Carroll conceded.

Under questioning from Moore, Carroll also acknowledged that he didn't record any of the conversation that took place on the way to the burial site, nor did Barbee tell them on videotape anything about where the bodies were buried.

"So from that videotaped interview, you wouldn't have known whether the bodies were in South Carolina or Denton, Texas, would you?" Moore asked.

"He did say off 407. That's on videotape," Carroll said.

"But as far as the exact spot, that couldn't have been deciphered from the videotape," Moore stated.

"I don't remember that, no," Carroll said.

"And when you said in the bathroom that he was going to jail for the rest of his life, that there was a plan to kill Lisa, and Barbee couldn't do it, and Dodd asked him if he should hire a hit man, and he said, 'No, I can do it. I couldn't provoke her the first time,' you didn't put that in your report, did you?" Moore asked.

"No, I didn't. I'm never going to forget that, though," Carroll said with conviction.

"How many years have you been a police officer?"

"Twenty-three."

"And you're taught to put important things in a police report. That's a no-brainer, isn't it?" Moore said.

"Yes, that's true," Carroll stated simply.

Once Carroll left the witness stand, both the state and the defense announced they had no other witnesses. Tim Moore began his closing arguments by questioning the legality of a confession that took place after his client had asked for an attorney but was not granted access to one.

"The law says, as soon as a person in custody is being interrogated, who has had his Miranda warnings, says, 'I want a lawyer,' interrogation should cease. That's the law. And it didn't cease. Whatever came after he said that came as a result of Mr. Barbee's Fifth Amendment right being violated.

"And that's why we're asking you to suppress anything that happened after he asserted his right to a lawyer," Moore argued.

Moore thanked the judge and took his seat at the defense table. He had done his job in arguing for his client's rights. But Moore was thinking of Carroll's surprise testimony that Barbee had confessed to him in the restroom. Moore knew he had more work to do to protect his client.

Kevin Rousseau stood to address the court.

"Your Honor, the case law is clear regarding invocation of right to counsel. It must be clear and unequivocal. His statement at best was not clear.

"Clearly what happened was the defendant said something regarding counsel. The detective was well within his rights—in fact, he made the appropriate decision to clarify whether or not Mr. Barbee wants an attorney and wants to stop the interview," Rousseau stated.

The fourteen-year prosecutor argued that Barbee's invocation of right to counsel was not obvious, due to Barbee's question to Carroll if that would be a bad thing.

Judge Gill appeared to be unclear as to when Stephen Barbee asked for an attorney in relation to when the confession took place.

Rousseau explained there were two different occasions when Barbee gave details of the murders of Lisa and Jayden Underwood. The first took place in the bathroom, with only Barbee and Carroll present, and no recording of that incident was made. The second was after Barbee returned to the interview room, made an utterance concerning an attorney, and continued to discuss the details of the murders.

Judge Gill stroked his short brown mustache with his right index finger as he thought.

"It's a little clearer now," Judge Gill said. "If you have any cases you would like to cite me on the issue, the defense has already cited a couple."

"Yes, I do, Your Honor. I can have them back for you if you'll give me fifteen minutes," Rousseau responded.

"I want to do a little research, anyway, so I'm not going to decide the issue today," Judge Gill stated. "I'll decide it the first part of next week. We stand in recess for today."

Stephen Barbee looked toward his attorneys for an explanation, but Ray and Moore were already discussing the need for another motion of suppression to be filed with the court. They knew it was imperative that Detective Carroll's testimony regarding the so-called bathroom confession be withheld from the jury. The damning words of their client, which Carroll claimed were told to him in the Tyler PD restroom, would surely seal his fate.

Ignoring their client as he was led back to the holding cell and eventually back to the Tarrant County Jail, Ray and Moore left the 213th Judicial District Court to begin preparing another motion to suppress. The next time they would appear in court, they would know if they had succeeded in stopping admittance of the critical confession.

However the judge ruled, Rousseau was glad the suppression hearing was over. It had been a tremendous fight for the evidence related by Detective Carroll to be admitted.

Rousseau knew Barbee was unhappy with Bill Ray and Tim Moore, but if anyone suggested the defense attorneys didn't do a good job, they didn't know what they were talking about. The two men had been competent adversaries, and Rousseau knew that without any physical evidence putting Stephen Barbee at the scene, the prosecutor would surely have an uphill battle without the admission of the confession.

14

Ten days after Judge Robert Gill announced he would take the defense counsel's motion to suppress under consideration, he rapped his gavel against the wooden desk and called the suppression hearing to order. The judge's usual stern demeanor was present as he spoke to attorneys for both the state and the defense.

"Both sides wanted to continue the motion to suppress. Actually, there has been another motion filed, is that correct?" Judge Gill asked, looking toward the defense table.

Bill Ray stood and addressed the court, explaining that a second motion to suppress had been filed to encompass the surprise "bathroom" confession, which Detective Carroll had discussed in the preceding hearing.

"We didn't find out about it until he testified," Ray complained.

Stephen Barbee glared at Kevin Rousseau, believing the state had deliberately withheld the claim that he had confessed to killing Lisa and Jayden Underwood while standing in the Tyler PD restroom. Even if Judge Gill disallowed the videotape *after* Barbee had asked for an attorney, the state would be able to slip in the detective's rendition of

Barbee's so-called confession. Barbee's attorneys were now working feverishly to keep Carroll's testimony of that conversation out of his trial for capital murder.

Judge Gill asked, "Who is going to proceed?"

"I will stand on the evidence I presented at the beginning of this hearing," Rousseau stated, standing momentarily to address the court.

The judge instructed the defense to proceed, but before presenting any evidence for the court's consideration, Ray asked that "the Rule" be invoked.

Judge Gill looked to those persons sitting in the gallery.

"The Rule has been called for. That means, unless you are testifying, you have to remain outside the courtroom and outside the hearing of any witness who is testifying." Gill's eyes roamed the room to make certain all were listening to his instructions, and understanding them.

"Before and after you testify, you cannot discuss your testimony with any other witness or allow any other witness to discuss their testimony with you," Judge Gill stated firmly.

"Who is your first witness?" he ended.

"Ms. Barbee."

As Trish Barbee approached the witness stand, other scheduled witnesses began to leave the courtroom as instructed.

Bill and Jackie Barbee had taken seats near the rear double doors on the left side of the courtroom. When their former daughter-in-law walked toward the front of the courtroom, they felt pangs of regret, mixed with a twinge of anger. Although they were not close to Trish, barely getting to know her before their son was arrested, they knew Stephen was in love with her.

* * *

As Trish Barbee approached the witness stand, her long blond hair swung softly back and forth. Stephen Barbee unconsciously smoothed his plaid shirt and sat a little taller in his chair.

Barbee watched as his former wife began her testimony. Even though she had abandoned him, he still loved Trish. He would always love Trish.

Under questioning by Bill Ray, Trish acknowledged that in February 2005, one year prior to her appearing in court, she was married to Stephen Barbee, but they had since divorced. Ray asked Trish to run through the day she drove to Tyler with her children to watch Barbee work, going to Wal-Mart to meet with detectives, and following the officers to the Tyler PD.

Trish refused to look at her ex-husband, although Barbee couldn't take his eyes off her. Barbee still thought she was beautiful. He often wondered about Tanner and Taylor. Were they happy? How much had they grown? Did they hate him? Barbee's eyes moistened at the thought of all he'd lost.

Trish estimated they had arrived at the police department about 7:30 or 7:45 P.M. on February 21, 2005. She assured Ray that during the five and a half hours she sat in the police station lobby with her children, waiting on her husband, she had only spoken to one person by cell phone. That was Teresa Barbee. Trish stated she never saw Stephen Barbee or Detective Mike Carroll during that time. Kevin Rousseau had no questions for Trish and she was excused.

Stephen Barbee watched as Trish walked out of the courtroom, and out of his life forever.

When Tim Moore called Detective Mike Carroll for the defense to once again question him, Barbee rubbed his temples and closed his eyes. His head throbbed. The stress of the hearings had made his headaches more intense, and they were coming more frequently.

Before Tim Moore began his questioning, Detective Carroll was reminded he was still under oath from the previous hearing.

"I just wanted to clear up a few details from your prior testimony. You presented a report that you made regarding the taking of a statement from Mr. Barbee, back in February of last year. Is that correct?" Moore asked.

"Correct."

"When did you generate that report?" Moore asked.

Detective Carroll stated that he didn't recall, but he knew it was sometime after Detective McCaskill generated his report.

The answer wasn't sufficient for Moore. He pressed to know exactly when Carroll had written the report that he had referred to during the last hearing. A report that the defense had no knowledge of prior to Carroll's original testimony.

"Are we talking February of last year? March of last year?" Moore pressed.

"No, it was later than that," Carroll responded vaguely.

"May of last year?" Moore continued to probe.

"No, sir. It was later than that," Carroll stated.

"Is there any way to know when you wrote that report?" Moore asked with irritation in his voice.

"No, sir," Carroll replied, explaining he didn't date his reports when he prepared them.

"Okay. So it could have been last month?" Moore said.

"Yes."

"Could have been last month?" Moore repeated, surprise resonating in his voice.

"Yes," Carroll replied simply.

From the stand, Carroll clarified that he had added

corrections to his minimal notes, along with memories of his interview with Barbee, in just the last four to eight weeks. Carroll specified that he had inserted times and dates in the report after reviewing the videotapes recorded in Tyler.

Moore inquired if anyone else had taken a statement from Barbee, and when Carroll responded no, Moore wanted to know if anyone had ever asked him for a written report.

"No, sir," Carroll responded.

"When did you have an opportunity to tell either Mr. Rousseau or Ms. Bersano about these conversations you had with Mr. Barbee at the Tyler Police Department?" Moore asked, turning his body slightly toward the attorneys sitting at the prosecution table.

"The moment I knew they were the attorneys for the state."

Barbee clenched his fists tightly.

Carroll testified that he had conversations with the two prosecutors, but he had not provided them with any written notes.

Moore asked why he hadn't taken notes or recorded his conversation with Barbee while in the Tyler PD bathroom.

"Well, when you interview a suspect, there is a point where you are trying to gain their confidence and trust. You are not talking to a suspect about a murder case and start taking notes or whip out a recorder, because they're going to clam up and not talk to you. You want them to talk to you, so you want to do that openly and freely," Carroll explained.

"Well, you had just come from having a recorder in front of him, hadn't you? And you just came from having a video camera on him," Moore stated flatly.

"But you don't go to the bathroom with those things, sir," Carroll responded coldly.

Moore approached the subject of Carroll possibly lying to his client while talking with him in the bathroom. Carroll acknowledged that he may have told Barbee he had been seen in a videotape, that there were witnesses, and that Ron Dodd had implicated him as the murderer, even though Dodd might not have.

"You didn't want that on tape, did you, Detective?" Moore asked.

"I don't mind that being on tape, because I lie to people all the time in cases like this," Carroll replied complacently.

"The only way we have of verifying that is by you saying that it (the confession) happened, right?" Moore asked.

"Correct," Carroll replied confidently.

Moore asked Carroll if he had recorded Barbee pointing out on MapQuest where the bodies had been disposed of, or if he had added that information in his written report. Carroll responded no to each question.

When asked what Carroll had told Detective McCaskill and Sergeant John Thornton about the exact location of the bodies, Carroll said, "I gave them the description that he gave me, which was off 407, through a gate. Shortly past the gate there was a pool of water. Stay to the left of the water. Go over two barbed-wire fences, and you'll see a freshly dug grave with debris on top."

"None of that is in your report, right?" Moore asked.

"Correct."

"The directions you gave to Thornton were not sufficient to find the bodies, were they?" Moore inquired.

"I don't know if he tried my directions. It was late," Carroll said.

"Well, you gave them directions, and they didn't find them because of those directions, did they?" Moore pressed.

"The answer is, I don't know if they tried to. So I don't know," Carroll reiterated. "They didn't find the bodies. I know that."

"Pass the witness, Your Honor. That's all I have," Moore announced before taking his seat beside Barbee and Ray.

Kevin Rousseau ran his long, slender fingers through his dark hair before rising to address the witness.

"Regarding the details of the conversation between yourself and Mr. Barbee that happened in the bathroom, you do reference those details in summary form in your statement. And although you didn't make a report at the time, you did tell me shortly, in the very early days of this prosecution, even before the first of March of last year, is that right?" Rousseau asked.

Even before Mike Carroll could respond with an affirmative answer, Stephen Barbee was tugging at the sleeve of one of his attorneys.

"That proves they withheld evidence," Barbee whispered, but again he was hushed by his attorneys, who were concentrating on the detective's testimony.

Through Carroll, Rousseau established that Detective Dick Gallaway had been in charge of the investigation, but shortly after the case was closed, Gallaway had been reassigned within the Fort Worth Police Department. His reassignment had some effect on the normal report gathering.

When questioned concerning any lies Carroll may have told Barbee, Carroll explained that he tried to convince Barbee that he had evidence that Ron Dodd had talked about seeing the bodies in the back of Underwood's car, and that Barbee was at the car with the bodies.

"I may have exaggerated it a little bit. That Ron Dodd had actually admitted something, that maybe Ron Dodd said that Stephen Barbee killed them, and Ron Dodd knew nothing about it. That Stephen Barbee was the lone suspect in the case, and that Dodd was going to be only a witness in this case, and things like that," Carroll said.

Rousseau made the point that such tactics are not designed to get a false confession, but rather to get a suspect to tell the truth. Carroll affirmed the statement.

"When you went to the scene the next day, Stephen Barbee showed you exactly where the bodies were, right?" Rousseau asked.

"Correct."

After only a few more questions Rousseau passed the witness, and Tim Moore announced he had nothing further. Mike Carroll left the courtroom as Stephen Barbee stared at the yellow legal pad in front of him, and Barbee's mother cried softly at the rear of the courtroom.

Bill Ray stood and announced the next defense witness would be Richard Cashell, a detective with the Tyler Police Department. Cashell informed the court that he never interviewed Barbee while he was at the Tyler PD, that his job was to operate the recording equipment at the end of the hall from where Barbee was being held. Cashell also testified that he pulled up MapQuest on the computer when Barbee was asked to denote where the bodies of Lisa and Jayden Underwood had been buried.

"Did you ever take Mr. Barbee to the restroom?" Ray asked.

"I believe I showed them, Detective Carroll and Mr. Barbee, where it was, but I didn't personally do anything," Cashell replied.

"Where did you show them it was?"

"I took them around the corner. It's in another portion of the building. The restroom isn't exactly close to where my desk is. It is a little bit of a walk, probably forty to fifty feet away. Near the lobby," Cashell explained.

There was a lengthy question-and-answer session concerning exactly which bathroom Barbee had used, and if Cashell had changed the location of the restroom in question from the first time he had spoken to Ray.

"Back when we talked to you before, you didn't mention anything about this conversation at your desk with Mr. Barbee and the MapQuest at all, did you?" Ray asked with annoyance in his voice.

"No, sir."

"In fact, you said on the tape you never had a conversation with him," Ray stated.

"All I did was click the mouse. I didn't know anything about the case. I don't know anything about the area," Cashell replied in defense.

Showing obvious annoyance, Ray passed the witness.

Kevin Rousseau approached the Tyler detective and handed him a paper marked as State's Exhibit Pretrial Number 3. He asked Detective Cashell if he recognized the exhibit.

"Yes, sir. That's the floor plan for the first floor of the police department," Cashell responded.

Rousseau asked the detective to point out where the interview rooms were located, the lobby, and the restroom in the secure area where Detective Carroll had taken Barbee, and where he claimed the defendant's confession took place. Cashell complied, stating again that he didn't recall if he had taken Carroll and Barbee to the bathroom, or if he had just given them directions.

Then Rousseau asked Cashell to explain the events that

occurred when Detective Carroll took Barbee to his desk so they could get directions to the burial site.

"So basically you were there because it is your desk," Rousseau stated.

"Yes, sir. My desk, and I am the only one that can sign on to the computer," Cashell responded.

"So the conversation, was it like an interrogation or an interview of a suspect at that point?" Rousseau asked.

"No, sir, it didn't seem to be. It was just give-and-take, asking questions of each other. Again, my only part was to move the mouse because I had no part in the investigation," Cashell stated as he twisted nervously in the witness chair. "I certainly never anticipated that my involvement would lead to anything other than providing a facility for them."

Cashell wished he hadn't had as much involvement in the case as he did. The detective didn't like being called to testify in a case of capital murder for which he had no jurisdiction. It was time away from his duties in Tyler, and he had little, if any, information to offer that Detective Carroll couldn't testify to directly.

"Was the information being dragged out of Stephen Barbee, or was he fully participating in the conversation?" Rousseau asked.

"He seemed to be fully communicating, and seemed to be wanting, even eager, to help," Cashell said.

On redirect examination Bill Ray asked if Stephen Barbee said anything, while the witness was in the room with Barbee, other than where the people were located. The defense attorney wanted to know if Barbee reported how the murders were committed or what had happened to the car. Cashell said no, Barbee had only given directions to a location he personally didn't know.

Cashell breathed a sigh of relief when Ray stated he had no other questions and he could return to his duties in Tyler. But Cashell's discharge was quickly withdrawn when the assistant district attorney told him to hang out for a few more minutes. Cashell left the courtroom to wait in the hall. He hoped he would not be recalled and could head east, out of Tarrant County, and away from the unpleasant proceedings of the homicide trial.

"We'd like to have Detective Thornton," Ray informed the court.

John David Thornton took the stand, telling the court he was a sergeant with the City of Fort Worth, now assigned to the homicide unit, and Detective Mike Carroll's supervisor at the time of the Underwood case.

"How important was it to the police department to try and find Lisa Underwood's car and her and her son when she was missing before she was found?" Ray asked.

"It was very important," Thornton said.

"Did the chief want this case resolved as quick as possible?" Ray prodded.

"Everyone wanted it resolved," Thornton said, realizing Ray was insinuating they were told to solve the case regardless of who took the fall.

"Is it a fair statement that y'all got a directive . . ."

Rousseau was on his feet. "Your Honor, I'm going to object. For the purpose of this hearing, it's irrelevant."

Showing obvious annoyance, Ray turned and addressed the court.

"Well, it's not, Judge," Ray stated, his voice laced with mockery.

Mr. Rousseau was quick to refute Ray. "It is irrelevant—"

The judge stopped both attorneys' arguments. "Can I just rule?" Judge Gill asked sharply.

"Yes, Your Honor," Rousseau quickly responded.

"Overruled," Gill announced.

Rousseau quietly took his seat.

"Was this a case that y'all were directed to handle twenty-four/seven until it was solved?" Ray continued.

"That was my impression, yes," Thornton answered.

In response to Ray's questioning, Thornton stated that Detective Carroll called him at about 11:00 P.M. and told him Stephen Barbee had confessed. Thornton explained it was a brief conversation, and they hadn't taken time to discuss any specific details. Thornton reported he had already gotten sketchy information from Detective McCaskill, who had been interviewing Ron Dodd, concerning the general area where the bodies could be found. Thornton stated it was around 2:00 or 3:00 A.M. when he received specific information concerning where the bodies were located. He was told by Detective Carroll, who had gotten the directions from Barbee himself.

Thornton testified that Captain Cordell had gone to the burial site during the night, and although he had walked within twenty feet of the shallow grave, he hadn't located it at that time. It was during the daylight hours when Stephen Barbee had provided exact information that they had finally located the bodies of Lisa and Jayden Underwood.

"If Barbee had decided at five o'clock in the morning on the twenty-second, 'I'm not going to talk to the police anymore, I'm not going to say another word,' it is your position that you would have found the bodies based on what you already knew?" Ray asked.

"Yes, it is," Thornton replied with confidence.

"You walked within twenty to thirty feet of where the bodies were?" Ray asked.

"Yes, sir."

"When did you do that?"

"That morning."

"And you didn't find them?" Ray asked.

"No. We didn't go on the other side of the barbed-wire fence," Thornton explained.

Ray continued his questioning concerning the search for the grave. He indicated that, even after several conversations with Detective Carroll, they were unable to locate the bodies until Stephen Barbee himself took them to the location.

"Our position was to let Mr. Barbee come and show us exactly where they were," Thornton stated. "If that didn't work out, we were prepared to make a search of that area, and, in my opinion, we would have discovered the bodies. We would have found them," Thornton stated emphatically.

"Even though you didn't find them and you were looking for them," Ray remarked.

"There were two of us walking an area which was probably, initially, ten acres. So with the number of people we had coming out, the number of dogs we had coming out, we hadn't flown the helicopter over yet, we hadn't done any of that yet. There were just two of us making a walk-through of that area," Thornton responded.

Ray had no other questions for Thornton, and he returned to his place at the defense table.

Rousseau gave a quick glance to Dixie Bersano before asking Thornton his first question. "You could have started a full-scale search at first light, couldn't you?"

"Yes."

"Did you withhold doing that because you expected Barbee would be there to show you where the bodies were?" Rousseau asked.

"Yes."

Barbee fumed, shaking his head in disagreement. He dug his pencil point deep into the legal pad.

After another half-dozen questions concerning the location of the Underwoods' grave, Rousseau excused Thornton.

John McCaskill was the next defense witness. The questioning of McCaskill centered on his interview with Ron Dodd at the Tyler Police Department.

"He had an idea of where Mr. Barbee had last been seen with the remains of Lisa and Jayden Underwood," McCaskill testified.

McCaskill told the court that he, Detective Jamison, and Ron Dodd left the Tyler PD about 9:50 P.M. and headed for FM 407 in Denton County in an effort to locate the grave site. McCaskill characterized Dodd as cooperative.

"Did you keep up with all the things that happened and incorporate your notes into that report?" Ray asked.

"Only for my part, yes," McCaskill stated.

"Y'all have a directive from the city that tells you are supposed to do that in any criminal investigation. Is there not a general order to that effect?" Ray asked.

"I'm not sure if it's a general order or not, but it's pretty much a standard practice," McCaskill responded.

"If you took a confession from somebody, you wouldn't forget to write that down for a year, would you?" Bill Ray asked, making a not-so-subtle reference to Mike Carroll's failure to write his report for months after hearing Barbee's confession.

"Well, it would have to be memorialized in some way," McCaskill said, without answering the question directly.

"Did Ron Dodd show you where he had seen the

bodies?" Ray asked, abandoning questions on reporting procedures.

"Yes, sir."

"How close was it to where the bodies were ultimately found?" Ray asked.

"Probably a few hundred yards," McCaskill said.

Through McCaskill's testimony, Ray established it was 1:00 A.M. when the two detectives arrived in Denton County with Ron Dodd to look for the burial place. McCaskill stated that at the time he was unaware of a brush pile obscuring the site, that there were actually two lakes in the area, and that the bodies would be located near two fences to the left of one of the lakes.

Following McCaskill's brief questioning by Ray, he was excused without any questions from the prosecution.

Continuing the parade of police detectives, Bill Ray called Detective Richard "Dick" Gallaway, lead investigator on the case.

"When did you first hear that Stephen Barbee confessed to the commission of the murders of Lisa and Jayden Underwood?" Ray asked.

"That would have been close to midnight, the twenty-first of February," Gallaway replied.

When asked if he prepared the arrest warrant after hearing Barbee had confessed, Gallaway stated he had already prepared the majority of the warrant, prior to getting the news about the confession. Gallaway simply added the information about the confession to the existing affidavit.

Gallaway acknowledged that he had heard that Stephen Barbee and Ron Dodd had conspired to kill Lisa Underwood, or to have someone else kill her. He also acknowledged that *that* information hadn't been included in the arrest warrant, since Detective Carroll hadn't told him until sometime later in the investigation. Gallaway admitted that no part of that story ever made it into any police department report.

Continuing to question Gallaway on the subject of Barbee's statement concerning Dodd's role in the case, Ray asked, "Would you agree with me that if a person confesses to a detective in a bathroom about a plan or motive to commit a capital murder, that would be important in that person's murder trial?"

"That's true, but motive was not necessarily what we were going after," Gallaway said.

"And it is also part of y'all's policy to document, write down, what somebody tells you if they talk about killing somebody?" Ray questioned.

"Yes, sir."

"Y'all didn't do that in this case, did you?" Ray said with a slight sneer.

"I would assume it wasn't done, if it's not in the file," Gallaway responded calmly.

"You have never seen a document from anybody that says anything about Mr. Barbee confessing in the bathroom, have you?" Ray asked.

"I don't believe so," Gallaway said.

Rousseau had few questions for the detective, finally asking, "On the DVD you watched, Barbee acknowledged he's not going to say anything about what Ron did. Isn't that right?"

"Yes, sir."

* * *

Finally the pretrial hearing was near an end. The defense had no additional witnesses, nor did the prosecution.

Bill Ray leaned toward Tim Moore, whispered momentarily, then rose to address the court.

"As I set out in my motion, Judge, today, what we are here to talk about is what I have set out as the bathroom confession, the office confession, and the police car confession.

"As Detective Carroll testified in our last hearing, the defendant was under arrest at the time he went to the bathroom. It is therefore our position that that would bar admission of the bathroom, the office, and the police car confessions because it is not memorialized in writing or recorded by any electronic means.

"In the event that the court or the prosecutor takes the position that what was obtained in any of those three statements led to other evidence or led to the discovery of fruits of the crime, it is our position that didn't happen, and there is nothing that was obtained in any of those three statements that talks about the murder of Lisa Underwood, except in the bathroom confession, and that doesn't talk about where the bodies were.

"So it is our position that all three of those statements should be suppressed.

"In addition, the police car confession occurred after Mr. Barbee invoked his right to counsel. It is also our position that all questioning was instigated on the part of the police, and was not as a result of the defendant making subsequent inquiries or reinitiating contact.

"That's all I have. I'm done."

It was the prosecution's turn to sum up their objection to the suppression of the confessions of Barbee.

"Your Honor, our position remains that there was never a clear and unequivocal invocation of counsel. The detective did the only appropriate thing under the circumstances, which was to inquire, in fact, what he was asking," Rousseau began.

"I will dispute Mr. Ray's assertion that the detective said that he was under arrest when he went into the restroom. That's simply not backed up by the record.

"If the court decided there was an invocation of counsel, I would say there was a reinitiation of contact by the defendant.

"It is our position that Barbee led them to the bodies, and that every word out of his mouth at the Tyler PD is admissible as evidence."

Rousseau returned to his seat next to Dixie Bersano.

It was the judge who would decide if Barbee had invoked his right to counsel, and if the taped confession could be heard by the jury. Judge Gill would also determine if the bathroom confession would be admissible. Rousseau wasn't worried. He felt confident he had made a persuasive argument to the court. The self-assured prosecutor was certain that within the month Stephen Barbee would be headed to the Texas death row.

Judge Gill looked to the defense table, then to the prosecution. "I find that there was an unequivocal invocation of counsel at the point where the DVD was reinitiated and the defendant made the statement 'I would like to get one'— that at the time he made the statement, he was in the custody of law enforcement officers.

"I find further that the statements made by the defendant in the restroom, which have been referred to by both sides as the bathroom confession, are admissible because they contain assertions of facts or circumstances that were found to be true, and which conduced to establish the guilt of the defendant. The bathroom confession, to me, is not distinguishable from what's been referred to as the office confession. I believe they are one continuous conversation and that the statements made by the defendant while he and the detectives were looking at the MapQuest program and trying to plot the location of the bodies are also admissible.

"I find that after the invocation of counsel, all questioning of the defendant should have ceased so that further statements made by the defendant after that point are inadmissible up to the point where they were returning to Fort Worth the next day and the defendant reinitiated contact with police on the subject of the investigation by stating that he would like to take the detectives to the bodies. Again, those statements at that time are admissible."

. The stage was set. Although nothing after Stephen Barbee stated he thought he might need an attorney would be seen by the jury, the damning bathroom confession would be introduced by Detective Carroll.

Kevin Rousseau was pleased. It had been a hard-fought battle, but he would be able to present Barbee's confession to the jury.

Stephen Barbee was dejected and angry. Although he continued to deny the existence of a bathroom confession, it would be a huge part of his trial. It would fall to the jury to decide if the confession had indeed taken place. Only Carroll and Barbee knew for sure.

15

Bill Ray and Tim Moore were feverishly preparing for Barbee's murder trial scheduled to begin just five days after Judge Gill's decision to allow the bathroom confession into evidence. While they concentrated on countering the damning testimony that would be presented by Detective Mike Carroll, Amanda Maxwell was completing a compilation of primary and secondary mitigation themes. The attorneys would need the information in the event that Stephen Barbee was found guilty of capital murder.

In 2003, the U.S. Supreme Court ruled that all cases of capital murder must have a mitigation investigation completed. Known as the Wiggins Act, the ruling armed defense attorneys with information that could be beneficial in citing any explanatory circumstances that led the defendant to the act of capital murder.

The High Court ruled that defense counsel should take into account all facts discovered during the mitigation investigation, including medical history, educational history, employment and training, social and family history, prior adult and juvenile records, as well as religious and cultural influences. The court stressed the importance and substantial role of the defense counsel to raise any mitigation factors at the time of sentencing.

Bill Ray had chosen Amanda Maxwell to gather this information and present it to him and Tim Moore for their consideration.

After interviewing a number of persons known to Stephen Barbee and gathering all records pertinent to her investigation, Maxwell prepared a psychosocial history of Barbee and presented her findings, along with primary and secondary themes of mitigation that could be used by the attorneys in defense of their client.

The primary themes included developmental delay, closed-head injury (a trauma to the brain that did not penetrate the skull), bipolar disorder, and hydrocodone abuse. The fact that Barbee had no prior criminal history, a good work record, and tragic family circumstances were secondary themes that could be raised at the penalty phase of trial.

Maxwell felt confident about her findings, being certain that they would be of help to Stephen Barbee in his quest to avoid death row.

Ray and Moore had more than Maxwell's findings to consider—they were also diligently reviewing all witnesses they planned to present. Stephen Barbee's name prominently appeared on that list.

Personally, Barbee was nervous about testifying on his own behalf. He wanted the chance to tell the jury his version of the events of February 18, 2005, but he feared he would say something that might hurt, rather than help, his case. Barbee expressed his concerns to his mother, who turned to Tina Church for advice.

"Don't let him take the stand," Church urged Jackie Barbee. "The prosecution will twist his words, use them against him. Nothing good will come from Stephen testifying."

Barbee informed Ray and Moore that he refused to take

the stand. It was yet another wedge driven between client and counsel.

On the morning of February 21, 2006, Kevin Rousseau and Dixie Bersano entered the empty courtroom of Judge Robert Gill.

The judge's bench loomed at the front of the courtroom, like an isolated island waiting to be inhabited. The empty witness chair to the right of the judge's bench, as the prosecutors faced it, waited ominously for the caravan of witnesses that Rousseau and Bersano would call.

Dixie Bersano, well groomed in a conservative suit complementary to her co-counsel's, looked toward the empty jury box. It had taken more than a month to select the four-man, nine-woman jury, which included one alternate. Soon the double row of upholstered swivel chairs would be filled with those jurors.

Bersano walked to the prosecutor's table, where Rousseau now sat, and set down a large three-ring binder filled with notes neatly tabulated for quick reference. She would soon take her place next to the lead prosecutor. Bersano took in one last glance around the courtroom, looking at the defense table across the way, the American and Texas flags on each side of the judge's tall-back leather chair, and the rows of empty benches that would soon be filled with law enforcement, media, family, and the usual courthouse gawkers.

It had not gone unnoticed by either of the assistant district attorneys or the defense counsel that the trial of one of the most publicized cases in recent Tarrant County history would begin on the one-year anniversary of the confession of Stephen Barbee for the murders of Lisa and Jayden Underwood.

Within thirty minutes the defense counsel, bailiffs, and court reporter had taken their places. The gallery seats were filled. Bill and Jackie Barbee sat at the back of the courtroom, as they had done during the suppression hearings. Sheila Underwood sat in a place at the front of the courtroom, near Rousseau and Bersano, normally reserved for law enforcement. Having not granted any interviews, and looking little like her daughter, Sheila was able to attend the trial unidentified and undisturbed by others.

Judge Gill entered and sat alone at his desk, where a number of law books lay unopened amidst stacks of papers.

The judge looked up, glancing from one table of attorneys to the other. The jury was not present—there was still a bit of unfinished business to be completed.

Kevin Rousseau addressed the court, stating that the state had taken the video recording made of Stephen Barbee at the Tyler PD, cut the tape—omitting statements made by Barbee after invoking his right to an attorney—and had added typed words at the bottom of the tape so that it would be easier for the jury to understand his spoken words.

Bill Ray was quick to stand and announce two objections. First, the attorney objected to the jury seeing the video of Stephen Barbee alone in the interview room when he stated, "My God, what have I done," and to the jury viewing the videotape of the exchange between Trish and Stephen Barbee, which should be marital privilege.

The second objection was to the jury being provided words attached to the video recording by the prosecution.

"That objection is overruled," Judge Gill stated. "I will let the state play the DVD with the transcript along the bottom. I will give the jury an instruction regarding the transcript, the fact that they will not be able to use it during deliberations."

Judge Gill also overruled the objections of hearsay

and marital privilege, as well as a later objection by Ray to the state's list of expert witnesses.

There was a short pause in the proceedings as the jury was ushered in and took their places in the jury box. The panel included two airline employees, a few teachers, and some realtors, among others.

Judge Gill turned slightly to his left in order to face the panel. "Good morning, ladies and gentlemen," he began, his black robe neatly fastened just under his knotted tie, and a rare smile on his face. "We're ready to start the trial. I have to place you under oath as jurors. Please raise your right hands."

Jackie Barbee's eyes were already beginning to mist. With all the adversity she had faced in her life, this was the most difficult. She looked toward her husband, the pain of cancer marring his face, then toward her son. As though there had been words spoken between them, Stephen Barbee looked back at his mother and attempted a reassuring smile.

Sheila Underwood stared at Barbee. This was the final lap of a year-long marathon—a race to justice. Sheila was confident the state would be victorious. Stephen Barbee would be convicted and sentenced to death.

The jury sworn in, Judge Gill continued with his instructions. He explained that the defendant would enter his plea to the indictment, and then each side would have an opportunity to make an opening statement, which would be their chance to outline the facts they felt they would prove during their portion of the trial.

Jurors listened intently as the judge declared that after the opening statements, the state would call any witnesses they wished to call; and when they rested, the defense would be given the opportunity to do the same.

The last instructions Gill made was for jurors to not be influenced by sympathy or prejudgment against the state or the defense; that they would not be allowed to take notes during the proceedings; and that if they listened carefully to the testimony coming from the witness stand, he felt certain they would have no difficulty during deliberations.

"The state may read the indictment," Judge Gill announced as the courtroom fell completely silent.

Prominent in a dark suit, white shirt, and conservative tie, ADA Kevin Rousseau stood, faced jurors, and, as instructed by the judge, read the indictment of Stephen Barbee for murder.

Once Rousseau completed the reading, Judge Gill turned to the defendant and stated, "Mr. Barbee, to the indictment you may plead guilty or not guilty."

Moore and Ray stood, placing their hands under Barbee's arms to gently encourage him to rise and address the court.

Facing Judge Gill, Barbee responded, "Not guilty, Your Honor." Then Barbee and his attorneys took their seats and waited for the prosecution to begin their case.

After placing the indictment papers on the prosecution table, Rousseau strolled confidently to the front of the jury box and began his opening statement.

In the back of the courtroom, persons seated near Jackie Barbee could hear a faint whimper as her son's murder trial began.

"Ladies and gentlemen, it's been a long time coming to this point, but this is what we've been working toward all these weeks. I need you to prepare yourselves because you're going to see, and you're going to hear, some very disturbing things, because this is a bad case."

Sheila Underwood took in a deep breath. The trial she had been waiting for, for a year, was finally beginning.

"About one year ago, almost exactly one year ago, Lisa and Jayden Underwood's lives were taken from them," Rousseau began. "Before that time Lisa and Jayden Underwood lived in a little house alone—a single mom, thirty-four years old, and her seven-and-a-half-year-old son.

"Jayden's father wasn't really in the picture. He had contact with his father, but his father lived in another state. He saw Jayden only periodically, every now and then.

"So it was really just the two of them. They had a nice little life, though. They had Lisa's mother, Sheila Underwood, who lived nearby. They had Marla Hess, Lisa's aunt, who lived in Wichita Falls. They were very, very close and saw each other frequently. And there was the other family.

"There was the family that centered around Lisa's business. Lisa was half owner of Boopa's Bagel Deli, right up there on Western Center Boulevard. Maybe you've been there, maybe you haven't. Good food," Rousseau added offhandedly.

"She was co-owner of that business with Holly Pils, a young woman about the same age as Lisa. It was named Boopa's, *B-o-o-p-a-s,* after Jayden. That's Jayden's nickname, given to him when he was just a baby. Jayden considered that business to be his too, because his name was on it.

"Boopa's was the center of the extended family. Friends and coworkers sort of had that place as a second home. It was not a McDonald's. This was a very important place in their world."

Rousseau paced in front of the jury box, making eye contact with each panelist during his presentation.

"Everyone was excited on February eighteenth of last

year because Lisa was pregnant with her second child. She was seven-and-a-half months pregnant. She was going to give birth pretty soon."

There was a muffled murmur in the gallery from those visibly shaken by the thought of the murdered expectant mother and her unborn child.

Rousseau continued, undaunted. "February nineteenth, a Saturday, Lisa's friends and family were gathered because it was Lisa's baby shower. A rainy day, so they left a spot right in front for her. They knew Lisa was coming. She was bringing Jayden. She was very excited. She hadn't gotten to have a baby shower with her first baby, seven and a half years ago. So she was very excited, planning to be there. She was going to get there at five minutes to four because the party was supposed to start at four P.M.

"They waited, and she didn't show up. And they kept waiting, and she didn't show up. She never showed up.

"Pretty soon, calls start being made, because they're nervous, they're concerned, they're worried. And before very long, the police are called. The police go into the house and they find blood on the floor. And ultimately they find blood on the wall and on the furniture and on the garage floor. And Lisa's vehicle is gone. And Jayden's shoes are there. He's seven and a half. He's growing fast. He only has one pair of shoes because he grows so fast. They're there. So wherever they are, Jayden doesn't have his shoes.

"Of course, the police start asking questions. Who did she know? Who did she associate with? Who's the father of her child? And that's when the defendant's name comes into this equation. Because Lisa had dated the defendant back in 2003. They dated some, not a lot. It was never an exclusive, long-term deal, but they dated some. It ended.

"Then Lisa started dating another man, Ed Rogers. She dated Ed exclusively. They were a couple. Toward the end of the time she and Ed Rogers were dating, she started seeing the defendant again. She saw him on a few occasions and she became pregnant. This was in the summer of 2004."

Rousseau moved smoothly around the courtroom, pulling the jury into the story. His flawless delivery had the thirteen men and women captivated as they hung on every word.

"Lisa believed the baby was the defendant's, Stephen Barbee's. However, she notified both men. She told them both about the pregnancy, and she told them both that it could be theirs. But Lisa also told them both, she believed it was Stephen Barbee's.

"Stephen Barbee was not married at this time. Stephen Barbee was dating someone, but he was not married. Now, he got married months later in December. He got married to a woman named Trish, who had two children of her own. He had a nice little life going there," Rousseau said with some sarcasm.

"But communications between [him] and Lisa continued, and it was clear to him that Lisa expected him to take responsibility for this child, at least to the extent of providing insurance. The bagel shop was getting by, but they weren't getting rich. They couldn't afford personal insurance.

"The defendant could. He ran two companies. That was too much for the defendant, though.

"You're going to hear from police officers that very quickly in the investigation they contacted the defendant to find out what he could tell them, and it was very little."

Rousseau told the jury about a Denton County deputy stopping a man, not a quarter of a mile from where Lisa's car was found, and that they would see a videotape showing that man to be Stephen Barbee. The assistant district attorney continued the story by informing jurors that detectives then went to Tyler, where Barbee had been working, to interview him. In that videotaped interview they would see a cooperative Stephen Barbee, a helpful Stephen Barbee, until he got caught up in his own lies.

"He will admit on that videotape that he was the man on the Denton videotape, that he was the man stopped by the Denton sheriff's deputy. He will also admit the connection between him and Lisa.

"Ultimately Detective Mike Carroll will tell you that during a break he escorted the defendant to the restroom and in that restroom a conversation took place. The defendant confessed to him that on the evening of February eighteenth, he had Ron Dodd, his employee and friend, drive him to Lisa's house for the express purpose of murdering Lisa. That he did, in fact, murder Lisa, and that when Jayden came in the room, screaming, he murdered him too. He loaded their bodies in the back of Lisa's Dodge Durango and drove them north, to southern Denton County. He dug a little hole. He [dragged] their bodies across two barbed-wire fences, buried them in that hole, and he covered that hole with brush."

Sheila Underwood's face remained stoic. She had been told all the gruesome details of the deaths of her daughter and grandson in preparation of this moment. Nothing Kevin Rousseau would say during the trial would be a surprise.

"You're going to see the defendant on videotape in a room alone where he's racked with fear. And you will hear his own words, saying, 'My God, what have I done?'

"You will see his wife, Trish Barbee, come into the room. She sits down in that room and he confesses to her that he did this killing. The police aren't in the room. He and his wife are alone together. He admits that he killed this woman. He didn't say anything about the little boy, because she didn't know about the little boy yet."

Stephen Barbee stiffened with anger. He would later point out that he never told his wife he didn't do it, only that it was an accident. He also informed them that he didn't know Trish didn't know about Jayden's death.

Rousseau began winding down his opening statement.

"And finally, folks, you're going to hear that the next day, exactly one year ago, he confessed.

"The next morning the Fort Worth PD takes him back to Fort Worth and he directs them to where Lisa's and Jayden's bodies are buried.

"We're going to bring you all that evidence, ladies and gentlemen, and more. And when it's done, when you're done hearing these unpleasant things and seeing these unpleasant things, I'm going to ask you to return the only verdict that makes any sense in this case. And that man sitting at the end of that table"—Rousseau pointed toward Barbee—"is guilty of capital murder in the deaths of Lisa and Jayden Underwood.

"Thank you."

Rousseau took his seat next to Dixie Bersano as she nodded approval of his presentation. He had made a compelling opening statement. The jury had been attentive, almost spellbound. Rousseau was more confident than ever of a conviction.

The prosecutor sat back in his chair and waited, along with the rest of the courtroom, to hear the defense's opening statement. Would they be able to match his determination? His persuasiveness? All Rousseau could do was wait and watch for the jury's reaction.

16

There was restless movement in the seats by observers as they anticipated the shift from the prosecution to the defense. But the watchers quickly settled down as Judge Gill asked, "Does the defense have an opening statement?"

"Your Honor, I'll exercise my privilege to withhold until I've heard the state's case." As soon as the words were out of Bill Ray's mouth, Stephen Barbee's head snapped toward his attorney, surprised they wouldn't make an opening statement. He quickly redirected his attention to the table before him.

Stephen and his parents had all been informed that the judge would be watching their reactions during the trial. Ray had stressed they not talk, turn their heads, roll their eyes, or make any facial expressions that the judge would consider disruptive. They all sat quietly, waiting patiently for the trial to begin.

Holly Pils, David Brawner, and Paula Hernandez, all scheduled to testify, were called into the courtroom, sworn in by the judge, and instructed to wait outside until called. As Judge Gill had done during the suppression hearing, he instructed the witnesses that they were under the Rule, and told them not to discuss the case or their testimony with anyone.

Officer Paula Hernandez was the first state's witness to be called. The attractive, thirtysomething female officer walked from the back of the courtroom, past Sheila Underwood, and took her place in the witness chair. She was so soft-spoken, Dixie Bersano had to ask Hernandez to speak up so that the court reporter would be able to hear her testimony and record it.

Hernandez had married during the year since the Underwood murders. She was known as Paula Fredrick at the time she was a parole officer on the north side of Fort Worth. She routinely responded to service calls in her assigned area, between the hours of 2:00 and 10:00 P.M.

On February 19, 2005, Hernandez, who had been working another call, heard the request for an officer to go to Boopa's Bagel Deli concerning a missing person. She immediately responded.

Hernandez told the court that after speaking to Holly Pils, Sheila Underwood, and a couple of others at Boopa's, she drove to Lisa Underwood's house on Chaddybrook. Sheila Underwood unlocked the front door, and Officer Hernandez reported she then entered Lisa's house.

"Where did you go?" Bersano asked.

"The first place I went was straight out the back. I was checking all the windows to see if maybe any screens had been pried off or anything had been damaged, and I didn't find any of that. No signs of forced entry," Hernandez stated.

"What did you do after that?" Bersano coaxed.

"I went inside and went straight to check all the bedrooms and checked in all the bathrooms to see if I could find anybody."

"Did you notice anything out of the ordinary when you were inside the house?" Bersano asked.

"About five to seven minutes after I'd been looking around, I spotted a stain on the carpet," Hernandez began.

Through a series of questions the officer informed the jury panel that she found Jayden's bed rather messy, but she didn't know if that was normal. Hernandez explained that she found a stain on the carpet near the coffee table. She moved the table and discovered an even bigger stain, approximately three feet by four feet.

At that point Dixie Bersano returned to the prosecution table, picked up a photo of the interior of the Underwood home, and introduced it into evidence. At Bersano's direction Officer Hernandez identified objects in the photo, including two glider rockers, a couch, and the coffee table discussed earlier.

"Was there anything significant about the stain?" Bersano asked.

"Yes. Along the edge, where the coffee table had been right here," Hernandez said as she pointed to a spot on the photo after stepping down from the witness chair, then joining Bersano in front of the jury, "it appeared as if it had a white crusty look to it. So I bent down to see if it was still damp. I used the back of my hand because I didn't want to touch it in any way. It looked like somebody had cleaned it, and maybe a vacuum run over it, after they tried to wash it, like a soap film or something."

Hernandez explained that she then stood by the front door so that no one would go in the house and disturb the crime scene. She stated that not until the crime scene officers arrived did she go back into the Underwood home.

Officer Hernandez's last act on the night the Underwoods were discovered missing was to string crime scene tape around the perimeter of the Underwood yard.

The officer's last involvement in the case was on the day Lisa Underwood's Dodge Durango was located in southern Denton County. Hernandez had been summoned to the location to maintain contact with the vehicle as it was loaded on the tow truck and transported to the city pound on East North Side Drive.

"Can I have one moment, Judge?" Dixie Bersano asked. "Yes."

Bersano crossed the courtroom floor, leaned over the table where Rousseau sat, and spoke in a hushed tone. Her blond hair fell gently over one eye.

Turning back to address Judge Gill, Bersano announced, "We'll pass the witness, Judge."

Tim Moore stood and walked toward Paula Hernandez, immediately addressing the issue the defense had determined to emphasize throughout the trial.

"Officer Hernandez, did you make a report about your involvement in this incident?" Moore asked.

"I didn't type a report, no," Hernandez replied.

Hernandez explained she was the assist officer and normally the sheet officer, or the original officer who gets the call, will prepare the report. However, in cases such as the Underwoods', the Major Case Unit would do the report.

"Is that kind of a Fort Worth Police Department policy, as far as report writing and who is to complete what report?" Moore asked.

"No. There's no written policy. It just depends on the detective who gets the case," Hernandez responded.

After establishing that Hernandez had completed a twenty-six-week police course and that report writing was a part of that training, Moore asked, "You put in your reports what you observed, when you observed it, kind of the who, what, when, where, how, and why of an investigation, right?"

"Correct," Hernandez said.

In his closing questions to the assist officer, Moore established that once Hernandez found the blood on the carpet, she allowed no one in the house to compromise the crime scene.

Officer Hernandez was excused, with Kevin Rousseau calling Holly Pils as the state's next witness.

Sheila Underwood watched as her daughter's business partner and best friend walked to the front of the courtroom to take her seat in the witness-box. Sheila knew it would be difficult for Holly to discuss the events that occurred prior to the disappearance of Lisa and Jayden, but she also knew Holly would do whatever she could to help convict their killer.

Thirty-four-year-old Holly Pils testified about her relationship with Lisa Underwood from the time Holly hired Lisa as an employee at Bruegger's Bagels, to going into business together at Boopa's. Holly admitted that neither she nor Lisa had ever been in business for herself, but together they figured out what needed to be done.

"Did you enjoy running the store?" Rousseau asked.

"Yes," Holly replied. "We enjoyed owning our own business. We worked very hard every day. We were just very proud."

Holly explained that Jayden was only about a year and a half when she and Lisa first met. When he was old enough to go to school, Lisa would take him to the bagel shop with her at six o'clock each morning, then on to school. The grief Holly felt was apparent on her face and in her voice as she spoke of Jayden.

Rousseau picked up a photo from a stack on the prosecution table and handed it to Holly.

With tears forming in her eyes, Holly identified the two people in the picture as Lisa and Jayden Underwood.

Stephen Barbee watched the question-and-answer session without reaction. He had only seen Holly at the bagel shop and barely knew her.

Holly confirmed that when she told the jury that although she didn't actually know Stephen Barbee, she knew that he and Lisa had a personal relationship. Lisa and Holly had been best friends, as well as business partners, and Lisa had confided in Holly about her feelings for Barbee. She also confirmed that Lisa hadn't introduced Jayden to Barbee.

Holly stated that Lisa had dated the defendant in the fall of 2003, but by the end of the year, the relationship was over.

"Who is Ed Rogers?" Rousseau asked.

"It's someone that Lisa started dating at the end of January 2004," Holly stated.

Holly explained that Lisa's relationship with Ed Rogers had begun after she and Barbee were no longer seeing one another. Holly disclosed that she knew Rogers better than Barbee because he was around a lot more than the defendant, and Lisa's relationship with him was exclusive.

"Was Mr. Rogers introduced into Jayden's life?" Rousseau asked.

"Yes, he was."

"How well did they get along?" Rousseau inquired.

"Pretty good," Holly said. "Ed had children himself, a little bit younger than Jayden."

Holly stated that Lisa and Ed had a fairly serious relationship until the summer of 2004. Then for a period of time, she was seeing both Rogers and Barbee. When she got pregnant, Lisa believed Barbee was the father. However,

Lisa and Jayden Underwood.
(Photo provided by Sheila Underwood)

Baby Jayden and Lisa Underwood.
(Photo by Sheila Underwood)

Lisa and Jayden
celebrate Jayden's
first birthday. *(Photo
by Sheila Underwood)*

Lisa Underwood stands in Boopa's Bagel and Deli, the shop she co-owned. *(Photo by Sheila Underwood)*

Jayden sits in "his" bagel shop where he greeted customers each morning. *(Photo by Sheila Underwood)*

Jayden and Lisa enjoy a fun day away from the shop. *(Photo by Sheila Underwood)*

Jayden graduates from kindergarten at age five. *(Photo by Sheila Underwood)*

Jayden at the beach.
(Photo by Sheila Underwood)

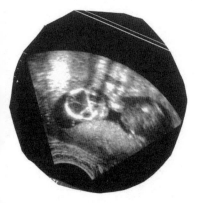

The sonogram of Marleigh, Lisa's unborn child. *(Photo by Sheila Underwood)*

Bloodstains on the carpet of Lisa Underwood's house had been scrubbed with soap and water, but they remained. *(State's evidence photo)*

The bloodstains found on the carpet had been covered by a coffee table. *(State's evidence photo)*

When the sofa was removed from the Underwood home, more dark blood was found just under the sofa's edge. *(State's evidence photo)*

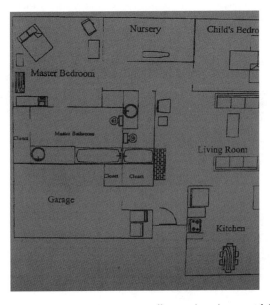

The Tarrant County District Attorney's office made a diagram of the Underwood home to present in court. *(State's evidence photo)*

Lisa Underwood's calendar, found in her home, showed a full schedule of activities, including a baby shower for her the day after her murder and Jayden's Blue and Gold Cub Scout dinner just a week after his death.
(State's evidence photo)

Lisa Underwood's blue Dodge Durango was found in a creek north of Fort Worth in rural Denton County. *(State's evidence photo)*

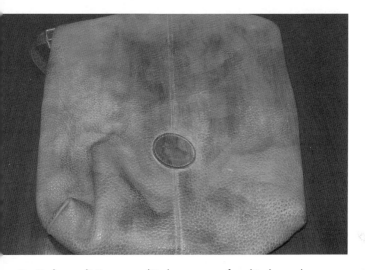

Lisa Underwood's Dooney and Burke purse was found in the creek near her abandoned automobile. *(State's evidence photo)*

Dried twigs and rotted tree branches were used to cover the bodies of Lisa and Jayden. *(State's evidence photo)*

Only Lisa Underwood's big toe, painted with bright red polish, could be seen peeking from the dried brush. *(State's evidence photo)*

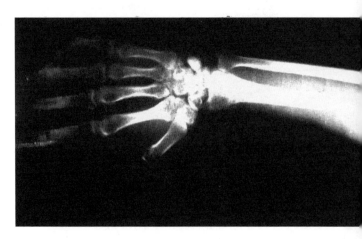

A fracture of Lisa Underwood's right arm was detected by x-ray.
(State's evidence photo)

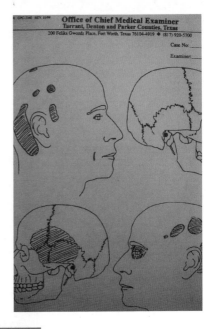

A chart prepared by the Office of the Chief Medical Examiner of Tarrant County depicted injuries to Lisa Underwood's skull. *(State's evidence photo)*

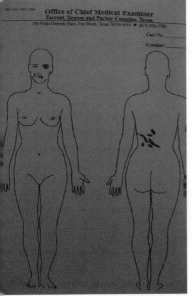

A second chart prepared by the Office of the Chief Medical Examiner and used during the trial to show bodily injuries to Lisa Underwood. *(State's evidence photo)*

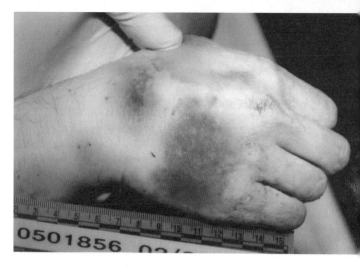

Bruising on Jayden's right hand indicates he fought his attacker.
(State's evidence photo)

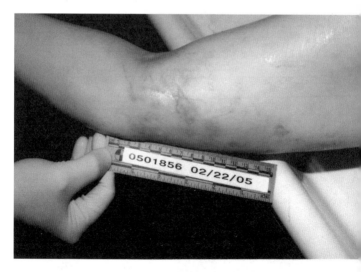

Jayden's legs showed signs of violent markings. *(State's evidence photo)*

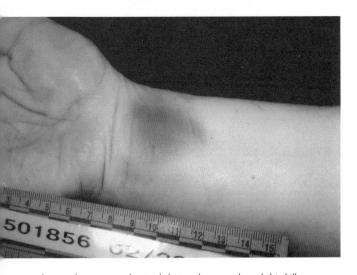

Jayden's right wrist was bruised during the struggle with his killer.
(State's evidence photo)

Stephen Barbee's mug shot was taken at the Smith County jail when he was booked for the murder of Lisa and Jayden Underwood.
(State's evidence photo)

The Barbee family at the marriage of Kathy Barbee. Left to right: Stephen and Jackie Barbee, Kathy Barbee Cherry, Mike Cherry, Bill and David Barbee. *(Photo provided by Jackie Barbee)*

Stephen Barbee played football in Azle, Texas, just west of Ford Worth. *(Photo provided by Jackie Barbee)*

Teresa Barbee was married to Stephen Barbee for seven volatile years. Teresa testified in court that Stephen was an abusive husband.
(Photo provided by Jackie Barbee)

Barbee married his second wife, Trish, just two months prior to the deaths of Lisa and Jayden Underwood.
(Photo provided by Jackie Barbee)

Trish and Stephen Barbee were happily married for only a short time.
Trish Barbee divorced Stephen shortly before his conviction for murder.
(Photo provided by Jackie Barbee)

Detectives Angela Jay and Mike Carroll remain close friends of
Sheila Underwood. *(Author photo)*

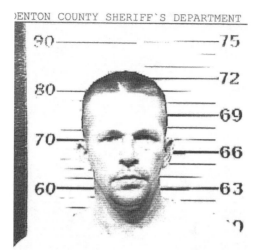

Rod Dodd was prosecuted by the Denton County District Attorney's office for tampering with evidence for his role in helping to dispose of the bodies of Lisa and Jayden. *(Photo courtesy of the Denton County Sheriff's Office)*

Kevin Rousseau, Felony Assistant District Attorney, was selected to lead the prosecution of Stephen Barbee. *(Author photo)*

ADA Rousseau selected Dixie Bersano to assist in the prosecution of Stephen Barbee. *(Author photo)*

Nothing is ever wholly lost. That which is excellent remains forever a part of this universe. R. W. Emerson

The Best and Brightest
Lisa, Jayden, & Baby Marleigh Underwood 2005

The Huguley Prayer Garden is a place for patients and visitors to stop, reflect and pray. *(Author photo)*

because she wasn't positive, she told both men about her pregnancy.

Switching to the week of the Underwoods' disappearance, Rousseau asked Holly to recap the events. She talked about Lisa and Jayden being sick that week and Lisa's inability to take any type of medication due to her pregnancy. Lisa had left work early on Wednesday, February 16, and missed work altogether on Thursday, February 17, and Friday, February 18. Although Holly didn't see Lisa on Friday, she had been in contact with her three times by phone, including once in an attempt to find out the name of Lisa's unborn baby for a baby shower in her honor the following day.

"How did you feel after that call?" Rousseau asked.

"I felt great. I was like, 'I can't wait for my best friend's baby shower. It's going to be fun.' There was a lot planned for it, and she was going to get lots of gifts. She was going to get everything she needed," Holly said.

"Did you ever talk to Lisa again?" Rousseau asked.

Holly took in a deep breath and swallowed hard. "No, I did not," she replied softly, sadness lacing her words.

The following day, Holly informed jurors, she had tried to reach Lisa, but her calls went straight to Lisa's voice mail. Lisa never answered. Holly hadn't been too concerned at the time, she knew Lisa had many things to do that day, including taking Jayden to a friend's birthday party.

Not until the twenty to twenty-five shower guests had been waiting more than fifteen minutes past Lisa's expected arrival time did Holly begin to worry. The empty parking spot in front of the shop reserved for Lisa due to the cold, wet weather remained empty. Holly testified that she then began to call area hospitals to see if Lisa had been admitted, while Sheila Underwood and a friend drove to Lisa's house to see if she was home and unable to answer the phone.

After Shelia returned to the shop, Holly notified police. It was about 4:30 or 4:45 P.M.

Holly detailed that after all the guests left the bagel shop and she closed up, she then drove to Lisa's house. By then, it was 6:30 or 7:00 P.M.

"When you got there, did you see anything that caused you concern?" Rousseau inquired.

"Yes. Jayden's shoes were on the fireplace on top of the hearth," Holly said, explaining that it was his only pair, because he outgrew them so fast.

Jurors listened intently to Holly's testimony. They showed no obvious reactions to the declarations, but the eyes of those jurors who were parents disclosed the sadness for the loss of a child so young he rapidly outgrew his shoes.

"You got there and other people are already there. Describe the atmosphere outside that house," Rousseau instructed.

"Everyone was scared. They wanted to know where Lisa and Jayden were. It was cold. We should have known where they were by that point," Holly responded.

"At some point did you return to the bagel shop?"

"Yes. It was after midnight."

"Did you go back to Lisa's house the next day?"

"Yes, I did."

"When did you finally leave, stop staying outside of Lisa's house?"

"When they found her car on Monday," Holly said.

"Did the police ever allow you to go into the house?" Rousseau asked.

"Yes. When they were done, they let us go back in," Holly said.

"Did Jayden wear glasses?" Rousseau inquired.

"Yes, he did," Holly said, explaining he needed them to see anything.

"Were his glasses in the house?"

"Yes. They were next to his bed," Holly responded.

"Is that where he kept them when he was sleeping?"

"Yes."

Rousseau had ended his questioning with the image of a small boy's glasses lying on his bedside table. An emotional illustration that indicated the youngster wouldn't be back to get them.

Bill Ray rose to question the witness and attempted to put her at ease.

"How are you doing, Ms. Pils? Do you need to take a break?" Ray asked pleasantly.

"No. I'm okay," Holly responded, shifting in her chair.

"Okay. I won't keep you very long," Ray said, smiling.

Ray reiterated Holly Pils's relationship with Lisa Underwood and that they confided personal information to one another.

Through Ray's questions Holly again stated that Lisa had been dating both Ed Rogers and Stephen Barbee in July 2004, and that in August of that year, Lisa had divulged that she was pregnant.

"Did Lisa tell you that she believed that the father of the child was Stephen Barbee?" Ray asked.

"Yes."

"Did that conversation come up on more than one occasion, as to who the father was?" Ray pressed.

"Yes."

"She told you Stephen is the father, Ed is not. Is that a fair statement?"

"She thought that he might be," Holly said honestly.

"Was there any kind of discussion between you and

Lisa concerning any kind of support for this baby?" Ray questioned.

Holly responded by stating that Lisa wanted health insurance for the baby, and she knew Lisa had discussed the issue with Barbee. Holly also told the court that she didn't know if Lisa had discussed the health insurance issue with Ed Rogers or not.

"Did Lisa ever indicate that she knew whether or not Mr. Barbee was getting married to somebody else?" Ray asked.

"No, she did not," Holly answered.

"You never heard that?" Ray asked.

"I never heard that," Holly stated firmly.

Bill Ray's questioning of Holly Pils was over, but her testimony wasn't yet complete. Kevin Rousseau had a few more questions for her.

"Was there a specific time that Lisa thought she had gotten pregnant?" Rousseau questioned.

"At the beginning of July," Holly said.

"It was because Lisa had spent time with him on a particular day?" Rousseau asked.

"Yes."

"And had you actually been caring for Jayden at the time that she had been off seeing Barbee that day?" Rousseau asked.

"Yes."

Holly Pils was finally excused and stepped down from the witness stand. Reliving the events of February 19, 2005, was a heartbreaking experience.

Judge Gill had been watching the jurors during Pils's testimony, and he determined that they needed a break. He announced that the court would be in recess for fifteen minutes, and that during that time jurors were not to discuss the case with anyone.

Kevin Rousseau and Dixie Bersano used the recess as an opportunity to review notes on their next witness. It would be the first person to put Stephen Barbee near the grave site of Lisa and Jayden Underwood, and therefore place Stephen Barbee's guilt in the minds of the jurors.

17

Judge Robert Gill was on the bench, the attorneys at their respective tables, and Stephen Barbee in his place as the jury filed in, following the short recess.

"Call your next witness, please," Judge Gill said to the prosecution.

"Officer David Brawner," Dixie Bersano announced.

Barbee recognized the officer, although he had only seen him in the dark of the early-morning hours of February 19, 2005.

Officer Brawner settled into the witness chair, wiping his hands on his brown polyester pants and straightening the neck on his khaki shirt. The Western-style uniform was worn by all Denton County Sheriff's Office (DCSO) personnel.

Brawner was aware of Bersano's own law enforcement record and respected her, not only for the position she now held, but for her twenty-year career with the Arlington PD. Nonetheless, the young officer, accustomed to working deep nights in a rural area with little contact with the public, appeared nervous in front of the court.

Brawner first explained that he had been employed by the Denton County Sheriff's Office for five years and was assigned to the patrol division. Brawner said he had graduated from the East Texas Police Academy in Kilgore, Texas, in 1998, and worked at the Lindale Police Department (LPD), about ten miles from Tyler, prior to taking the Denton County job.

The sandy-blond Brawner told jurors that on February 18, into the early hours of February 19, 2005, he was patrolling the west side of the county in a marked patrol unit. At the time he was wearing his Denton County sheriff's deputy uniform, including the familiar brown felt cowboy hat, making it easy to recognize him as an officer of the law.

"What's out in that part of the county?" Bersano asked.

"Not a whole lot. I mean, we have some trailer parks, some residential areas, but mostly it's farm roads, dirt roads, a lot of pastures. A country-type area," Brawner responded.

"What are you supposed to do on the midnight shift in the west portion of Denton County?" Bersano asked.

"My main responsibility is to protect lives and property. We do have a very big problem with burglaries in the area, so part of my responsibility is to check into suspicious circumstances, pedestrians, or vehicles," Brawner said, looking at the jury as he responded.

Taking the deputy back to February 19, 2005, Bersano asked Brawner if anything unusual happened while he was on duty.

Brawner testified that during his patrol he exited I-35W and drove down the access road toward Farm-to-Market Road 2449. At that time he saw a man walking northbound on the service road.

"At what time was that?" Bersano inquired.

"It was approximately three o'clock in the morning," Brawner said.

Brawner described the area where the person was walking as sparsely populated, with only a few small houses scattered in the vicinity. The region was mostly fields, farm-land, and wooded areas. The officer admitted it was very unusual to see someone walking in the locale at that time on a Saturday morning.

Most of the faces of the jury remained expressionless; however, there were a few whose brows were wrinkled in obvious confusion. They had no idea where the assistant district attorney was going with her line of questioning, but the relevance of Brawner's testimony would be clear very soon.

"So what did you do?" Bersano asked.

"I pulled my patrol vehicle behind the individual, activated my emergency overhead lights, which also activated my in-car video camera system, then I checked out with dispatch on a suspicious person," Brawner explained.

"When you pulled up behind him, did he react in any way?"

"He did react. The reaction to me was somewhat of a concern, because he just stopped. The individual never turned around, he just stopped. That was most unusual," Brawner responded, wrinkling his brow.

Brawner stated the man was wearing a dark-colored sweatshirt-style jacket, with hand-warmer pockets, light-colored jeans, and tennis shoes. The man's clothes were wet and covered in mud. The officer admitted the lighting was very poor, due to overcast conditions and no other light source other than his vehicle headlamps.

"Now you get out of the police car. You go up to this person. What do you do next?" Bersano questioned.

"When I approached the individual, I noticed he was covered in mud. My first question to him, was he okay? And his response was 'Yeah.' After that, I asked him for identification. He said that he got into an argument with a friend who lived in the housing addition he was walking toward. He stated he didn't have his identification with him because his wallet was at his friend's residence. So he gave me a name and date of birth," Brawner responded, looking at the jury, as he had been taught to do at the police academy.

"And do you recall what that name and date of birth was?"

"The name he gave me was David Weekley. I do have the date of birth here," Brawner stated, lifting the papers he had placed on the ledge in front of him.

There was a momentary pause as Officer Brawner looked through the report he had taken with him to court. Once he reviewed his notes, Brawner stated, "The individual gave me the name of David Weekley and the date of birth of March 16, 1967."

A couple of jurors glanced quickly toward the defendant. They had heard the name of David Weekley before, but they knew that the man sitting at the defense table bore no resemblance to him.

Officer Brawner gave details of how he returned to his vehicle and contacted dispatch to run the information the man had given him when he couldn't provide a driver's license number or Social Security number.

"Dispatch was unable to find any type of information by the name and date of birth given. No Social Security number, no driver's license number, or history—no criminal history. There was no information found whatsoever," Brawner stated, shaking his head.

"What did you think about that?" Bersano inquired.

"It's very unusual. The state of Texas has very good records of people, and it's very easy to locate this information," Brawner answered.

"What was the man doing while you were running the information?" Bersano asked.

"He was standing in front of my patrol vehicle. He never stopped moving. He was standing on the roadway, and he was scraping his feet on the pavement," Brawner stated.

Brawner described the man as Caucasian, approximately

five feet six inches, 160 pounds, short brown hair, with facial hair. He continued by telling the court that as soon as he opened his car door to again speak with the man, the pedestrian suddenly took off running. Brawner described notifying dispatch that he was in a foot pursuit, which eventually took him through a field of high grass and into a thick wooded area. He stated that the man became entangled in a barbed-wire fence for a few seconds, got up, and continued fleeing.

The deputy informed the jury that officers from other departments arrived to help in the apprehension of the man, but eventually Brawner couldn't keep up and lost him. Brawner described an all-out effort to locate the unidentified subject, including walking the area and using a handheld thermal-imaging unit, but their efforts were futile.

"What happened to the videotape?" Bersano asked.

"The videotape was logged into evidence two days later, when the vehicle was found. I was requested to bring the videotape to the same area where I had gotten into the foot chase with the individual," Brawner stated.

At that time ADA Dixie Bersano picked up an oblong plastic box from the table and placed the videotape that Deputy David Brawner had described to the jury into evidence. She then asked Deputy Brawner, "Officer, do you see the person that you stopped at three oh-six in the morning, on February 19, 2005, on the side of I-35, in the courtroom today?"

"Yes, ma'am, I do."

"Would you please point to him and describe what he's wearing?" Bersano instructed.

"From the left of this table, he is number five, sitting at the very end. He's wearing brown khaki pants, dark brown shoes, a multicolored brown shirt, and brown hair," Brawner replied, describing Stephen Barbee.

"Your Honor, may the record reflect that the witness has identified the defendant?" Bersano requested.

"It will," Judge Gill replied.

Sheila Underwood turned to look at Stephen Barbee's parents. Bill Barbee was looking down, his shoulders slumped, while his wife's eyes remained transfixed on their son. Sheila wondered if they understood the implication the deputy's identification of their son had on his guilt.

Sheila turned her attention back to Deputy Brawner as he began to recall the morning he was asked to assist in an evidence search. The deputy had arrived at the location of where Lisa Underwood's Dodge Durango had been found. He described the SUV as half submerged in a creek, the front end down and the back end up. Brawner was unable to estimate the depth of the water, but he did say the creek could not be crossed without getting wet. He admitted that when he completed his search, the bottom of his jeans were both wet and muddy.

With no objection from the defense, ADA Bersano placed into evidence a photograph of the area where the defendant was stopped in the early-morning hours of February 19, 2005. At Bersano's direction, Brawner stepped down from the witness-box and described for the jury what was visible in the photo.

Brawner pointed out that the defendant was stopped at 3:06 A.M. He pointed on the photograph to the direction Barbee began to run when he was confronted by the deputy.

"Is that an embankment there, on the other side of the roadway?" Bersano asked, pointing at the picture.

"Yes, ma'am, there is a slight decline in the hill, and then there's a barbed-wire fence here," Brawner said as he indicated that to the prosecutor.

"How did he get over the barbed wire?" Bersano asked.

"He ran right through it," Brawner stated. "He knocked

down a metal post holding the barbed wire up. It was enough force to knock it over, and he continued to run from that point."

The deputy pointed out that the man ran north, crossed over Vintage Road, and continued north into a wooded area, where he was ultimately lost.

"When you got called to the scene where the Durango was found, is that located in the photograph?" Bersano inquired.

Brawner replied, "Yes." He then pointed to the area where the SUV was found. "The Durango was found right here."

"The night you were chasing the defendant, did you ever make it down that far south?"

"No. I did walk down Vintage Road, about one hundred and fifty yards into this area," Brawner said, again pointing to the photo. "But I turned around and walked back, because he had run in the opposite direction."

Once Brawner pointed out where the Durango had been found, it was easy to see how close the deputy had come to finding the vehicle on the morning he had chased the defendant. At that point Dixie Bersano passed the witness on to the defense.

The deputy shifted in his chair, took in a deep breath, and readied himself to answer questions from the defense.

Moore, a man of average size with red hair and a confident air, reestablished Deputy Brawner's qualifications, then requested to see the report he had with him at the witness stand.

"When did you make this report?" Moore asked.

"The night of the foot pursuit."

"And who told you to make it?" Moore asked, setting the deputy up for his next question.

"I did it on my own."

"That's just a police officer's duty, isn't it?" Moore inquired.

"Yes, sir."

Moore drove his point home by having the deputy agree that although he would probably have remembered the events of that morning a year later, he wrote the report so that it could be referred to, if needed. Brawner also unknowingly helped Moore set up for the state's most explosive witness when he testified that these report procedures were taught at the police academy. When he wrote a report, he re-read it, even double-checked it, to make certain all events were included.

Jurors, who hadn't been present during the suppression hearing to hear the defense drill Detective Carroll for his recordkeeping, were unaware that Moore was using the deputy's testimony to shed doubt on Detective Carroll's credibility.

"On the twenty-first you get a call from the Fort Worth Police Department asking you to bring the videotape to where the Durango was located. Is that right?" Moore asked.

"No, sir. I was contacted by the Denton County sheriff's dispatch office and they told me about the situation that was happening on Vintage. What they told me was the vehicle that was involved in the AMBER Alert had been located, because they already knew I had gotten into a foot pursuit in the immediate area. And per our captain, he wanted me to respond to that location with the videotape," Brawner explained.

Brawner stated that while he was on the scene, the Fort Worth detectives watched the videotape, showed him a photo lineup, and that he had picked out a photo of Stephen Barbee as the man who had run from him.

"No doubt about that?" Moore asked.

"I'm one hundred percent positive. One hundred and ten percent," Brawner stated firmly.

"Thank you, Deputy. That's all I have, Judge," Moore announced.

ADA Bersano rose and addressed the court from behind the prosecution table.

"One question, Judge," Bersano said. "Deputy, from where you initially stopped the defendant, to where you spotted the vehicle in the creek when you were called to the scene, about how far is that?"

"Three hundred yards, approximately," Brawner responded.

"Okay," Bersano said. Turning from the witness to face the judge, she added, "No further questions, Judge."

Moore stood and addressed the court. "I don't have any other questions, Judge."

Judge Gill looked at the large-faced clock on the wall, then at the twelve jurors and the alternate.

"Ladies and gentlemen of the jury, we're going to break for lunch at this point. Please remember and follow your instructions while we're on the lunch break. We're going to break until one-fifteen. Let's be back outside the courtroom door right before one-fifteen and the bailiffs will meet you there. Have a good lunch."

At that time the jury stood and exited via a door adjacent to the jury box. Knowing Judge Gill expected punctuality, bailiffs warned jurors not to be late.

Stephen Barbee was taken back to the court's holding cell, where he would eat his lunch and wait for the trial to reconvene. His attorneys would confer on witnesses who had testified to that point, while their counterparts prepared for the state's afternoon witnesses.

* * *

When the lunch break was over, and the jury had taken their places, Judge Gill called court to order. At that time ADA Kevin Rousseau entered into evidence two photographs, then called his next witness.

Detective Troy Lawrence, dressed in street clothes rather than a Fort Worth PD uniform, took the stand. The Fort Worth detective informed the jury he had been called several times to the location where Underwood's Durango had been found, as well as to where the bodies had been buried.

Lawrence first arrived at the creek where Lisa's car had been ditched to secure her water-soaked purse, which had been recovered by Fort Worth Fire Department divers. They had snared the bag from the limb of a tree overhanging the cold waters and thirty feet below the bluff above. Lawrence said he retrieved a white piece of paper from the tan Dooney & Bourke purse, laid it out flat for it to begin drying, and dumped water from the handbag before turning it over to crime scene investigators.

Once the bodies of Lisa and Jayden were discovered, and prior to recovery, Lawrence said, he had been assigned to guard the grave site overnight.

In addition to these duties, Lawrence stated, as Fort Worth Police Department's computer forensic expert, he had also been asked to analyze Lisa Underwood's computer. Before his testimony could be continued, Bill Ray asked the court for a 705 hearing. The defense attorney wanted to question Detective Lawrence outside the presence of the jury in order to learn exactly what the detective would testify to that had been found on the computer, as well as any opinions he might plan to give.

Under the Federal Rules of Evidence, Judge Gill granted the 705 hearing so that the defense could determine the testimony and opinion Detective Lawrence would be giving. He asked the jury to be excused, until they would be called back into the courtroom.

Under voir dire examination Lawrence explained he planned to testify that Lisa Underwood's computer was logged on to AOL at 11:22 P.M. on February 18, and logged off at 12:02 A.M., February 19. Lawrence admitted he was unable to tell if the computer was turned off at that time, or if AOL had logged off automatically after ten minutes of nonactivity. The detective also stated he would testify that at 11:43 P.M. Lisa had logged on to the Birthplan.com website. Again, he was unable to determine exactly how long Lisa had actually been on the website.

Lawrence told Mr. Ray that he had also found two e-mails on the night of February 18, but he was unaware if the prosecution would be asking him questions concerning those e-mails.

Kevin Rousseau declared he didn't intend to question Detective Lawrence about the computer correspondence. Bill Ray announced he had no more questions and no objection to Lawrence testifying on the subjects discussed in voir dire.

The judge instructed the bailiff, "Bring the jury back out, please."

The uniformed officer did as directed and the jury filed back into their seats, unaware of what had taken place in their absence.

Kevin Rousseau continued his examination of Detective Lawrence, concentrating on Lisa Underwood's computer.

Lawrence testified he was asked to make a copy of the hard drive of Underwood's computer. He explained that because it was an older model processor, he had to install a special card in his own computer in order to attach the drive from Lisa's PC. He was then able to make an exact duplicate, and worked from that copy.

The detective repeated for the jury the information that had been heard in voir dire during their absence.

Rousseau presented State's Exhibit 33, a ten-page copy taken from the Underwood hard drive. The exhibit showed the Birthplan website Lisa had been visiting on the last night of her life, as well as a file accessed on the afternoon of February 19. The detective assumed that on February 19, since Lisa and Jayden had already been reported missing, the computer was being used by a family member.

After passing the witness to the defense, Bill Ray had few questions, but reserved the right to recall the detective, if needed.

Judge Gill excused the detective, but unlike the earlier witnesses who had been told they would no longer be needed, the judge informed Lawrence he was subject to recall.

Immediately after Kevin Rousseau announced his next witness, Dr. Marc Krouse, Bill Ray stood, buttoned his open coat, and informed the court that he would need a 705 hearing on Dr. Krouse. Jurors had been in the courtroom less than an hour when they were asked to leave again. Some began to think the trial would never end if a rash of 705 hearings were called. They could be there for weeks, rather than days, as first anticipated.

Those in the courtroom who knew Dr. Marc Krouse as the chief deputy medical examiner of Tarrant County were anxious to hear his findings from the autopsies of Lisa and Jayden Underwood. They wondered what pertinent facts the ME would share that could shed light on the final minutes leading to their tragic deaths.

18

Rousseau called Dr. Marc Krouse to the stand, then walked to the railing and leaned over as he spoke softly to Sheila Underwood.

"Sheila, you need to leave now. You don't want to hear the medical examiner's testimony," Rousseau said.

Rousseau wanted to spare the grieving mother from the gruesome details of the murder of her daughter and grandchild. And as if those particulars weren't enough, Dr. Krouse would also be discussing the death of Marleigh.

Tall, trim, with graying hair at his temples, the distinguished Dr. Marc Krouse took his place in the witness chair as Sheila Underwood quietly slipped out the rear door of the courtroom. Krouse had testified in hundreds of cases since joining the Tarrant County Medical Examiner's Office in July 1978. He had performed between thirteen thousand and fourteen thousand autopsies during that time.

Bill Ray had no problem with Dr. Krouse's credentials, having faced him in court a number of times. A true product of Texas, Krouse had graduated from Texas A&M University, Southwestern Medical School in Dallas, and then completed his residency at Baylor Medical Center, also in

Dallas. Krouse had the respect of prosecutors and defense attorneys alike.

Ray wasted no time in getting directly to the questions he had concerning the doctor's autopsy of Lisa Underwood. He asked for the doctor's opinions and the data supporting his opinions, concerning the cause of death.

"It is my opinion that the cause of death of Ms. Underwood was traumatic asphyxiation. The evidence supporting that was a number of abrasions and bruises of her face and lips. Evidence of compression of her teeth against the inside of her cheek, particularly the left. Some bruises under the scalp on both sides, but generalized hemorrhaging in the temporal muscle on the left side, and contusions of the back, external and occult bruising over virtually her entire back.

"Incidentally, and not related directly to the cause of death, she had a fracture of one of the bones of her right forearm," Krouse explained.

"Just to make sure I understand, you're here to say that the cause of death was traumatic asphyxiation?" Ray asked.

"Yes."

Ray thanked Dr. Krouse and was ready to bring the jury back in when Rousseau stated, "Just so we're clear, I also intended to ask Dr. Krouse about his autopsy of the fetus and his findings."

"Tell us your opinion first," Ray scoffed, directing his disparagement toward Rousseau and his question to Dr. Krouse.

"The woman was pregnant. She had a normal female fetus that appeared to be about seven and a half months or so gestational age. The size and weight was consistent with that. The development of the ears, growth of head hair, and development of creases on the palms of the hands and the soles of the feet were all consistent with that gestational age.

"The placenta was fine. No evidence of any abnormality. There was no evidence of direct injury or trauma to the fetus herself. We did find some bleeding internally in the head and chest cavity. That commonly occurs when a fetus dies of oxygen deprivation or asphyxia.

"So basically we have maternal asphyxiation resulting in fetal asphyxiation," the doctor stated.

"What's your opinion on the cause and manner of death, if that's different than what you already said?" Ray asked.

"The cause of death I put in the report as traumatic asphyxiation, primarily either compression or suffocation by occlusion of her nose and mouth, or a combination of those two events, and that the manner of death was homicide," Dr. Krouse replied.

The medical examiner's words hung in the courtroom like a dark, ominous cloud as the jury returned to hear his testimony.

Kevin Rousseau began his questioning as he most often did, by having Dr. Krouse state his qualifications for the jury. He also asked the ME to explain the type of cases handled by his department.

"In the Texas criminal code under Article 49, it is required that certain deaths be reported either to a medical examiner or to a justice of the peace in a county where there is not a medical examiner. This would include anyone who is found dead not attended by a physician or a nurse practitioner, anyone who dies under the same circumstances, anyone who dies under suspicious circumstances, where the cause of death might not be a natural disease process, and, of course, that can open up a huge can of worms. We get a lot of deaths reported under that clause of the law.

"Anyone who dies within twenty-four hours of admission

to a hospital, to a jail, or to any other custodial facility, their death must be reported to us because that interval is too short to allow accurate diagnosis of conditions in many cases. As a practical matter, custodial deaths are routinely reported to our office by the sheriff and the various police agencies.

"And then anyone who dies, regardless of their period of hospitalization, where the cause of death is known or suspected to be from a traumatic injury, drug ingestion, or other suspicious circumstance."

When asked why an autopsy would be performed, Dr. Krouse explained that it was to determine the cause of a person's death. Secondly, if it was a case such as drug ingestion or a poison, body fluid samples and organ or tissue samples must be taken to properly figure out what happened and when the event occurred. And lastly, to determine if it was a natural disease, like some cases of pneumonia, ruptured aneurysms, or an artery bursting inside someone's heart or chest or abdomen. Those were cases that could not be seen by simply looking at someone.

Dr. Krouse added that they also, as conclusively as possible, tried to make a positive identification of the body.

The doctor testified that the ME's office was notified on February 22 that a possible location of the bodies of Lisa and Jayden Underwood had been found. Dr. Krouse stated he arrived at the scene with the chief medical examiner, their anthropologist, Dr. Dana Austin, as well as a number of assistants, who would help with the recovery of the bodies.

"We disassembled a pile of brush and began working on a mound of dirt that lay beneath that mound of brush. In short order we were certain we had two human bodies," Dr. Krouse stated.

"We continued to remove the dirt, looking for any other

material that might be of some evidentiary value later. Upon
finally uncovering the bodies and making measurements
and [taking] photographs, I examined the two bodies in
their location, noted the conditions, and prepared to make
positive identifications. We then removed the bodies from
the shallow pit and examined that for tool marks or other
potential evidence," Dr. Krouse continued.

The doctor described the appearance of Lisa at the scene
as clothed, with her underpants down around her knees, and
a T-shirt that was damp, bloodstained, and tainted with dirt.
He added that some sleep pants or pajama pants were under
her body, and a pair of eyeglasses tangled in her hair.

"It was about four-fifteen P.M. when we got the body back
to the morgue, and we went over everything again," Dr.
Krouse said. "We wrapped her in a clean white cotton sheet,
took her back to the morgue, and our trace evidence ana-
lysts and I, along with a photographer present to take pictures, went over the body. Then I disrobed the body and
actually began my autopsy at about six P.M."

After stating that he cleaned the body, removing all for-
eign material and dirt, Rousseau instructed Dr. Krouse to
explain to the jury what his initial observations were of Lisa
Underwood's body.

Dr. Krouse reported that Lisa appeared to be in normally
nourished and fairly decent physical condition. At three in
the afternoon when he first looked at the body, there had
still been a little residual rigor mortis, or stiffening.

"Is that something that would fade away under different
circumstances?" Rousseau asked.

"Yes, once a body begins to decompose, that stiffening
disappears. After a person dies, your brain dies, your heart
quits, but your skeletal muscles actually continue to live. In
so doing, they generate a lot of lactic acid, along with some
other organic compounds that tend to drop the pH to make

the environment more acidic. At a critical point all the proteins in the muscle that normally run over each other to make them contract all gelatinize. They become gelatin, basically. It's like Jell-O setting up. That phenomenon is called rigor mortis. The body becomes very stiff and it may be very difficult to extend or move a limb."

From the expressions of the faces of jurors and an occasional nod, it was apparent they were following the medical examiner's detailed testimony.

"This persists until bacteria gets in there and the body begins to decompose and break down. Usually, under normal room temperature conditions, this is about twenty-four to thirty-six hours after death. In cooler conditions this can persist a long time. In our refrigerator, for example, which we keep, I think, at forty-two degrees Fahrenheit, rigor will persist for a week, easily. I've seen it persist even in exterior environments in cool temperatures at least five to six days. And there have been documented cases where someone disappeared in the wilds of Minnesota where rigor didn't appear until four months after death because of the cold conditions. So basically, cooling the body tends to cause rigor to persist."

The jury appeared to be enthralled by Dr. Krouse's testimony. They gave him their undivided attention as he spoke of medical conditions they had heard about, but most had never really understood.

In describing Lisa Underwood's injuries to the jury, Dr. Krouse stated she had sustained a left black eye, a small contusion on her lower lip, a small abrasion on her cheek, another abrasion on her left armpit, and several bruises on her lower left back, from the rib cage on down to where the left kidney sits on the back of the pelvis. There were a couple of bruises on her right arm, right at the base of her arm, her right elbow; and on her right wrist, at the base of her hand, were three small rectangular bruises.

At that time Kevin Rousseau introduced a number of photographs into evidence. Bill Ray asked the court for a chance to ask the doctor a couple of questions, which were basically inquiring as to when the photos had been taken.

In response Dr. Krouse stated the pictures had been taken during the autopsy of Ms. Underwood. With that, Bill Ray stated he had no objection to the introduction of the photographs into evidence.

Rousseau then presented two large blowup charts, the originals having been made during the autopsy at the county morgue. Dr. Krouse informed the court that the charts indicated detailed injuries to the head that photographs could not be taken of, including a number of bruises under the scalp and hemorrhage in the temporal muscle.

ADA Rousseau then asked Dr. Krouse to step down from the witness stand so that he could explain to the jury what each of the photographs and charts depicted.

Dr. Krouse stepped down as instructed, standing nearly as tall as the assistant district attorney. The doctor began describing each photo and the type of injuries Lisa Underwood had sustained.

When Dr. Krouse explained the type of wounds found on her back, he depicted them as a constellation of injuries that would be called blunt-force trauma.

"That is a force applied against a person's body sufficient to rupture blood vessels, either from compression or a blow and an impact," Dr. Krouse clarified.

"So the injuries there could be from some object striking her, correct?" Rousseau asked.

"Yes, they could."

"And they could also be from pressure with a knee in the back to cause that type of injury?" Rousseau inquired.

But before Dr. Krouse had a chance to respond, Bill Ray was on his feet.

"Excuse me before you answer that, Dr. Krouse. Judge, I'm going to object. He's outside the scope of what was brought up at the 705 hearing. Maybe we need to have another hearing," Ray stated.

"Sustained," Judge Gill ruled.

"Okay," Rousseau said, "then we do need to have another hearing. I thought we covered it. We need to go into this, Your Honor."

As with the prior 705 hearing, the defense would be able to learn what the medical examiner would be testifying to, prior to the jury hearing his remarks. The defense would have an opportunity to object and possibly keep a portion of his testimony out of the trial.

Judge Gill looked toward the jury and, after taking and expelling a big sigh, announced, "Ladies and gentlemen, another couple of minutes."

Once the jury had been taken to the jury deliberation room adjacent to the court, voir dire examination by both the state and the defense began. After several minutes the jury returned, and direct examination by the state continued.

As the prosecution continued, Rousseau again asked Dr. Krouse to step down from the witness chair. Rousseau held a stack of autopsy photos of Lisa Underwood lying on the cold stainless-steel examination table at the county morgue. Rousseau requested the doctor choose the photos he thought best depicted the injuries he would be describing to the jurors. Each of the photos selected by Dr. Krouse portrayed, in vivid color, the horrendous beating suffered by Lisa Underwood. And as the doctor spoke in medical terms of a fractured forearm and wrist, as well as a broken thumb, it was obvious the once-vibrant young woman had fought for her life with all the strength she had.

Holding a picture of an X-ray taken of Lisa's broken arm, Dr. Krouse stated, "You can see that the break not only goes all the way through the bone, both sides of the cortex are broken, but at a bit of an angle. It was caused by a bending or shearing force of the wrist."

Dr. Krouse then clarified that a shearing-force break would occur when the bone was struck with an object, while it was resting on something solid. Because in this case there was also a rectangular-shaped bruise accompanying the wrist break, the object had to have been shaped in that manner, the doctor believed.

As Kevin Rousseau began to question Dr. Krouse about injuries to Lisa's face, and the enlarged photo of her facial injuries was presented, there were faint signs of horror on some faces of the jury and spectators alike.

Lisa Underwood's features appeared swollen, discolored, and distorted. The photo image of the deceased woman was nothing like the animated, bright-eyed, smiling woman in a photo shown at the beginning of the trial. Rousseau was glad Sheila Underwood had left the courtroom prior to Dr. Krouse taking the stand.

Stephen Barbee averted his eyes from the pictures of the woman he had once dated, while his mother's tears began to streak her cheeks.

Next the medical examiner selected an enlargement of a chart regularly used in his work. For easy identification the doctor had previously circled each bruise that had occurred on Lisa's body in blue Marker on the chart. The Marker depicted bruises that ran from the base of her skull, across her shoulders, and down her lower back. In addition to those outwardly visible signs, Dr. Krouse stated there was internal bruising up and down both sides of her back.

"What caused that kind of injury you just described to her back?" Rousseau asked.

"This can be caused by an impact against or by a very broad surface, one where the force is distributed over a wide enough area that it's not damaging the skin, but indeed is damaging the underlying muscles and connective tissues. Or it can be caused by an external force over a longer period of time. It's impossible for me to distinguish those two," Dr. Krouse explained.

"So it could be being hit hard with a broad object or having a broad object pressed against you long enough to do some amount of damage?" Rousseau asked.

"Yeah."

"So you're not going to get this falling down in your living room?" Rousseau inquired.

"No, sir, not unless you have about a four-story living room you're going to fall out of," Dr. Krouse replied with a slight smile.

Dr. Krouse concurred with the prosecutor that the injuries were consistent with a person facedown on the floor, with the weight of another person's body sitting or kneeling on that person's back. The doctor added it would be even more likely if the person was struggling, because the one holding them down would be increasing the force in increments over different areas as they struggled.

When asked by Rousseau if this action would make it difficult for the victim to breathe, the medical examiner stated, "Yes. If a person is conscious and you're preventing them from breathing, they're going to try to relieve that situation."

"Sure. Would a person being seven-and-a-half months pregnant have any effect at all on the situation?" Rousseau asked.

Dr. Krouse explained that two things would be happening. First, the compression itself. Compression of the chest wall would make it very difficult to move significant amounts of air in and out. The second thing, the guts were being shoved up under the rib cage into the diaphragm and inhibiting diaphragmatic motion and inflating of the lungs. You need both things to inflate your lungs effectively.

He further stated that if the belly was compressed, it interfered with diaphragmatic motion, and if the chest wall was compressed, it interfered with rib cage motion.

"Either one of those could get you," Dr. Krouse said.

ADA Rousseau took his scenario one step further: what, if any, effect would it have if that same person's face was being pressed into the floor.

"The face being smashed against a surface probably doesn't have a lot of effect," Dr. Krouse stated.

He added that if there was neck compression, there would be some bleeding in the upper ends of the neck muscles that overlay the larynx and the voice box. Dr. Krouse acknowledged there was such bleeding found during the autopsy of Lisa Underwood.

"Would heavy bleeding from the nose, at the same time that's going on, further impact the ability to breathe?" Rousseau asked, taking the doctor down the path of death that Lisa Underwood traveled on February 19, 2005.

"It might obstruct the nasal airway to some degree, yeah," Dr. Krouse responded.

"And you can only breathe through your nose or your mouth, right?" Rousseau asked, straight-faced.

"Yeah, unless you're very specialized," Dr. Krouse said with a slight curve of his lips.

"Yeah," Rousseau said with a smile and nod of his head, acknowledging the medical examiner's attempt at humor. "So if your nose is blocked, that only leaves your mouth, right?"

"Yes, sir."

Rousseau had successfully set up the medical examiner for the next set of photographs, and additional clarification of the death of Lisa Underwood.

Looking at another chart made at the medical examiner's office, Dr. Krouse described injuries to Lisa Underwood's head that would not be visible in a photograph.

Those injuries included bruises to the right side of her head, just in front of the ear, as well as a large area behind the ear. There were additional bruises on the left side in the soft tissue, just above the temporal muscle and behind the ear.

All thirteen jurors concentrated on the chart Dr. Krouse was presenting as he explained the internal head wounds of Lisa Underwood.

"Then there is bleeding in virtually all of the temporalis muscle itself. It could be either a blow that is spread over a wide area that damaged fifty to sixty percent of the muscle. It's a pretty wide area of pressure," Dr. Krouse declared.

"The smaller bruises, can you tell us what type of force might cause those?" Rousseau asked.

"They're pretty localized. They present an impact point. If her head's striking an object, and since her head is this severe, he'd whack her real hard on a flat surface. It's not all that much of a hit—it's contacting it. The areas that damaged the scalp, behind the ears, are localized impact," Dr. Krouse said.

"Are those consistent with a hand gripping the back of someone's head?" Rousseau asked.

"That is one potential cause, yes. A very hard grasp of

somebody's head, particularly if they're moving against it, is going to multiply the force being applied. We occasionally see what we call fingertip bruises under the scalp," Dr. Krouse responded.

Rousseau paused momentarily before asking one of the state's most important questions.

"Doctor, looking at all of this," Rousseau said with a wave of his arm toward the state's exhibits, "your internal examinations, what you know of this case, is there anything that is inconsistent with Lisa Underwood being beaten, followed by or contemporaneous with her face being forced to the floor, while her assailant sat or kneeled on her back?"

"No."

"What was the cause of death?" Rousseau asked.

"Traumatic asphyxiation," Dr. Krouse stated.

Dr. Krouse explained to the jury that asphyxia death is one that occurs because of fatal oxygen deprivation to a person's brain. Traumatic asphyxiation is a specific term that's utilized in the forensic community to designate that a person has died because of compression, or other mechanical interference with their breathing. The medical examiner illustrated this statement by stating that traumatic asphyxiation could be an obstruction of the airway, like a hand or some object placed over the head or face, or even a plastic bag that they can't get off. It could also be the actual mechanical loading of the chest wall and belly, which he believed occurred in the Lisa Underwood case.

"Does the term include smothering?" Rousseau asked.

"Yes, smothering would be upper airway obstruction by external means, or even stuffing an object in the oral cavity or nasal cavity," Dr. Krouse responded.

"The allegation here is that Lisa's death was caused by smothering her with the weight of a body or with an object that is unknown, or by a combination of the two. Do you see anything that is inconsistent with that?" Rousseau inquired.

"No, sir, I do not."

"What was the manner of death?"

"The manner of death in this case is homicide," Dr. Krouse announced.

Rousseau asked the doctor to explain to the jury how long it would take for a person to die from oxygen deprivation.

Dr. Krouse informed the court that to die in this manner the brain, heart, or, to a lesser degree, other organs must be lethally affected. He stated it as most likely to be the brain, at which time everything would shut down. The doctor stated that it would take between two to three minutes, up to seven minutes to absolutely kill someone. He added that a person would probably lose consciousness within a few seconds, but if the blockage was removed, they would recover.

"So for this death to occur like this, it would take at least two to three minutes of pressure being applied?" Rousseau asked.

"That would be my opinion, yes," Dr. Krouse stated.

"Could this be an accidental death?" Rousseau questioned.

"I have not seen anything about this case that leads me in that direction," Dr. Krouse said.

The doctor's words rang in the ears of Trish Barbee, who was sitting in the gallery. Stephen had told her he didn't mean for Lisa to die. He said it was an accident; yet the doctor said there was nothing to make him believe her death was accidental. Had Stephen lied to her about everything?

Nearing the end of his questioning, Kevin Rousseau asked Dr. Krouse to describe the condition of the fetus Lisa Underwood was carrying at the time of her death.

Repeating what he had said during the 705 hearing, Dr. Krouse stated, "This was a healthy fetus. It appeared to be seven to seven and a half months or so gestation age. Size and weight were normal for that. The development of the ear cartilage was well along. You've got to be about five and a half to six months to even start ear cartilage. The basal cartilage was well developed. The creases on the palms and the soles of the feet were well developed.

"So we're looking at a near-term, definitely third trimester, fetus. It was a female. I found absolutely no external injuries. The placenta was in good shape. Everything that was required to keep this baby alive was there.

"Internally all we found was some blood leakage in the chest cavity around the lungs and some over the surface of the brain, and in the ventricles inside the brain. All of these being very common signs of oxygen deprivation in the fetus. So it's basically maternal asphyxiation leads to fetal asphyxiation."

"So this baby died because her mother died?" Rousseau asked.

"Yes."

Marla Hess, Lisa Underwood's aunt, looked at Stephen Barbee with indignation. The baby that her niece had been carrying at the time of her death would have been named Marleigh, partly named for her. The rage Marla felt was beyond anything she had ever experienced. She turned her stare from Stephen Barbee to his parents, wondering how they could believe their son hadn't taken the life of her beloved niece and the baby for whom the family waited with such joyful anticipation.

Rousseau glanced toward the jury. Having brought them to an emotional pinnacle, Rousseau passed the witness.

Bill Ray stood to address the medical examiner. Dr. Krouse had been on the stand for some time without a break, but he appeared relaxed and poised. Ray reviewed the doctor's testimony concerning obstruction of the airway and then stated that if duct tape was placed over a person's nose and mouth, there wouldn't have to be any compression at all, because they would be unable to breathe. Dr. Krouse concurred. Ray also asked that if that had been done, wouldn't it decrease the amount of time it took her to be asphyxiated? Krouse concurred with the defense.

Ray then focused on Lisa's pregnancy and asked Dr. Krouse if her physical state would have altered her ability to breathe, depending on how she was held.

Dr. Krouse agreed.

Moving on, Ray asked, "Did you find any injury that would indicate she was struck with any type of object? And I mean a board, a baseball bat, a piece of pipe, anything that a person might use as a weapon?"

"Some of the bruises on the external part of the back, over the lower left back, could possibly be a cylindrical object, like a pipe or bat. There's not a terrific pattern to them. But the injuries on her right arm have a distinct rectangular pattern to them. That arm was either forced against, flung against, or had something strike it that had a rectangular shape," Dr. Krouse stated.

"A piece of furniture?" Ray asked.

"That's fair to say, yeah. And one of those blows produces enough of a shearing force across her arm to break it," Dr. Krouse stated, as he had earlier in his testimony.

"Okay. She was certainly in a fight of some sort. I mean, she was in some sort of confrontation. She has a black eye and lots of other bruises. Would you agree with that?" Ray asked.

At that point Jackie Barbee looked toward her husband and shook her head, closing her eyes momentarily. The defendant's mother couldn't comprehend why her son's

defense attorney would want to point out the beating the
victim had taken, rather than casting doubt in the jury's
minds that it was Stephen who had waged the attack.

"The injuries I've seen are entirely consistent with an
altercation, probably one-on-one," Dr. Krouse responded.

Ray wanted to know how the doctor could determine
there had been only one assailant.

Dr. Krouse stated that for a person to have suffered a fatal
injury in an altercation against more than one person, the
injury distribution would be much greater and over a greater
part of the body.

When Bill Ray questioned Dr. Krouse about the possibility of an accident, the doctor explained that for an accidental death to be considered, they would have to have
evidence that the circumstances under which that occurred
were not initiated with the intent or with what they would
consider grievous or a gross degree of negligence. He stated
that in determining homicide—one person causing the death
of another person—they would consider intent or gross
negligence in the process.

In response to the ME's answer, Ray asked, "Well, you
said that the injuries that you found were consistent with an
individual holding Ms. Underwood down and stopping her
breathing. Would you agree that there's nothing you found
that shows what was going on in that person's mind [who]
was doing that?"

"Yes," Dr. Krouse simply said.

On redirect Dr. Krouse again testified that Ms. Underwood would have lost consciousness after a few seconds,
but would have had to be held down for two to seven minutes for death to occur. Mr. Ray argued the point on re-

cross-examination, with Dr. Krouse admitting that it could have been as little as thirty seconds, but unlikely.

With the image of a pregnant Lisa Underwood lying on the floor of her Fort Worth living room and her assailant pushing her face into the floor until her death, and the death of her baby, Judge Gill called for a welcome fifteen-minute recess.

19

Following the fifteen-minute recess called by Judge Robert Gill, testimony of the Tarrant County chief deputy ME continued to ring in the ears of courtroom observers.

Before her death Lisa Underwood had suffered a ruthless beating that left her with a black eye, a bloody nose, a broken arm, and multiple bruises. But the thing spectators remembered most was that it had taken between two and seven minutes for Lisa Underwood to die, and that the fetus she carried had died along with her.

A stern-faced Judge Gill rapped his gavel for the court to come to order as the gallery waited with anticipation to see who the next state's witness would be.

Kyle Sullivan, a Fort Worth police officer assigned to the Crime Scene Unit, walked with confidence to the front of the courtroom and took his seat in the witness chair. The ten-year veteran of the FWPD, who appeared to be in his middle thirties, was accustomed to testifying in court, as displayed by his demeanor on the stand.

Officer Sullivan, a blood pattern analyst, had been called to the Underwood house on February 19, 2005, to examine a stain found on the living-room carpet. Sullivan had performed a presumptive blood test to determine if the stain was indeed blood, as suspected. When the stain turned pink after applying phenylphaline, he knew for certain it was blood.

Sullivan testified that as soon as he had determined the nature of the stain, he notified the Missing Persons Unit, then cleared the house and laid down paper on the floors so as not to disturb any potential evidence. Meanwhile, a search warrant for the residence was obtained.

Kevin Rousseau asked the crime scene officer if he had noticed any forced entry when he first arrived at the Underwood house.

"No signs of forced entry," Sullivan remarked.

"Did you notice any other possible bloodstain in any other location, other than the living room?" Rousseau asked.

"Yes. Inside the residence we immediately recognized what we thought to be blood on an entertainment center, on the top shelf and the bottom shelf, on the west, east, and north walls of the residence, and on the fitted couch cover, along the north wall," Sullivan stated.

Checking his notes, Rousseau asked Sullivan if there was anything odd about the furniture in the house.

"The coffee table inside the living room was in an awkward position," Sullivan responded. "It was in a north/south position, and it was a little off center. It just didn't look like it fit in the living room."

In long strides from the witness-box to the prosecutor's table, Kevin Rousseau picked up a videotape and offered it as Exhibit 54. With no objection from the defense, it was presented into evidence.

Rousseau pushed the tape into the video player and waited for the crime scene footage to begin. When there was no response, Rousseau continued to fiddle with the machine, his irritation with the malfunctioning player mounting.

Within minutes the frames of the video ran, showing the

interior of Lisa Underwood's house. The camera lingered on the front entry and door, revealing that there had been no forced entry, just as Officer Sullivan had testified.

As the video showed the interior of the garage, Rousseau asked if the visible discolorations on the garage floor were bloodstains.

The veteran investigator stated they believed some may have been blood, but there were also furniture stains and a can of stain nearby, insinuating that the stain may have come from that source.

Rousseau pushed the television and VCR out of the way, picked up a stack of still photographs, and returned to his witness.

Once Officer Sullivan had identified the photos as ones he had taken at the Underwood house, Rousseau entered them into evidence as State's Exhibits 36 through 50.

Sullivan identified the first photograph as the living-room floor, where numbers had been placed in random areas. The officer explained the numbers coincided with presumptive blood tests he had performed at each spot.

"How do you go about doing that?" Rousseau asked.

"We use Q-tips and distilled water. You place two drops of distilled water on a Q-tip to get it wet, and then in a circular motion, you try to get as much of the substance on the Q-tip that you can," Sullivan explained.

"Can you tell us if there's anything unusual about these bloodstains?" Rousseau asked.

"Yes. It's a saturated bloodstain on carpet. It appears an attempt has been made to clean, or wipe up, the carpet. Where you have a dark area here," Sullivan said, pointing to a portion of the photo, "where a stain, pool, or saturation was, and then as it gets farther away, it gets lighter in color. Something's being wiped out of the carpet."

The crime scene investigator explained that in order for

the carpet to have been saturated with blood, the person had to have been on top of the carpet while bleeding.

The next photo showed a bloodstain on one of the living-room walls. Sullivan explained that the blood had been transferred from a bloody object or person onto the wall by touching it, versus blood being cast off from an object onto the wall. The stain had also been transferred in a down-ward motion, evidenced by feathering at the edges, as well as a higher volume of blood at the top and diminishing toward the bottom of the stain.

Sullivan also identified a photo that depicted blood trans-fer on the inside front doorknob and dead bolt, and another that showed a bloody crooked line on the garage floor that appeared to have been made by bloody hairs.

Sullivan had taken swabs of each area where blood had been found in the Underwood house, and air-dried them for later testing.

Over the days immediately following the report of Lisa's and Jayden's disappearance, Sullivan stated that the Crime Scene Unit processed the house for additional evidence. They took the contents from each drain in the house, vacu-umed contents from the sofa cover and other areas of the residence, seized sheets off the master bed, and trash from each room in the house. Latent, meaning hidden, finger-prints were also collected throughout the residence.

The investigator stated that the processing of the house took place over several days. At night, in order to insure the integrity of the crime scene, a police officer was posted at the front door of the residence, and another at the back door.

"What did you do that Monday morning?" Rousseau asked.

"Monday, February 21, 2005, I met with Major Case de-tective Gallaway. We went to the suspect's house and looked in the trash," Sullivan reported.

There were a few restrained chuckles from the gallery

before Sullivan admitted they found nothing of significance in the rubbish. But Stephen Barbee's expression revealed he saw little humor in the police going through his trash.

While in front of Barbee's residence, Sullivan and Gallaway received a call notifying them that Lisa Underwood's Dodge Durango had been located. Sullivan looked at jurors and informed them he and Gallaway immediately drove to Denton County to help with evidence collection.

"We would like to have found the vehicle with the keys in it," Sullivan explained, "because we knew we were going to have to transport it to our auto pound. We wanted to roll up all the windows to prevent any evidence from blowing away."

"So what did you do?" Rousseau asked.

"What we ended up doing was to have it pulled out and we collected all the loose items in the car. Then we vacuumed all the driver's-seat area, the driver's floorboard, passenger-seat area, all throughout the car," Sullivan testified.

Rousseau requested the investigator open the plastic bag he had taken to court with him, handing Sullivan a knife to break the seal, and asked him to pull out the contents.

Sullivan put his hand in the transparent bag and brought out a set of car keys. He explained they were the keys that fit Lisa's car, and had been found in the shallow water of the creek, near where the car had been ditched. From a second sack the officer retrieved a brown handbag. Sullivan stated that the purse, along with the contents belonging to Lisa Underwood, had been found in one of the two creeks near where Lisa's and Jayden's bodies had eventually been found.

Suddenly a cell phone rang, interrupting the court proceedings. Jurors looked around the courtroom as Judge Gill's stare focused on Kevin Rousseau.

"Your Honor, I apologize. I turned this off," Rousseau said, looking a bit embarrassed as he reached in his suit pocket to retrieve the ringing phone and quickly silenced it.

Rousseau was lucky—there were judges who would have fined the assistant district attorney, or anyone else in the courtroom, $100 for the preventable interruption. But Judge Gill ignored the situation, nodding for Rousseau to continue with his examination of Officer Sullivan.

Sullivan ended his direct testimony by telling the jury that the Durango was taken to the Fort Worth PD auto pound, secured, and processed by another crime scene officer.

At that time Rousseau passed the witness to the defense for questioning.

Tim Moore walked to the front of the courtroom and stood in front of Officer Sullivan. Moore's reddish hair stood out under the fluorescent lights. He began his questioning as the defense team had done in the past by asking the witness if he had prepared a report regarding the incident.

After Sullivan testified that he had actually prepared two reports during the course of events, Moore asked him if they were pretty detailed. He also asked if he had been taught to be as detailed as possible.

"Well, what the report is mainly for is so you'll remember how the scene existed. And it's as detailed as you need it to be so you remember it," Sullivan stated.

Moore continued to make his point, which would be revealed much later in the trial, by asking a series of questions concerning report writing. The crafty defense attorney had the witness agreeing with every question regarding accuracy and timeliness in the process of preparing reports.

The remainder of Moore's cross-examination pertained to the number of fingerprints lifted from the Underwood house and the Durango, as well as the number of swabs taken from each crime scene location. Sullivan informed the court that he and the other three crime scene investigators took all trace evidence collected to the Fort Worth Crime Lab for further processing.

On redirect examination Kevin Rousseau went straight to the essence of the defense to inform jurors of the procedures followed by Fort Worth officers on the subject of reports. Rousseau knew Moore and Ray would do all they could to later discredit Detective Mike Carroll and would attempt to use his failure to write an account of Barbee's confession as a tool to sway the jury in their favor.

"It's the job of the crime scene officer to write a report, correct?" Rousseau asked Sullivan.

"Yes, sir."

"When you did patrol work, did you ever get involved in a homicide investigation?" Rousseau questioned.

"Yes, sir."

"And in those cases, was it your responsibility as a patrol officer on the scene to write a report?" Rousseau asked.

"Yes, sir."

"Did you frequently give your notes or tell your findings to a detective who later wrote the full report?" Rousseau asked.

"Yes, sir."

"Is that the way it's done at the Fort Worth PD?" Rousseau inquired.

"Yes, sir."

Believing he had neutralized any questions jurors might have concerning report procedures of the Fort Worth PD, Rousseau left the subject and returned to the collection of blood swabs at the house on Chaddybrook.

His remaining questions were few and the responses short; then he announced, "I pass the witness."

Tim Moore had no additional inquiries for Officer Sullivan and he was excused.

Judge Gill announced he was suspending testimony for the day and instructed jurors to go home, get a good night's sleep, and return at eight-thirty the next morning for another full day of testimony.

As Kevin Rousseau and Dixie Bersano stood and watched the jurors depart for the evening, Rousseau's eyes followed one female juror in particular. The young woman, maybe nineteen or twenty years old, appeared sympathetic to Stephen Barbee as she glanced at him occasionally during trial. Rousseau knew this could be a problem. He wanted a unanimous guilty verdict, and he had to have one for Barbee to get the death penalty, which Rousseau believed he deserved.

20

The second day of trial, Stephen Barbee entered the courtroom smiling. He waved to his parents and appeared almost jovial. Sheila Underwood, back in court to watch the proceedings, gawked in stunned surprise.

Is he on drugs? Sheila wondered. Barbee's demeanor was significantly different from when the trial began. *Did he see in the previous day's testimony a glimmer of hope?* Sheila thought back to the witnesses called by the state just the day before. No, she believed they had done an excellent job of setting up the case against Barbee. She leaned back against the wooden pewlike bench and waited for the judge to rap his gavel, calling court to order.

The first witness was Laurie Scheieirn, another Fort Worth Police Department crime scene investigator. The ten-year veteran of the Crime Scene Unit was first enlisted to help with the Underwood case when called to the location of the missing Dodge Durango. There Scheieirn photographed a license plate found in the creek, then tagged and bagged it for evidence after its recovery.

Scheieirn next explained she was sent to the northbound service road of I-35W, near Exit 82. Detectives had located a fence T-post that was bent over. The officer stated there appeared to be a couple of pieces of blue denim attached to some of the barbs of the wire fence. As she had at the creek bed, Scheieirn said, she photographed the potential evidence, diagramed it, and collected the two pieces of cloth, the T-post, and a section of the barbed wire attached to the fence.

Officer Scheieirn also testified she had been part of the Crime Scene Unit sent to the grave site of Lisa and Jayden Underwood. There she snapped photographs of evidence that was discovered while the grave was being unearthed.

ADA Rousseau asked the officer to step down from the witness stand and identify a series of photographs at the grave site for the jury. Standing next to the tall assistant district attorney, Scheieirn was considerably shorter. She looked up at him as he asked her to first ID a picture of the grave when a few of the larger limbs had been removed. A close-up of the same shot depicted a piece of duct tape, with hairs attached.

Another photograph revealed a second piece of duct tape in close proximity to the first. Each piece of tape had been discovered after the first layer of large limbs had been removed from the makeshift tomb.

Officer Scheieirn stepped back to the witness chair and took her seat. Rousseau passed the witness to the defense for cross-examination.

Not one person in the courtroom was surprised when Bill Ray immediately began questioning Officer Scheieirn concerning her procedures for documenting her work, just as the defense had done with previous witnesses. He commented that the officer's report was so detailed she had even included the longitude and latitude of where the bodies were found.

"Why did you make such a detailed report?" Ray asked the officer.

"It is important to be able to document the scene for the detectives, the prosecutors, and for the jury so that if you don't have photographs or additional evidence, you could, so to speak, paint a picture with words by using your report so everybody would understand what you saw at the scene that day," Scheieirn replied.

"Y'all have general orders in the police department that require you to make reports when you do something that a report is needed [for]. Is that a fair statement?" Ray asked.

"Yes, it is," Scheieirn agreed.

Ray gave the former patrol officer a scenario of stopping a DWI driver who admitted to drinking a twelve-pack of Miller Lite. He then asked, "Would it be good police work not to make a report when the person confessed to you?" Ray asked.

"No," Scheieirn admitted.

Ray looked smug, having made his point.

Neither Ray nor Rousseau had any further questions for Scheieirn and she was excused.

Dixie Bersano rose and announced to the court that the state's next witness was Connie Patton.

Bill Ray immediately informed Judge Gill he wished to conduct a 705 hearing.

As soon as the judge dismissed jurors, Ray began his questioning.

Connie Patton, a senior forensic biologist at the Tarrant County Medical Examiner's Office, had been specializing in DNA testing for fifteen years. Patton explained that DNA was the genetic biological material people inherit from their biological mother and biological father. She stated that as a forensic analyst she could extract this genetic material and develop a unique profile to compare it to known individuals. Since there is DNA in all human biological material, the forensic biologist said, she could use blood, semen, saliva, vaginal fluid, tissue covering the internal organs, hair, or bone to make the determination.

It was Patton's responsibility to test the swabs collected at the Underwood house on Chaddybrook.

The soft-spoken witness, in her midforties, stated she took swabs from the top and bottom shelves of a blond-toned entertainment center, the tub of the master bath, a green couch cover, a maroon-and-white blanket, a section of living-room carpet, tissue paper, and some fabric threads, all positive for blood when presumptive tests were performed.

Patton had also tested two sexual assault kits, one taken from Jayden Underwood, the other from Lisa Underwood. The kits, also known as rape kits, were generally used for gathering and preserving physical evidence following a sexual assault, which can then be used in criminal prosecution.

The kits included a collection of receptacles such as cups, envelopes, plastic bags, and tubes, as well as disposable items, like cotton swabs, napkins, and pipettes, and tools, including a sterile comb for pubic hairs and sheets.

If one or both of the Underwoods had been sexually assaulted, and semen could be detected and collected, it would have made identification of their assailant easier. However, semen had not been detected in either of the kits.

There was a collective sigh of relief from members of the gallery. The beatings Jayden and Lisa had endured had been appalling; if they had been sexually assaulted, it would have been unimaginable.

Connie Patton, having been instructed to speak louder so that every juror wouldn't miss her testimony, explained that all DNA tests that produced positive results had come from Lisa or Jayden Underwood. Other samples were inconclusive.

Stephen Barbee, who had been focused on the tablet in front of him, looked up at Patton with a slight upturn of his lips. He understood what the biologist had said—*his* DNA had not been found anywhere in Lisa Underwood's house. He believed that fact would go a long way in convincing the jury he hadn't committed the murders.

Patton testified that the hair fixed to the two pieces of duct tape found at the grave site was hair belonging to seven-year-old Jayden Underwood.

At that point Ray was finished with his 705 hearing questions and the jury again returned to their seats in the courtroom.

As Connie Patton's testimony was heard by the jury, and she detailed each piece of evidence tested for DNA, Stephen Barbee sat quiet and attentive.

For the first time the jury learned sexual assault kits taken from both Jayden and Lisa were negative. They were also told that none of the DNA located in the house and in Lisa's car was that of Stephen Barbee or Ron Dodd.

Having completed her queries, Dixie Bersano passed the witness to Bill Ray for questioning before the jury.

Ray asked Patton about two pairs of blue jeans she had tested for the presence of blood: one pair found to the east of an exit ramp, off I-35W, and the other of unknown origin. Patton reported the pants were negative for the presence of blood.

Bill Ray then turned Ms. Patton's attention to the duct

tape found at the burial site, asking her if any DNA had been found on either of the two pieces of tape.

Patton explained that she personally swabbed the tape, taking a collective sample by swabbing every area of each strip, then performing her tests. Again, she had not found any DNA on either portion of duct tape.

"So is it fair to say that nothing you were able to find— DNA-wise, epithelial cellwise, or bloodwise—matches a profile from Mr. Barbee or Mr. Dodd?" Ray asked smugly.

"Those individuals were excluded from all profiles that were obtained," Patton responded.

Ray smiled slightly as he turned toward the jury and announced, "I believe that's all. Thank you. Pass the witness."

"Judge, may I approach?" Kevin Rousseau asked before walking to the bench.

"We'll take a stretch break at this point," Judge Gill addressed the jury. "About fifteen minutes."

Out of respect for the jury members, everyone in the courtroom stood as jurors filed out, just as they had each time jurors entered and left.

Murmurs began softly, then rose in volume as more spectators learned the name of the next witness scheduled to be called by the state. They knew he would be presenting the most damaging testimony of the capital trial for murder.

After taking a break from the confines of the courtroom, Sheila Underwood returned to her seat in the front row, next to the jury box. Kevin Rousseau walked over to where Sheila sat, leaning over the rail that divided spectators from lawyers, judge, and jury.

"Are you doing okay?" Rousseau asked.

"Yes," Sheila said, taking in a deep breath.

Rousseau smiled at Sheila before returning to the prosecution table.

Stephen Barbee walked back into the courtroom from the holding cell behind the bench. He had taken a bathroom break and had a drink before returning to his spot at the defense table. He ignored the stares of both his former wives sitting in the gallery, but as usual, Barbee smiled at his parents and gave a little wave before sitting. He appeared relaxed and more confident following his attorney's cross-examination of the DNA expert. Barbee leaned back in his chair and waited. His posture soon changed, though.

Stephen Barbee's shoulders suddenly stiffened, his chin became rigid, and his fists clenched as he heard Kevin Rousseau's words ring in his ears.

"Your Honor, we'll call Detective Mike Carroll."

21

With an air of assurance, Mike Carroll walked into the Tarrant County courtroom of Judge Robert Gill. Clad in a well-tailored suit that complemented his lean body, Carroll gave a nod of acknowledgment to Sheila. He had promised Sheila Underwood that he would do all he could to help the district attorney's office secure a conviction. Now it was finally his turn to tell the jury the story of Stephen Barbee and their discussion at the Tyler Police Department.

Stephen Barbee sat quietly, avoiding eye contact with Carroll and the smile that Carroll was giving him. He made no attempt to hide his contempt for the twenty-three-year seasoned police officer. Barbee hated Carroll.

Kevin Rousseau glanced toward Barbee, a sneer of anticipation on his face as he approached the detective. Carroll was the prosecution's key witness, the bombshell that would explode Barbee's claim of innocence. First the cagey prosecutor would neutralize all the questions the defense asked of former witnesses regarding recordkeeping. Rousseau knew those questions were designed to discredit Carroll. He planned to deal with the dispute head-on.

Carroll began, what would be a lengthy testimony, by

explaining he first became involved in the Lisa and Jayden Underwood case after Lisa's Dodge Durango was found abandoned in Denton County.

"For the most part the case at that time was being worked by a Major Case Unit. They investigate kidnappings and officer-involved shootings. They were investigating the scene at that time. They were the lead detectives. We (homicide) were there just to assist them. So we kind of sat around, and they filled us in on what they had. They were bringing different people in, and at some point in time, we were asked to go to Tyler to interview some people that they had talked to over the weekend, Stephen Barbee and Ron Dodd. So we were asked to go to Tyler and interview them, and that's what we did," Carroll said, explaining his initial involvement in the case.

Carroll stated that Dick Gallaway, as a member of the Major Case Unit, was at first the lead detective on the case. It was Detective Gallaway's responsibility to produce a report.

"Did you, at some point in time, communicate with Dick Gallaway about what your experience was in this case?" Rousseau asked.

"Yes."

"Did you, at some point, also type up some notes for your own use?" Rousseau asked.

"Yes," Carroll replied with a smile.

"What caused you to do that?" Rousseau inquired.

"Well, normally, the notes we type up, we type up for court. I may do something that I'll pass on to another detective, and his job is to document that information. I will type up information for myself, and a lot of times I will give that information to the detective, either my handwritten notes or my typed notes. But in most cases it is used for my memory to testify in court, so I typed that stuff up. Because I had interviews and did things that nobody else did, because it was a short period of time, but I wanted to document that so I wouldn't forget it here in court," Carroll stated confidently.

Although Barbee failed to look at Carroll, he was seething inside. He believed Carroll was lying, that he hadn't written any notes at all and was relying on a one-year-old memory for his appearance before the jury.

The detective continued testifying about the notes made on the Underwood case, stating that as the trial drew closer, he conferred with Detective McCaskill, reviewing his notes on the case as well. Carroll admitted McCaskill's notes were more detailed, but that there were some discrepancies in time compared to his own notes. Carroll explained he then went back to the audiotape or video recordings, which always contain the time and date, to make a more accurate timeline of the events of the case. Throughout his testimony Carroll maintained a slight grin of assurance.

"It is part of your responsibility to sometimes interview suspects. What is your objective when you are interviewing a suspect?" Rousseau asked from his chair at the prosecution table.

Detective Carroll turned his body slightly toward the jury, looking at them pleasantly as he spoke. He exhibited the confidence he had in the case and his work.

"The objective in a suspect or a witness, no matter who you talk to, is to get the truth, and that's the objective. We always assume that witnesses are going to be honest and forthright with us. Suspects are not always honest, so we use a lot of tools, sometimes deception, to try to get to the truth," Carroll stated.

Barbee took in a deep breath in an attempt to restrain his anger. Carroll did lie to him during their interview, and Barbee didn't believe it was a commonly used tool of the police department. He believed it was an all-out effort by Carroll to trick him.

Moore and Ray glanced at their client in a way that reminded him of their warning before trial began: "Don't show any emotion. Don't make any remarks. Just sit quietly."

Rousseau's next question surprised Barbee.

"Isn't there a danger of getting a false confession when you lie to somebody?"

"When we talk to someone, we know certain facts. We know they know those facts, so we tell them the facts. Sometimes we exaggerate the facts, because we want them to tell us something we know to be factual—they know to be factual—but that no one else would know. So we tell a deception.

"For instance, I may say that someone saw you commit a crime, but no one did. You know you were there and you committed the crime, so you think about it and say, 'Yes, someone could have seen me.' And then you'll tell the truth. But we withhold certain information because we want them to tell us. There are certain things that only the person who committed the crime would know. So we withhold information so they can tell us that, to verify that they do know and they are telling the truth," Carroll summarized.

"So when you're doing this, it needs to be a mixture of truth and lie," Rousseau stated.

"Yes," Carroll agreed, a slight smirk on his face.

Rousseau asked Carroll about the incident that occurred in Denton County involving Deputy Brawner and the unidentified person he stopped in the early-morning hours of February 19, 2005.

Carroll described a photo lineup that was presented to Deputy Brawner that included a picture of the defendant. Although Brawner had identified Stephen Barbee as the man he had stopped and questioned, his identification wasn't certain enough for Detective Carroll to make an immediate arrest.

"Explain that," Rousseau said.

"When you show a witness a photo spread of people, you want them to be certain. You don't want to arrest the wrong man. So if I show a photo spread and you look and say, 'Well, that kind of looks like him, but I'm not sure,' you don't arrest a person with that kind of iffy pick. So I put a number to it, 'Like on a scale of one to ten, where do you think you are?' If they say seven, six, or eight, that's not good enough. You wanted it to be ten, real sure, or nine point five, or something real close," Carroll explained.

"It wasn't good enough for you to arrest Barbee, but was it good enough to cause you to be more suspicious of Mr. Barbee?"

"Yes."

Carroll acknowledged that he had known Barbee had been connected to the investigation prior to Deputy Brawner's encounter.

The detective testified that at the direction of his supervisor, he and Detective McCaskill drove to Tyler, Texas, where Barbee was known to be working, in order to meet with him.

They picked up Detective Brian Jamison at the airport, where he had flown in by helicopter, found out Jamison had arranged to meet with Barbee and Ron Dodd at the Tyler Wal-Mart, and drove to that location.

Carroll explained that he talked with Trish Barbee, attempting to find out when she saw her husband last; McCaskill spoke with Ronald Dodd; Jamison talked with Barbee. The decision was then made to take Barbee and Dodd to the Tyler PD, where they could interview them in a comfortable place with access to video and/or audio equipment. Carroll also wanted to be able to sit across from the suspect in order to see his eye movements and body movements.

While sitting in the plain eight-by-eight-foot room with Barbee and Jamison, Jamison read Barbee his Miranda rights, Carroll stated.

Once Rousseau established that a video recording had been made of Barbee's interview, with the help of the Tyler Police Department, Rousseau entered it into evidence.

"We'll make the same objections we made at pretrial," Bill Ray announced, standing to address the court.

"Overruled."

Jackie Barbee's wrinkled brow revealed confusion and dismay. Jackie was confused by the legal system and the intricacies of the procedures. Tina Church had attempted to prepare her for the court proceedings, but Jackie had difficulty following all the banter. And it was for that very reason that Church had begun The Other Victims Advocacy. She knew most defendant supporters had no knowledge of how the judicial system worked, and most had never been inside a courtroom.

Sheila Underwood, unlike Jackie Barbee, knew just what was happening. She had been coached by Mike Carroll and Kevin Rousseau on everything to expect in court. When Sheila turned to look at Jackie Barbee, she saw puzzlement in her face. Sheila suspected that Mrs. Barbee was confused by all that was happening.

Judge Gill turned his attention to the twelve jurors and one alternate. He informed them they were about to see a videotape that contained, along the bottom of the tape, a segment of scrolling text that constituted a transcript of the conversation that would appear on the videotape and audiotape. He warned them that the transcript was only for their use in court—it was not evidence—and they would not be allowed to have the transcript during deliberations.

But before he began playing the interview for jurors, Rousseau asked Detective Carroll to explain what Stephen Barbee told him concerning his whereabouts in the early-morning hours of February 19, 2005.

Barbee pushed his pen into the lined tablet on the desk, not only writing the word *HEARSAY,* but pressing it indelibly into the paper.

"We assumed he would lie about what he did that night. At the scene we learned that the person running from the officer may have cut his leg," Carroll stated.

Carroll continued by testifying they were fairly confident that Stephen Barbee was the person who had run from the Denton County deputy. So, while they were taking photos of Barbee's injuries, Carroll said, "We have a picture of a white male fitting your description running from an officer in Denton County. Now, if that wasn't you, you have no problem. But a Denton County deputy is going to come and look at this videotape and look at you, and if it's you, then you do have a problem."

Carroll explained that what he told Barbee wasn't true—in the sense that there was no Denton County deputy coming to look at the video, they had already done that. Carroll admitted it was a false statement made in an attempt to get the defendant to tell them the truth about fleeing from the deputy. And he did.

Mike Carroll smoothed his brown mustache before telling jurors that in addition to the video recording, which had no time or date stamp, he had a backup cassette recorder on which he mentioned the time of the interview.

"After stopping the video recording to take photos of

the defendant, what time did the tape begin again?" Rousseau asked.

"At eight-twenty PM. It was a short break," Carroll responded.

"Were there any noteworthy injuries on him?" Rousseau asked.

"Yes."

"What were they?"

"We saw injuries like those on his arms (scratches). They were also on his legs," Carroll stated.

Rousseau asked the experienced officer to explain what happened in the interview room when he left to find out what Ron Dodd was saying to Detective McCaskill down the hall.

Carroll again looked to the jury and stated that while he was out of the room, Detective Jamison and Barbee got into a heated argument. Detective Cashell, of the Tyler PD, had gotten Carroll's attention in the hall and told him of the situation between Jamison and Barbee.

Explaining that they wanted to keep Barbee cooperative, Carroll said that he went back to the interview room to ask Jamison to leave, but he was already coming out of the room.

"Then I began calling my supervisors back in Fort Worth about trying to get someone in Denton to see if we could get a warrant for Barbee's arrest for running. He'd confessed to running from the police, which would be either a Class A misdemeanor or a third-degree felony," Carroll stated.

Carroll described leaving Barbee alone in the interview room and going to McCaskill and asking what Dodd had said during their discussion.

"I wanted to know about what Dodd said, because quite often when you have two people involved in some type of an incident, one might start to confess on the other because they feel their responsibility is not as important, not as serious. So you want to hear what that other person says. It might give you some leads to go back and interview the other person with," Carroll explained, again grinning during his statement.

When Rousseau asked Carroll to relate what he had learned from Detective McCaskill concerning what Ron Dodd had told him, and Carroll remarked that he gave them information about where the bodies might be, Bill Ray objected on the grounds that it would be hearsay. Judge Gill agreed, sustained the motion, and advised the jury to disregard the last statement made by Detective Carroll. At that point in the two-day–long trial, Bill Ray asked for a mistrial. Judge Gill denied his request.

Barbee would later complain that Carroll was about to tell the court that Ron Dodd was the one who told them where the bodies were, when his attorney asked for a mistrial.

During the exchange between Bill Ray and Judge Gill, Sheila Underwood again looked toward Barbee's parents. Jackie Barbee still had a look of complete perplexity. It was more apparent to Sheila that Jackie Barbee was unschooled in court proceedings, as she herself would have been, had it not been for Rousseau and Carroll.

"What did you go in and say to Stephen Barbee?" Rousseau asked Carroll.

"I went in and said, 'Does FM 407 sound familiar to you?' And walked out," Carroll replied.

Carroll stated that he again left Barbee alone. He just wanted to plant a seed and give Barbee time to wonder how much Carroll knew about the case, after all. Carroll had also left photos of both Lisa and Jayden Underwood in the room with Barbee. He wanted Barbee to think about the lives, and deaths, of the two innocent people in the photographs.

Sheila Underwood again looked at Stephen Barbee for any sign of remorse, but she found none as he kept his eyes averted from Rousseau and Carroll.

"Did you manage to get him to a restroom?" Rousseau asked.

"Yes."

Barbee's reaction was decidedly visible as he lifted his head and stared through narrowed eyes at his accuser. Barbee knew what Carroll would be telling the jury, and he was livid. Ray and Moore had managed to keep a portion of the videotape out of court, but Carroll's testimony was going to be heard by the jury.

"Did you have a conversation with him in that restroom?" Rousseau asked.

"Yes."

"Tell us how that happened," Rousseau prompted.

"Well, that conversation started because by now I have heard more conversations, so I approached Stephen Barbee with, 'Dodd's going to lay this whole thing in your lap, that Dodd is basically saying you are a cold-blooded killer,'" Carroll stated.

The assistant district attorney asked if during the course of that conversation, anything Carroll said to Stephen Barbee was a lie.

"Well, part of the stuff about Dodd saying he was a cold-blooded killer, he was going to lay this whole thing in your lap, he (Dodd) had nothing to do with it, he was scared of Barbee. Those kinds of things. Those things that made it seem like Dodd had no responsibility in this whatsoever, and I pretty much convinced him—misled him—to believe that Dodd was an innocent guy here and he was the true suspect, and the *only* suspect in the case."

Barbee and his parents had a hard time believing that officers of the law could legally lie to a suspect and get away with it.

Rousseau asked Carroll why he misled the defendant.

"That's one of those tools we use to try to elicit the truth. Usually, if you find out that your best friend, or your friend, is starting to say that you did something that you did, or maybe you didn't do, you are going to come in with, 'No, it was his idea,' or 'No, I did this but not that,' to correct what I'm saying. And that's exactly what happened in this case," Carroll said with conviction.

"Did you tell him anything else to try to get him to be more open with you?" Rousseau asked.

"Yes. I also told him about the family needing closure, that Lisa's family needed closure. He started making comments about being locked up the rest of his life, at this point," Carroll said.

Barbee was working hard to keep the stoic look his attorneys advised him to retain during the trial. All he wanted to do was stand up and shout at Carroll, "Liar!"

Bill Ray stood and addressed the court. "Excuse me. I'm going to object to the entire conversation in the bathroom from this point forward, based on objections we made at pretrial."

"They are overruled," Judge Gill said without hesitation.

Rousseau, who had waited for the exchange between the defense counsel and the judge, said, "Go ahead. He began telling you?"

Carroll told the jury that Barbee had said he was going to jail for the rest of his life. The detective said Barbee told him he lost a family member and he knew what it was like not to have closure.

The detective and suspect had also talked about Ron Dodd's involvement and blaming the whole thing on him. Carroll informed the jury that Barbee said Dodd actually created a plan to go kill Lisa.

According to Carroll, Barbee thought Lisa was going to ruin his family, his relationship with his wife, Trish. Lisa wanted his name on the birth certificate and she wanted money for the baby's care. Barbee acknowledged that at the time he did think the baby Lisa was carrying was his child, so he and Dodd devised a plan.

"Barbee was going to drop his car off at Dodd's house. Dodd was then going to take him to Lisa's house, which is what they did. He said he was going to go into Lisa's house, try to pick a fight, but he couldn't do it. She wouldn't pick a fight with him. So he leaves the house and calls Dodd on the phone and says come pick him up, which Dodd did. He picked him up and took him away.

"The plan was that once he killed Lisa, he was going to put her body in Lisa's Dodge Durango and take it up north. Dodd was going to follow and then, when they had disposed of the body and the vehicle, Dodd would take him back home," Carroll detailed.

Carroll testified that Barbee told him that when he left Lisa's house, he called Dodd and said, "I can't do it. I can't go through with it." According to Barbee, Dodd then made the comment "Do we need to hire a hit man?" Barbee said no, that he could do it, so Dodd took him back to Lisa's house.

Although most jurors remained transfixed on the face of Mike Carroll, several pairs of eyes darted toward the defendant, seeking any reaction. They saw tears in his eyes.

"Did he describe what happened?" Rousseau asked after

Carroll stated Barbee was able to provoke Lisa into a fight the second time he was at the house.

"Yes. He said during the fight he wrestled her down to the ground, facedown into the carpet, where he held her face into the carpet until she stopped breathing," Carroll stated.

"Did he say anything about Jayden?" Rousseau asked.

"He did. He said that while he was in the process of killing Lisa, Jayden came in, crying. He said he looked up and Jayden was standing there.

"So I asked him, 'How did you kill Jayden?' He said, 'I walked up to him and I placed my hand over his mouth and nose and held it there until he stopped breathing,'" Carroll said.

The courtroom was totally silent, except for the keyboard clicks created by Bill Ray on his laptop computer. The vision of seven-year-old Jayden seeing his mother on the floor of their living room, and of Stephen Barbee putting his hand over the child's mouth until he no longer breathed life was a shocking image.

Tears spilled from Jackie Barbee's eyes. *No, it's not true. Stephen loves children. He could never do such a thing,* Jackie thought. She wanted to stand before the court and shout it out, but Ray had given her and Bill specific instructions to show no emotion during the trial.

Nancy Kearly, a good friend of the Barbees, and the wife of the pastor at Gospel Outreach Church, where Stephen Barbee had taught children's Sunday school, squeezed Jackie's hand. Kearly also believed Stephen Barbee incapable of ever hurting a child. And she knew she would later get her chance to tell the jury so.

Detective Carroll, his balding head beginning to glisten

under the bright lights, continued telling the jury the events of February 19, 2005, as told to him by Stephen Barbee.

Carroll said Barbee had told him he had attempted to clean up the living room, using some solvent from the house. Barbee denied vacuuming the carpet, but he had admitted trying to cover up a blood spot with a piece of furniture.

Regarding the burial spot, Carroll stated that Barbee was very specific on his directions to the location, and the detective reiterated to the jury the exact description of the site, as Barbee had related it to him.

Rousseau retrieved an enlarged photo from the stack nearby. The ADA approached his witness and, showing him the photo, asked if the aerial shot depicted the location where Lisa's and Jayden's bodies had been recovered.

After verifying that it did, Rousseau asked if Carroll and Barbee were still in the bathroom during this entire conversation.

Carroll replied "yes," and during a series of questions from Rousseau, he continued to describe the events, as Barbee had told them to him.

Barbee said Dodd had provided the shovel used to bury the bodies. The defendant admitted driving Lisa's vehicle to the location, but denied driving it into the creek, as it had been found.

"I drove it to the area, but stopped just short of the creek," Barbee had told Carroll.

"Did you talk to him in the bathroom about putting this on tape? About recording it?" Rousseau asked.

"Yes," Carroll replied, indicating that Barbee agreed to be taped later.

"Was there anything specifically, though, that he did not want to talk about on tape?" Rousseau questioned.

"Yes. He didn't want to talk about Ron Dodd's involvement on tape in any way," Carroll said.

The detective told the court he and the suspect had been in the bathroom talking for forty-five minutes to an hour before he took Barbee to the office of Detective Cashell, from Tyler, so they could use his Internet access. In Cashell's office they had pulled up MapQuest so that Barbee could show them the roads he had traveled to dispose of the bodies.

"By now, it's a couple or three hours since you first started talking to him, right?" Rousseau asked.

"Correct."

"So it's getting into the middle of the night, right?" Rousseau questioned.

"Yes."

"Did anyone come into the bathroom while you were in there with him?" Rousseau asked.

"No, sir."

"Were you taking notes during the time he was telling you all this?" Rousseau asked.

"No."

"Why not?"

"Well, when you are interviewing somebody in a case, particularly as serious as this case, your whole objective is to make them think you care about them, that you understand what they did. And so you are saying a lot of things to comfort him, commiserate, to listen. I know I'm going from that point to record it later on, but I don't want to alienate him before we get to that point, so you want to win him over.

"If I would have taken out a tape recorder or a pad and start taking notes at that point, he starts to feel that we're not friends—you don't care about me. This is about getting him to trust you, to like you. Once you get to that point, then you take him to the room—and you do anything to make him mistrust you, he stops talking.

"So you want to wait until the last possible minute before you do the tape recorder. You have that conversation just relaxed to get him comfortable, to get him to trust you, to like you. Once you get to that point, then you take him to the room and you do the interview on tape," Carroll explained.

After a few questions relating to the MapQuest itself, Rousseau asked to approach the bench for scheduling purposes.

Within seconds of speaking to Judge Gill, the judge announced a lunch break until 1:15 PM.

Outside the courtroom Jackie Barbee was surrounded by the press. They shouted questions and shoved microphones in her face. She may have been confused and anxious in the courtroom, but outside she was afraid.

When Jackie finally broke away from the media, she quickly called Tina Church. Jackie voiced her anger at Detective Carroll, her frustration at the justice system, and her fear for Stephen.

Church did all she could to calm Jackie Barbee. Church had been through this many times with the families of defendants. It was a long, often gut-wrenching process to take them from arrest, all the way through execution. The anxiety she heard in Jackie Barbee's voice was all too familiar.

When everyone had returned from lunch, Rousseau was again asking questions of Mike Carroll.

"After you left Detective Cashell's desk, where did you go?" Rousseau asked.

"We went back to the interview room," Carroll replied.

"Was the interview captured on video—DVD?" Rousseau asked.

"Yes."

"I'm sorry, my habit is to say 'videotape,'" Rousseau said as he handed Carroll a DVD and asked if it was the tape made at the Tyler PD on the night in question. When Carroll stated it was, Rousseau then admitted it into evidence, over the objections of the defense.

Judge Gill again instructed the jury that they could not use the transcript of the tape during their deliberations.

Kevin Rousseau's long, thin fingers pushed the DVD into the player, pushed the start button, and he stepped back as the images of Stephen Barbee and Mike Carroll appeared on the television screen.

Mike Carroll took a quick look at Barbee before his dark eyes focused on the TV monitor, while Barbee's gaze remained fixed on the table in front of him.

This portion of the video interview showed Stephen Barbee alone in the Tyler PD interview room crying. The first words jurors heard were Barbee speaking out loud, "God Almighty, what have I done?"

The exclamation drew gasps in the courtroom.

In seconds Trish Barbee could be seen entering the small room, slamming something on the table and asking her husband loudly, "You got her pregnant?"

"I'm sorry," Barbee said, crying. "My life's over."

Sheila Underwood winced. *Just like Barbee to think only of himself,* she thought. *He never considered Lisa and Jayden's lives, only his own.*

"God, Steve, was it worth it?" Trish asked.

"I didn't mean to," Barbee sobbed.

Through his tears Barbee told Trish that he was afraid she would leave him if she found out about Lisa Underwood's baby. He claimed he only went to Lisa's house to talk to her, but everything spun out of control.

Everyone in the courtroom watched as Stephen and Trish Barbee sat entwined, both crying uncontrollably.

Several times Barbee begged his wife to forgive him and asked her not to leave him. Then—clearly spoken—Barbee asked, "Does this mean we're breaking up?"

That question brought forth audible sighs and groans of anger from friends and family of the Underwoods.

Trish promised to stick by her husband, but it was common knowledge that she had obtained a final divorce decree just prior to the beginning of Barbee's trial.

When the TV screen was once again blank, Rousseau asked Carroll if at some point he had left the room, leaving Barbee alone.

Carroll responded that he had, but explained that the recording equipment continued to run. At that point Carroll went to speak to Trish Barbee, telling her that her husband had confessed to killing Lisa, and he asked her if she wanted to talk to Stephen.

"Did you tell her before she entered that room that he had confessed to killing Jayden?" Rousseau asked.

"No."

Barbee never confessed to premeditated murder, telling his wife that it was an accident—he hadn't meant for Lisa to die.

From there, Carroll stated, Barbee was booked into a Tyler jail cell, Carroll took a nap in the Tyler bunk room, and Dodd was transported back to Fort Worth by Detectives McCaskill and Jamison. Carroll explained that he and Barbee were later driven to Tarrant County by a fugitive officer.

"Barbee said, 'When I take you to the bodies, I don't want to see the bodies, and I don't want the media to see me,'" Carroll reported.

Carroll explained that they had set up a diversion, where

on his signal everyone who was at the known area of the grave site would jump in their cars and speed off in another direction. They assumed the media would follow—and they did, leaving the actual burial place devoid of anyone but the officers assigned to guard it.

According to Carroll, Barbee directed them to the exact location of the bodies by a series of instructions.

Rousseau handed Carroll three photographs and asked if they depicted the scene, as he had described it. When he answered yes, Rousseau entered them as state's evidence.

"Could I get you to step down for a minute, please," Rousseau said to Carroll.

Mike Carroll left the witness-box and stood by Kevin Rousseau. Carroll, a tall man, approximately six feet, was still shorter than the prosecutor.

The first photo the detective identified was of the two barbed-wire fences in the area of the grave; the second was of the grave itself, before the debris was removed; the third was after removal of the debris and dirt, with both bodies exposed.

Sheila Underwood's eyes focused on the wooden divider between her and the inner courtroom. She didn't want to see the photo of Lisa and Jayden in the makeshift grave.

Rousseau asked Carroll where Barbee was, following the unearthing of the bodies.

"At that point, at the moment we found the victims' bodies, I had Officer Thornhill take him to jail," Carroll replied.

"Thank you, pass the witness," Rousseau announced.

Tim Moore stood and walked toward Carroll. The detective had been on the stand the majority of the day, but he appeared to be as fresh as he was earlier that morning. He smiled at the approaching attorney. In twenty-three years on the Fort Worth police force, Carroll had testified hundreds of times. He knew how to make a jury understand his case, and he knew how to keep from being rattled by a defense attorney.

By now, Mike Carroll and everyone in the courtroom knew the defense's strategy, so it was no surprise when Tim Moore began his cross-examination by asking, "I noticed in the video you had a tape recorder in your pocket. Is it a routine thing you do when you want to talk to somebody about their potential involvement in a crime to audiotape them?"

"No, sir."

"Would it be safe to say you take notes instead of audiotaping?" Moore asked.

"Yes."

Moore asked Carroll if he tape-recorded his conversation outside Wal-Mart with Trish Barbee. When he admitted he had, Carroll said, "The purpose of audiotaping an interview is that sometimes you have a situation where you don't have access to a typist. It could be that I'm interviewing somebody in jail, or an odd location, like the field. You just can't sit down with someone and type it up, so it's just better to have a tape recorder to record that conversation. It's just more convenient."

"It's more reliable too, isn't it?" Moore asked, a sign of a slight leer on his face.

"I don't know about reliability, but some people think it is, yeah," Carroll said coolly, again smiling at the lawyer.

Moore inquired about Detective Gallaway, as the lead detective, and his task to make a report of the incident. Carroll admitted that neither Gallaway's nor Detective McCaskill's reports reflected his conversation in the bathroom with the defendant; therefore, he generated his own report.

When asked when Carroll had written the report, he stated, "December '05."

"So it would have been some ten months after the incident?" Moore asked, emphasis on *ten months*.

"Yes."

Moore asked Carroll if anyone had requested he write the report, and Carroll said no. He had read McCaskill's account early on and had typed up a couple of paragraphs about his men's room interview with Barbee. The detective stated he created the full report in December after seeing that Detective Gallaway's statement was lacking those details. He again stated he had also adjusted times and dates he found to be inaccurate in one or both of the other detectives' information.

"Let's talk specifically about this bathroom interview and let me make sure that the jury is clear. We are talking about this confession that you say Mr. Barbee told you in the Tyler Police Department bathroom?" Moore asked.

"Yes."

"This is after you have interviewed him for an hour or so, and you have taken some pictures of his injuries, and I believe you even lied to him a little bit?" Moore said snidely.

"Yes."

"And then he says he wants to go to the bathroom, and Cashell takes you and Mr. Barbee to the bathroom. Okay? Now, you didn't pick up your little tape recorder and take it with you, did you?" Moore asked, sarcasm dripping from his words.

"No," Carroll said, smiling.

"And there certainly wasn't any video equipment in that bathroom, was there?" Moore asked.

"No," Carroll replied, continuing to grin as he spoke.

For the first time Stephen Barbee smiled. He liked the way his attorney was questioning his nemesis.

Carroll stated he hadn't asked Detective Cashell to stay in the bathroom with him and Barbee as a witness, nor did he plan to get a confession when Barbee asked to be taken to the bathroom.

Moore asked if the plan Carroll claimed Barbee said he and Dodd had hatched to go over to Lisa's—then he backed out from—was discussed in the bathroom. When Carroll said it was, Moore wanted to know why it wasn't in his final report. Carroll insisted it was, just not in detail.

"Well, if you look in your report on page five," Moore said as he flipped open a copy of Carroll's report, "you said he went on to explain how and why he killed both Lisa and Jayden Underwood."

"Correct."

"You didn't put any details about what he and Ron Dodd were planning, did you?" Moore asked.

"No."

Moore pointed out that everything else was memorialized on videotape or audiotape, except for that portion of the interview, which only came from Carroll's memory. Carroll hadn't put any of those details down for Gallaway, but the detective insisted he had informed Gallaway verbally.

Moore continued pointing out various details of Carroll's written report, such as times and even the address of the Tyler PD, and that something as important as Barbee's description of a plan he and Dodd had made to kill the victims had been left out.

It was obvious the defense attorney was making every effort to discredit the detective.

Moore questioned Carroll's tactic of not utilizing a tape recorder or taking notes so that Barbee would think he cared about him. Then he asked if accusing Stephen Barbee of being a murderer, on videotape, right before taking him to the bathroom, would endear him to the suspect.

"No," Carroll said, almost laughing.

"So you changed tactics right there?" Moore asked.

"Yes."

"What made you change the tactic?" Moore asked.

"He was focusing on the fact that he'd run from a police officer, and I wanted to get him back on track. Running from police is a minor issue. He was seen near a woman's car, a woman who had disappeared, and he lied and ran from police. So I wanted to get him back on track, thinking this was a murder investigation," Carroll stated.

Carroll said once the defendent confessed, Barbee began crying. He told Moore he had informed Barbee he would tell the district attorney he had cooperated, which he did, because he wanted Barbee to remain cooperative until the bodies were found.

"Did he tell you he held her (Lisa) down too long, and she stopped breathing?" Moore asked as his final question.

"Yes, yes."

Under redirect examination Rousseau asked Carroll if Dodd had given them enough information to find the bodies of Lisa and Jayden Underwood. Carroll stated Dodd directed them to the general area, but they didn't actually find the exact location of the bodies until Stephen Barbee took them to the grave site.

The questioning of Detective Mike Carroll, which had taken hours, was finally over. He walked from the witness stand, giving Sheila Underwood a smile on his way to the back of the courtroom.

* * *

Outside the Justice Center, Trish Barbee, who had been in the courtroom all week watching her ex-husband's trial, spoke to the press.

"What punishment do you want Stephen Barbee to get?" a reporter asked.

"I'd rather not say," Trish responded with animosity in her voice.

"My deepest sympathies go out to the Underwood family," Trish said. "She (Lisa) didn't deserve that. Nobody deserves that."

22

Detective Mike Carroll's testimony had accomplished what prosecutors had hoped for. He had convincingly reported it had been Stephen Barbee who ran from police near where Lisa Underwood's vehicle had been ditched in the early-morning hours the day she was reported missing; that he had led authorities to the exact location of the graves; and that it was Stephen Barbee who was responsible for the untimely deaths of Lisa Underwood, her son, Jayden, and her unborn daughter.

As Carroll walked past Barbee, he exhibited an expression of sheer satisfaction. Barbee refused to look at his accuser, but under his breath he muttered, "Fuckin' liar."

Following the emotional testimony of Carroll, Judge Gill called a stretch break. Sheila Underwood escaped the horde of newspeople as she hurried outside the Tarrant County Justice Center, where she grabbed a smoke and settled her nerves.

Jackie Barbee was not so lucky. She was bombarded with the media asking questions concerning her reaction to the detective's testimony. Emotionally drained, Jackie was unable to speak. With the help of friends, she pushed her

way through the crowd as she wiped tearstains from her
cheeks. Jackie and her friend Nancy escaped into a restroom on another floor of the Justice Center, waiting there
till the fifteen-minute break had elapsed.

When Judge Gill rapped his gavel on the large, dark
wooden bench to resume court, Sheila Underwood was
visibly absent. As spectators had left the courtroom following the departure of the jurors for the midafternoon break,
Kevin Rousseau had spoken with Sheila at the rail.

"Sheila, Dr. White from the ME's office will be testifying next about Jayden's injuries," Rousseau said softly.

The prosecutor had to say no more. Sheila picked up her
handbag as Rousseau offered his office to her as a refuge
until Dr. White completed his testimony, but Sheila chose
to leave the building for a needed respite.

Inside the courtroom, away from the cold, damp February air blowing outside, spectators took their seats, wondering what else the prosecution had in store.

Like Dr. Krouse, Dr. Lloyd White was employed as a
Tarrant County deputy medical examiner. Unlike Krouse,
White had only been with the ME's office for a year, although he had been a forensic pathologist for more than
three decades.

Just as gallery viewers were wondering why another
pathologist was set to testify following Dr. Krouse's lengthy
testimony from the previous day, Rousseau asked a question
that stiffened many a back of those watching the proceedings.

"Doctor, did you perform an autopsy in this case on the
body of a little boy named Jayden Underwood?"

Dr. White informed the court he had completed Jayden's
autopsy on February 23, 2005.

"Would you tell us, please, what injuries, if any, did you

observe on the body of Jayden Underwood?" Rousseau
instructed.

"Yes. There was a one-half-inch bruise on the upper left
back. There was a one-and-one-half-inch abrasion, or
scraped area, of the skin on the upper right back, just below
the top of the shoulder. There were scattered approximately
two-inch scratches in various directions over the back of the
right arm. That is, above the elbow, and the right forearm
below the elbow. There were a few scratches in the hip
region in the back. There was a very small scratch on the
back of the left calf."

Dr. White paused momentarily as he took a breath and
adjusted his glasses. Then he continued.

"There was a discoloration around the right eye, associated with hemorrhage into the membranes of the eye. There
was also revealed, after removing the scalp, a large contusion, or bruise, on the right side, above the right temple in
the scalp.

"Additionally, there were areas of contusion throughout
the edges of the lips, upper and lower, extending into the
mucosa, the lining of the lips, and also on the gums of the
underlying teeth.

"There was a small amount of blood-tinged fluid in the
mouth and also over the surface of the left lung. I saw petechiae. There were small pinpoint hemorrhages that are
associated with increased pressure in the chest and are
sometimes seen with asphyxial death, or death due to lack of
oxygen, associated with increased pressure in the chest," Dr.
White reported.

Rousseau asked what many in the courtroom were wondering. "What is petechiae?"

"Petechiae are little pinpoint hemorrhages that are actually the size of a pinpoint. We see them around the face and
sometimes on internal organs in association with asphyxial

death, such as strangulation, where the neck is constricted. We see them in the legs when a person has been hanged and the legs have been suspended. They can also be seen in heart failure and other natural causes as well," Dr. White explained.

"So it's caused from pressure on the pulmonary system?" Rousseau asked to clarify.

"Correct."

"The injuries to the lips and gums, what type of force causes that type of injury?" Rousseau asked.

"Those are caused by some sort of compression, some object put over the area of the mouth, pressing on the mouth and compressing the lips against the underlying teeth," Dr. White replied.

The pathologist stated that Jayden's injuries were inflicted prior to loss of life. He determined asphyxia by smothering to be the cause of death, and the manner of death was homicide.

The faces of the jurors remained expressionless. Rousseau wanted to invoke emotion in them. He would now like for the jury to see Jayden Underwood, not as the adorable little boy he first showed them at the beginning of the trial, but as a battered and bruised homicide victim.

To accomplish this goal, Rousseau entered into evidence a series of enlarged photos taken during the autopsy of Jayden Underwood. He then asked Dr. White to identify the four pictures.

Dr. White stated the photographs accurately depicted Jayden's injuries, which he had described for the court. He explained that some of the discoloration of the body was postmortem change.

Kevin Rousseau then gave Dr. White three scenarios: (1) Jayden being killed by someone placing their hand over his mouth and nose; (2) having his face pressed down against a flat surface; (3) having his face pushed against a surface that gives if you push against it, such as a couch or a carpeted floor. Rousseau then asked if any one of the scenarios was more likely. Dr. White stated, "No." He agreed they were all *equally* likely.

Jackie Barbee turned to her friend Nancy.

"There's no way Stephen could have done that. He wouldn't. He loves kids," Jackie said, her eyes again damp with tears.

"I know," Nancy replied, taking Jackie's hand. "He didn't hurt that child."

On the other side of the courtroom, Sheila Underwood's friends were relieved she had decided to stay away from this portion of the trial. Seeing Jayden's lifeless body lying on the stainless-steel table at the morgue was more than any grandmother should have to endure.

Rousseau passed Dr. White to the defense.

Bill Ray was the defense counsel who would question Dr. White, just as he had questioned Dr. Krouse. His first question addressed an issue the prosecution had not raised.

"Did you find any evidence that Jayden Underwood had been tied or bound with any type of tape?"

"I did not find any such evidence," Dr. White replied.

"No evidence of tape over his hands or head, or whatever, and that tape pulled off?" Ray asked.

"Tape can be applied and pulled off without leaving any marks on the body, but there wasn't anything specific in my findings that would suggest that that had taken place," Dr. White stated.

Having asked and had answered his most important question, Bill Ray stated, "That's all I have. Thank you, Dr. White."

Dr. White's answer still left questions concerning the

origin of the duct tape found at the grave site that contained strands of Jayden's hair.

Kevin Rousseau stood and addressed the court.

"No further questions. Your Honor, we'll rest."

Bill Ray stood parallel to Rousseau.

"Your Honor, we need to take up a brief matter outside the jury's presence," Ray stated.

Once all jurors were in the jury room and the door had closed, Bill Ray began his plea to the court.

"Your Honor, at this time the defendant would move for an instructed verdict (a verdict granted by the court) for two reasons. First of all, as technical as it might sound, there hasn't been any evidence that either Lisa or Jayden Underwood were killed or transported in Tarrant County. We move for an instructed verdict on that basis."

"Denied," Judge Gill responded without hesitation.

"Thank you," Ray said. "We also move for an instructed verdict for the offense of capital murder, in that the only credible evidence indicates that the defendant, on the murder of Lisa Underwood, did not act intentionally or knowingly, so therefore it is not capital murder."

"Denied."

"Thank you," Ray responded.

Bill Ray then announced he would be calling Ron Dodd to the stand, and due to the fact that it was his understanding Mr. Dodd would be taking the Fifth, Ray planned to question him outside the presence of the jury.

Ron Dodd walked into the courtroom, averting his eyes from his former friend and employer at the defense table, and took the witness stand.

Barbee stared at Dodd, wondering what he would say. Barbee considered his former friend to be a silver-tongued devil able to sell anything to anybody. Barbee wondered what he would try to sell the jury.

As Bill Ray expected, when he asked Dodd if he was to question him about the deaths of Lisa and Jayden Underwood, and any involvement he might have had in the events of February 18 and 19, 2005, concerning the murders and burial, was he planning to take the Fifth, Dodd replied, "Yes."

Barbee was not surprised Dodd pled the Fifth. If he had agreed to answer questions, the court would learn he had a history of assaulting women, including Teresa. It might cause the jury to look at Dodd for the murders of Lisa and Jayden.

"That's all I have in light of his plea," Ray stated.

With no questions from Rousseau or Bersano, Dodd left the courtroom, as he had entered, avoiding the angry eyes of Stephen Barbee.

Barbee unconsciously rubbed his head. The persistent pain reminded him of the steel beam Dodd had let slam into his hard hat, causing him months of severe headaches. Barbee was more convinced than ever that it was not an industrial accident, as Dodd had claimed. Barbee believed Dodd had tried to kill him. Because of that incident and Dodd leaving him stranded the night of the murders, Barbee had become afraid of Dodd.

Ray had one more piece of business he wanted to place on the court record while the jury was outside the courtroom.

"Judge, at this time I would like to put something on the record with Mr. Barbee," Ray said.

"Go ahead," Judge Gill responded.

Bill Ray requested that Barbee remain seated at the

defense table and to speak loudly as he answered his questions.

"It's the time in the trial for us to either present witnesses or rest. Do you understand that?" Ray asked his client.

"Yes."

"And I have explained to you that you do not have to testify if you don't want to. Do you understand that?" Ray asked.

"Yes."

"And I have explained to you that you could testify if you want to, and you understand that?" Ray questioned.

"Yes."

"And we have talked about if you testified, the prosecutor would be able to ask you any question that he believed relevant about this case. Do you understand that?" Ray continued.

"Yes."

"I also explained to you that any inconsistent statement that you have made to another person, if you were to say something up here inconsistent with that, the prosecutor would be able to talk about those things. Do you understand that?" Ray asked.

"Yes."

"And, specifically, there has been a portion of a statement that Judge Gill has suppressed and this jury hasn't heard. And if you were to testify and you were to say something inconsistent with what was in that statement, in all likelihood, at least a portion of that would become admissible before the jury. Do you understand that?" Ray asked.

"Yes."

"Knowing all that, do you want to testify in this case, or are you telling the court that you do not want to testify?" Ray asked.

Although Ray had encouraged Stephen Barbee to take the stand in his own defense, Barbee remembered what Tina

Church had advised while they talked by phone. Stephen Barbee replied, "I do not."

Ray announced he had no further questions for his client, but that he intended to call one witness.

Judge Gill gently rocked back in his high-back chair while the jury filed in.

"The defense calls Stanley Keaton," Ray announced.

Stanley Keaton, working for Professional Investigations and Associates, had been hired by the defense to serve subpoenas in the case. Keaton testified that he had served a subpoena on the city of Fort Worth for cell phone records of Detective J. T. McCaskill, Detective B. A. Jamison, and Detective Mike Carroll for all calls made February 21 through February 22, 2005. Bill Ray submitted the cell phone records as Defense Exhibit Number 2.

Keaton also acknowledged that he served a second subpoena on the city of Fort Worth for all police department manuals and general orders relating to taking statements and confessions from witnesses and suspects, in effect on February 18, 2005, as well as all revisions. Those records were admitted as Defense Exhibit Number 4.

Without any further questions or offering any explanations of the cell phone records or police procedural manuals, Bill Ray rested the defense's case.

Stephen Barbee turned and looked at his parents questioningly. *Is that it? Is that my defense?* he wondered. His mother's expression told Barbee she was as confused as he was. Barbee thought, *Why didn't Ray tell the jury about the discrepancies between the cell phone records and the testimony in court? Why didn't my attorneys point out the Fort Worth policy on confession and how it was handled in my case? Why offer proof of subpoenas without any explanation?*

Barbee shook his lowered head, hopelessness marring his face.

Both Kevin Rousseau, for the prosecution, and Bill Ray, for the defense, announced they were ready to close their cases.

Judge Gill turned to the jury as he spoke.

"Ladies and gentlemen of the jury, both sides have rested and closed. That's all the testimony you will hear in trial. I will get the charge ready and have it ready to go for y'all tomorrow morning at nine o'clock.

"When we reconvene tomorrow morning at nine, I will read you the court's charge. You'll hear the summations of counsel, and then the case will be yours for deliberation.

"Have a good evening. We'll see you tomorrow morning at nine o'clock."

As the gallery began to vacate the courtroom, conversations focused on the closing statements that would be heard the following day. After such a short defense, spectators wondered what Bill Ray and Tim Moore would say in an attempt to save their client. It was certain Kevin Rousseau would come out with "guns blazing" to insure a conviction of capital murder.

23

The next morning, February 23, 2006, dozens of court spectators, along with regular employees, filled the distance between the two banks of elevators on the ground floor of the Tarrant County Justice Center. It would take several minutes for each person to arrive at his final destination.

· Stephen Barbee entered the courtroom ready for his attorneys to fight for his freedom. He was nervous, yet hopeful that he would be able to walk out of the Tarrant County Justice Center a free man.

Sheila Underwood, dressed in one of her plain, yet fashionable, suits, was back in her front-row seat. This was one portion of the trial she had no intention of missing. Sheila had waited a year to see Stephen Barbee convicted for the brutal murders of her daughter and grandson.

Jackie and Bill Barbee were also present. They had been at the trial each day to support their son and believed firmly in his innocence. Nancy Kearly was by Jackie's side, just as she had been throughout the trial. Nancy squeezed Jackie's hand as Judge Gill took his seat and greeted the jury.

Judge Gill informed jurors he would present the charge to them following the summations of both the state and the defense. He then announced each side had twenty minutes to make its presentation to the jury, and instructed the state to begin.

Kevin Rousseau stood, buttoning his dark suit jacket, and looked at Sheila Underwood, giving her a slight nod, and crossed the courtroom to stand before the jury.

"Ladies and gentlemen, I can stand up here all day long telling you why this man is guilty of capital murder, but I don't have a great deal of time, so I'll get right to it," Rousseau began.

Tears immediately came to the eyes of Jackie Barbee. She took a deep breath, but nothing would help stop the flow of fearful tears that streamed down her cheeks.

"I told you, and we have proven, that he had a motive to do this killing. And in his own words, in his explanation to his wife, you heard that motive, and he also explained it to the detective, Detective Carroll. He explained quite clearly that he thought he was going to lose everything. He thought that he was going to lose his new wife.

"And remember, from Trish's own mouth she explained in that video that you saw that they were not married at the time that Lisa got pregnant. He thought Lisa was pregnant with his baby, and that his new wife would not understand that he cheated on her when they were dating five months before they were married. He thought he was going to lose her. That's why he intended to do the killing," Rousseau said as he walked back and forth before the jury.

Rousseau stated that Barbee had committed the murders—because they knew he had dumped Lisa's Durango in a creek not three hundred yards from where he ran away from Deputy Brawner three hours after the last activity on Lisa's computer.

The assistant district attorney reminded jurors that Barbee had lied about being in Denton County.

"He lied until Detective Carroll made him confess. Until Detective Carroll told him that a man was coming to look at [the] video, and it was sure looking bad for him. That's when he started squirming," Rousseau said.

Rousseau reminded the jury that Barbee had confessed to the police, even though the defense would like them to disregard the confession, because it wasn't written down.

"He told you Ron Dodd took him over there. If Dodd hadn't taken him there, then where was his own vehicle? He needed Lisa's car because his car wasn't sitting out front. That corroborates the detective's version.

"He confessed to his wife that he committed this killing. Now, does it surprise you that he lessens his involvement, that he backed off, that he didn't say, 'You know what? I went in that house and I brutally slaughtered this pregnant mother and her child.' Does it surprise you that he wouldn't tell his wife that?" Rousseau asked rhetorically.

Rousseau described Barbee's action as that of a child who got caught, when he told Trish, "I didn't mean to. Oh, please, oh, please, don't leave me. Please don't stop loving me."

"He was reduced to the simpering coward that he is," Rousseau said with malice in his words.

Stephen Barbee sat with his head down, crying.

"And finally he led police to their grave. Overwhelming evidence of guilt. This is not a whodunit. You know who did it, and you know why."

Rousseau then explained that there were two lesser included offenses they could render: murder and manslaughter. He agreed Barbee was guilty of those, but stressed he was guilty of so much more. He was guilty of capital murder.

Rousseau had decided prior to the beginning of the trial not to prosecute Barbee for the death of Marleigh. Although

Texas law would have allowed the prosecution to charge Barbee with capital murder of the unborn fetus, the deaths of both Lisa and Jayden also constituted capital murder. Rousseau felt bringing Marleigh into the equation was a potentially divisive issue for jurors. He needed a unanimous decision—he didn't need to give the jury too much to ponder.

To prove his point, Rousseau first reminded jurors of Barbee's conversation with Detective Carroll in the bathroom at the Tyler Police Department. Barbee had said, "I held her down too long, and she died." But Rousseau recapped for jurors that in the same conversation Barbee told the detective that he went over there with the specific intent of killing Lisa, and that he then killed Jayden when he was screaming.

Rousseau stated that, secondly, Barbee had lied to his wife, telling her he had gone over there to talk to Lisa. That he had made a bad decision. And that he just wanted Lisa to stop hitting and kicking him.

"From his description it sounds like he's lucky to be alive. 'It was an accident. I held her down too long.'

"Lisa Underwood was in her home in the middle of the night before one of the biggest days of her life. She's very, very pregnant. She's wearing her pajamas. She's finally got that hour or two or three of precious time that mothers have alone after their child has gone to bed, and her child is sleeping in the next room in their own home.

"She's been sick for a week with the flu. How much of a fight can she put up? How interested do you think she was in jumping on this poor man? And if he just went over there to talk, why did he forget his car? Why would he be concerned about his car being out front? Why would he need a ride to her house under cover of darkness in the middle of the night with no way to leave? Why?

"Ladies and gentlemen, this is not an accidental killing followed by an intentional killing. Killing like this takes work. First you have to get them down. You have to close off the oxygen supply and keep it closed off for two to three minutes at a minimum. That takes work.

"This was not an accidental killing followed by an intentional killing. This was two intentional killings committed in the exact same manner. Identical method used to kill both victims. The only difference between the two victims is the first one was a little bigger. The first one took a little more. He had to deliver a good beating before he could kill that mother. You know, mothers in their own home when they are fighting for their lives and the lives of their children don't go down easy.

"He has to pay for what he has done. Do not let him go. Thank you," Rousseau said in a dramatic finish.

As Kevin Rousseau turned from the jury box, he looked at Sheila Underwood. Sheila smiled, closed her eyes, and nodded. Rousseau had done the job he had promised her he would do. She felt certain they would have the conviction they wanted.

Bill Ray strolled toward the jury.

"I want to tell you before I start, I wish, and I think everyone in this room wishes, we weren't here. There is nothing in this case that can bring back the lives of Lisa and Jayden Underwood, and her unborn child.

"And I have seen the pain associated with their family. I don't know these folks, but I know who they are, and I would give anything if we weren't here today," Ray said with sincerity.

Ray told the jury they had taken an oath to determine

Stephen Barbee's involvement and what was going on in his mind.

He stated that there were four verdict forms, but contended there were only two that the evidence supported.

"What I mean by that is if you look at the evidence in this case, what you saw on the DVD player, what you heard from the electronic equipment, the exhibits the prosecutor introduced, the testimony of the witnesses and the exhibits I introduced, that is the evidence in this case and that is what you have to make your decision with, and nothing else," Ray stated.

Ray told jurors that as strong as their emotions about the case might be, that was not to be considered. Looking from one of the twelve jurors and one alternate to the other, Ray said, "The charge tells you that the definition of 'intentionally' is it must be your conscious objective or desire to achieve or cause the result.

"The definition of 'knowingly' is that your conduct is reasonably certain to cause the result."

Ray told the jury that if they looked closely at the evidence in the case, and applied the two definitions he had given them, in order to find Stephen Barbee guilty of capital murder, they would have to find he had intentionally or knowingly caused the death of Lisa Underwood, and—in the same transaction—intentionally or knowingly caused the death of Jayden Underwood.

The defense attorney reminded the thirteen members of the panel that in the pretrial interviews, they all had stated that if they had an intentional killing on one hand, and on the other hand they didn't, they had all said in no uncertain terms they would find a person not guilty.

Ray made a point of telling the jury trust was the most important thing in the trial, and assured them he had done nothing that would cause them not to trust him.

For the first time Ray explained the importance of the exhibits he had entered into evidence during his direct examination. First were the cell phone records. Ray stated that when the jurors scrolled through the lists in the jury room, they would find that Detective Carroll had called Detective J. D. Thornton at least ten times during the hours of 11:30 P.M. on February twenty-first and the next morning.

Ray reminded them that on the stand Carroll had testified that he knew from what Stephen Barbee had told him in the Tyler bathroom where he would be able to find the bodies of Lisa and Jayden Underwood.

"Yet, as many times as he called Detective Thornton, his boss, he didn't tell him. If he had, they would have found those people. He said he knew exactly where they could be found, based on the conversation with Stephen Barbee," Ray said.

"And here is the crux of all of it. The second set of records is a subpoena for the manuals and general orders relating to taking statements and confessions from witnesses and suspects in effect on February eighteenth, and all revisions of 2005. The chief of police, Ralph Mendoza, has put out a list of rules. And the rules say, document what you've done.

"I daresay that in your own business, in your own life, that if something extremely important happened to you, that you wouldn't wait nine months before you told anybody about it.

"And that brings us to motive. The problem is the only evidence of the motive that you've heard from the courtroom is from a detective who, in spite of the fact that he had an interview in front of a machine with the capability to record exactly what was done, and watch the personal emotions and the voices of everyone, he chose to conduct a forty-five-minute interview standing next to a couple of urinals. That's where the motive came from. And the motive doesn't get told for nine months," Ray stated.

The counsel for the defense then made a shocking statement. He reiterated what Dr. White had said, that Jayden Underwood could have been killed only one way. And Ray told the panel he took the doctor at his word. But then Bill Ray stated, "As hard as it is to say, the evidence from the courtroom shows that Stephen Barbee killed Jayden Underwood. There is no evidence to the contrary."

Ray attempted to sway the jury by stating that the problem in the case for capital murder was that Stephen Barbee didn't have the conscious objective or desire, nor did he know his conduct was reasonably certain to cause the result, referring back to the two definitions he had previously given the jury.

Ray told the jury panel that the only motive for the defendant to take Lisa Underwood's life came from Detective Carroll. Then, as if an afterthought in the middle of his closing statement, Ray began talking about how there was nothing wrong with the police misleading a suspect or putting two suspects in different rooms to compare notes. Ray referred to that as good police work. But he did have a problem with Carroll's testimony—the detective had smiled.

"He sat up there in that chair and he was proud of those things," Ray said, pointing to the witness-box.

"The motive in this case is the most important part, and the only motive you have comes from the detective who doesn't write a single word of that down for almost ten months, and smiles at you. Was he lying to you? It certainly doesn't bother him to lie to achieve his results."

Ray asked the jury if Detective Carroll looked any different when he spoke to them than when lying to a suspect. He told them the answer was no, suggesting that Carroll had lied when testifying.

Ray again told the jury that how Jayden Underwood died was conclusive, but, based on Dr. Krouse's testimony, they couldn't be sure what happened to Lisa. He proposed that a person intent on murder would have gone in the house, shot the victims, and left the scene. Ray contended that someone who had planned to kill wouldn't have left two or three crime scenes, and then taken the police to where the bodies were buried.

"We have a horrible, horrible, horrible thing that has happened," Ray said.

"Something happened in that house. Kevin said it both ways. How is a sick young lady going to fight? She's not. Then he turns around right before he sits down and says she's going to fight until she can't fight any more.

"It's not a one-sided fight. There are two people involved. Stephen Barbee's own words to his wife matches. He told Trish Barbee he held her down too long. That's exactly what matches the testimony of Dr. Krouse. And as hard as it is to do, I submit to you that the evidence in this case—the conclusive, beyond-a-reasonable-doubt evidence—does not support an intentional or knowing murder for Lisa Underwood. Was he there? Yes. Did he hold her down? Yes. Did he know or intend that she was going to die, or was that his conscious objective? The answer is no.

"Thank you."

Ray walked back to the defense table. He had done his job.

The burden of proof rested on the state. Therefore, they would have the last word directed to the jury. Dixie Bersano, her blond hair contrasting against her dark suit, stood to address the panel of citizens who would ultimately decide the fate of Stephen Barbee.

"Ladies and gentlemen, this was a horrendous, horrible crime," Bersano began. "Two generations of a family were snuffed out on February 19, 2005. And there was a plan to kill those two people.

"Why? What was the motive? Holly told you what the motive was. Lisa wanted insurance for her baby—the baby that she thought this man was the father of. She wanted insurance. No talk of child support. If she put that baby on his insurance, this man knew Trish was going to find out, and he couldn't have that.

"He had weeded all these women out of his buffet line, and he had picked Trish, and he wasn't going to lose Trish [because] of Lisa and Lisa's unborn baby."

Dixie Bersano then recapped the plan that Barbee had told police about. Ron Dodd was to drive him to Lisa's house and he was going to kill her. But, Bersano said, Barbee couldn't do it and he left. He then decided he could get himself worked up enough to kill Lisa, and he had Ron Dodd drive him back to Lisa's house. Bersano told the jury that Barbee went to Lisa's with the intent to kill her so that he didn't have to put the baby on his insurance.

Bersano explained the rest of the plan was to put Lisa's body in her Durango, dump the body, dump the Durango, and have Dodd pick him up. But, Bersano said, the plan went terribly wrong.

"While he was killing Lisa, Jayden was there. He wasn't gone for the weekend with [his] grandma. Jayden comes in, screaming, because some stranger—Lisa had never introduced him to this man—was killing his mommy. He was screaming. He was a witness.

"He turns to Jayden and kills him by smothering him. What to do now? 'My plan isn't working. Well, the Durango is big enough. Let me load the bodies into the back of the Durango. I have got two bodies instead of one. Go up I-35, dump the bodies in a shallow grave.' It wasn't even that deep. You saw Lisa's toe."

Members of the jury, as well as spectators in the audience, recalled the photo of the grave that was presented by Kevin Rousseau. Among the limbs and brush atop the bodies of Lisa and Jayden Underwood, one painted-red toe stuck out. It was an eerie remembrance.

Dixie Bersano continued with her summation.

"He dumps the Durango. Gets muddy and wet from the creek, where he dumped the Durango. Go meet Ron Dodd. The plan is working.

"Well, lo and behold, whoops, we have a problem. Denton County is out patrolling, and out in the middle of nowhere, they run across this man who says he's David Weekley. It's a problem. What to do? He runs from the police, and to their credit, they put up a search. That officer chased him, and 'Oh, no, I'm leading him to the Durango.' He makes a ninety-degree turn, and somewhere north of there, he meets up with Ron Dodd. The plan is complete," Bersano stated with emotion laced with sarcasm.

The female ADA then reminded the jury that on the Monday following the murders, Barbee took his wife and kids to Tyler. Barbee went on with his life after ending the lives of two others, as though nothing had happened.

Bersano stated that Barbee's plan of murder had fallen apart because of a "pesky video" in the Denton County deputy's car. She emphasized how that video put him near the dump site of the Durango and the burial site of the bodies.

Bersano then reminded the panel that Dr. Krouse testified that Lisa had bruising and deep injury down both sides of her spine from compression of one hundred pounds or more; that a person would become unconscious after six to eight minutes; that they don't die, they become unconscious.

"That pressure had to remain on her, compressing her

chest down on the floor for a minimum of two to three minutes, maybe up to six to eight minutes," Bersano explained.

Bersano questioned Barbee's contention that he didn't intend to kill Lisa, when he obviously kept the pressure on for a long, long time. In addition, Dr. Krouse testified that injuries to her head were consistent with fingertips holding her head down in the carpet. Bersano pointed out Lisa had been beaten. She had a broken wrist from something coming down on her wrist. She was fighting, but she didn't make it. Bersano told jurors they didn't have to agree exactly how Lisa Underwood was killed, just agree unanimously that she was smothered by one of the means cited by Dr. Krouse.

The attention was then turned to Jayden.

"Dr. White told you there were injuries on Jayden that occurred before death, and injuries after death. Can you imagine the terror of a seven-and-a-half-year-old little boy coming in, finding his mommy was being killed? He didn't have his glasses on. He couldn't see without his glasses. They were beside his bed. He went in there to save Mommy, and he was killed," Bersano stated, pulling at the heartstrings of many in attendance.

Dixie Bersano wrapped up her summation by telling the jury that both Lisa and Jayden Underwood had been intentionally killed.

"The state is asking you to come back with a verdict of guilty of capital murder—the killing intentionally or knowingly of two individuals in the same transaction. Lisa and Jayden."

Bersano paused momentarily at the jury box's rail, letting her words sink in; then she returned to her place next to Kevin Rousseau.

* * *

Both the state and the defense had done all they could—one to secure a conviction, and the other to seek freedom for Stephen Barbee.

There appeared to be a collective sigh of relief from the gallery. This had been no ordinary trial, but one filled with the emotions only the deaths of a seven-year-old and an unborn child could muster.

Judge Gill released the alternate juror from service, issued the charge to the remaining twelve, and dismissed them to the adjacent jury room for deliberations.

Sheila Underwood slipped out of the courtroom, while the Barbees remained in their seats, watching their son escorted from the courtroom by armed officers.

Jackie Barbee nervously wrung her hands as her husband labored to rise from his bench seat. Bill's health was deteriorating, and the stress of the trial was contributing to his discomfort. Standing, Jackie cradled her arm under Bill's and helped him to his feet. Ignoring the questions from the media, Jackie steered Bill toward the elevator and escorted him downstairs, where he, like Sheila Underwood, had a smoke to calm his nerves.

No one knew how much time it would take for the jury to deliberate the fate of Stephen Barbee. Most spectators took time to grab a soda, a coffee, or even a quick snack in the first-floor lounge before returning to the courtroom to wait. Spectators sat visiting with one another, sharing their predictions of the outcome of the trial, until they heard the sound of the familiar buzzer announcing the jury had a message for the court.

Ninety minutes after retiring to the jury room, a message was sent to Judge Gill that the jury had reached a verdict.

Kevin Rousseau and Dixie Bersano, confident they would get the conviction they had worked for, were in their offices preparing for the penalty phase of the trial when they received word the jury had reached a decision.

Kevin Rousseau smiled. He knew that when a jury reached an early conclusion, it was normally a judgment in favor of the prosecution, but Rousseau was not one to take anything for granted. He was still concerned with the one female juror he had watched during their presentation. The young woman had looked at Barbee many times during the proceedings. Did she find him attractive, as so many women had seemed to? Rousseau could only hope he had convinced her of Barbee's guilt.

People hurried into the courtroom to take their places as word that the jury was returning had spread throughout the courthouse.

Stephen Barbee was led back into the courtroom and was seated next to Tim Moore, with Bill Ray on the far side of the table.

A somber Judge Gill took his seat. He spoke in an imposing voice to both the prosecution and the defense.

"The jury has notified us they have reached a verdict. Are both sides ready to receive it?"

Kevin Rousseau stood and addressed the court. "Yes, Your Honor."

"The defense is ready," Bill Ray announced.

Tim Moore gently took Stephen Barbee's arm and lifted it, to indicate he was to stand, as he himself stood up.

Judge Gill turned his attention to the jury.

"Has the jury reached a verdict?" Judge Gill asked.

The foreman of the jury stood and spoke to the judge.

"Yes, it has," he stated.

"Is that verdict unanimous?" Judge Gill inquired.

"Yes, it is."

"Hand the charge to the bailiff," the judge instructed.

The courtroom was silent in tense anticipation. No one

spoke. No one moved as the bailiff handed the charge to Judge Gill. The judge looked at the piece of paper handed to him by his bailiff, giving no indication of how the verdict read.

Stephen Barbee averted his eyes away from the twelve people who had decided his fate. He thought of his parents, of Trish, and of the mistakes he had made leading him to that moment.

Sheila Underwood clung tightly to a friend sitting next to her, lending her support as she had throughout the trial. Sheila wanted to hear the words "guilty of capital murder." She would accept nothing less for her daughter, grandson, and unborn granddaughter.

Jackie Barbee held tightly to Bill as he bowed his head in prayer. A godly man, Bill Barbee had prayed throughout most of the trial. He asked God to free his son and help him escape the injustice of the accusations against him.

Reporters sat with pens poised over tablets, ready to take down any utterances from the defendant or reactions from others.

Finally, after what seemed like an eternity, with no expression or inflection in his voice, Judge Robert Gill announced, "'We the jury find the defendant guilty of the offense of capital murder as charged in the indictment.'"

Judge Gill looked toward Rousseau, and then to Ray.

"Does either side wish to have the jury polled?" Judge Gill asked.

Although the prosecution did not request that each individual juror be asked if that was his or her verdict, the defense did want to make certain that all twelve persons agreed.

One by one, Judge Gill called the name of each juror and asked if "guilty" was his or her verdict. Twelve times he received "yes" as the response, including from the young woman whom Rousseau had worried about.

Stephen Barbee hung his head in emotional defeat. He believed his attorneys had done little to disprove the prosecution's case. He could only hope at this point that they put up a substantial fight for his life, for the jury would now be asked to decide if he would live in prison for the rest of his life, or die on the execution gurney.

24

An announced lunch break was an appreciated interruption from the tension-filled atmosphere of the courtroom. Stephen Barbee had been found guilty of the murders of Lisa and Jayden Underwood. The jury was told to return at 12:45 P.M., when the trial would reconvene. It appeared jurors had little trouble reaching a guilty verdict, having taken a mere ninety minutes to come to their decision. The next time they entered the jury room to deliberate, a man's life would be at stake.

After everyone returned to their seats for the punishment phase of the trial, and following Judge Gill's announcement that the state could proceed, Kevin Rousseau called Teresa Barbee.

It was one of the few times Stephen Barbee looked at a witness that would be testifying against him. He had once loved Teresa, and even after their divorce, they had remained business partners and friends. But Barbee had had time to think during the year he had been incarcerated, awaiting trial. He was now convinced Teresa had conspired with Ron Dodd to get rid of him.

Ron had allowed the steel beam to strike him in the head at the job site, and phone records showed Teresa had been in communication with Ron during the night of the murders. Barbee was now certain he had been set up by Teresa and Ron. Why else would Ron have abandoned him at Lisa's house, and again at the burial site in Denton County? Barbee also knew it was Ron Dodd who had called police with the anonymous tip that he was responsible for Lisa's and her son's deaths. *Why?* Barbee pondered. *Why would they do it?* Then he remembered the life insurance policy he had taken out, with the businesses as beneficiaries, and Teresa had convinced him to sign the businesses over to her. Barbee stared at Teresa; mistrust and contempt filled his brown eyes.

Teresa took her seat, pushing the microphone back from her face slightly. Teresa Barbee and Trish Barbee were very different. Teresa fought a weight problem, where Trish was petite. Teresa had long, very dark hair; Trish was a blonde. Teresa had an active role in the businesses Stephen had built, but Trish had no interest in any of her husband's business affairs.

The two Mrs. Barbees didn't get along. Stephen believed Trish had been jealous of Teresa, for no other reason than the house Teresa retained after their divorce. Trish had asked him several times to build her a house of comparable size, which had led him to purchase a parcel of land for just that purpose shortly before his arrest.

Teresa Barbee was the prosecution's most valuable witness in their effort to gain a death sentence.

ADA Dixie Bersano began questioning Teresa Barbee, first focusing on her personal relationship with Stephen Barbee, then leading her to their business operations.

Teresa described Four Seasons as a thriving tree service, while she portrayed Cowboy Cutters as a financial strain.

She contended she begged Stephen not to take over Cowboy Cutters.

Stephen Barbee shook his head slightly. He had always asserted it was Teresa who insisted on obtaining the business, as well as taking on an active role.

Bersano asked Teresa why things started falling apart after the acquisition of Cowboy Cutters.

"With Four Seasons there was no overhead. It was easy. We had just built our house. We were supposed to spend '03 having a child. It took a lot of money to get Cowboy Cutters, and we went into almost a million dollars in debt when he bought the company. It was an everyday situation at Cowboy Cutters. It didn't make any money. We charged everything on our credit cards. We got a loan and started paying. There were a lot of struggles. Bad decisions with the demolition crew and we got into debt. We tried to work them both. Then Four Seasons started having problems," Teresa stated.

Stephen Barbee had told his parents they were in debt because of Teresa's overspending. He told them she spent $65,000 decorating their house. She had to have a swimming pool. She was spending it faster than he was making it.

When Bersano asked if there had been any physical assaults against her by Stephen during their marriage, Teresa stated there had been four.

"She's lying," Stephen said, leaning toward his attorneys.

"Stop that," Ray said. "The judge is looking at you."

Stephen Barbee sat back, frustration covering his face.

Teresa described the first assault as an incident that occurred before they were married. She couldn't remember what the argument leading up to the physical altercation had been about, but she and Stephen had ended up fighting on the bed, and someone called the police.

The first Mrs. Stephen Barbee stated the second altercation

happened while they were living in the metal building on their property, prior to the completion of their house. Teresa could not recall what had sparked the argument between them, and once more someone else had called the police. She stated Stephen had pushed her up against a door and had his hands around her throat. As with the first incident, Teresa sustained no injuries. She testified that after the police left, she refused to allow her husband back in their apartment, and he had spent the night in his truck.

In describing the next quarrel between herself and her former husband, Teresa insisted Stephen hadn't hit her, but admitted he was mad and had begun slamming doors and knocking stuff off the walls. Teresa explained that when Barbee had knocked a shelf off the wall, a large-jarred candle had hit her in the head. She insisted it was *not* intentional.

"When I came to, I was nauseated and I had blood on my head," Teresa stated.

Teresa contended she went to look for Stephen and found him eating ice cream in the apartment portion of the metal building. She claimed she asked Stephen to take her to the hospital, but he thought she was faking and refused.

"How did you get to the hospital?" Bersano asked.

"I drove myself," Teresa said.

"Were you in any shape to drive yourself to the hospital?" Bersano inquired.

"No. I woke up and I was in the ditch in our front yard in the car," Teresa explained.

Teresa stated that after she finally made it to the hospital, she told the nurse what had happened, and the nurse called the police. She informed jurors that she was told she had a "real bad concussion," and had been advised to stay overnight.

"Did anyone show up at the hospital for you?" Bersano asked.

"Yes, Stephen did."

"What kind of mood was he in when he got to the hospital?" Bersano asked.

"He was mad because he thought I called the police," Teresa responded.

In describing the final incident of alleged abuse, Teresa yet again claimed she didn't recall what they began arguing about, but she knew they were outside at the time.

"I started screaming at him," Teresa said. "I don't remember too much of what he said. I just remember what I said. I just said that if you want to hit me, hit me. You always say that you do. If you feel like a man, hit me."

Teresa claimed Stephen then struck her repeatedly, bruising her arm.

"I was saying, 'Does that make you feel better? Does that make you feel like a man? Do you feel good? Is this what you wanted?'" Teresa testified, her voice shaky and her eyes tearing.

"Why did you stand there and let him do that to you?" Bersano asked.

"Because he was so angry. I don't know why. I just was egging him on and telling him, 'If you feel like this is what you need to do, then do it.' I put my fists up and said, 'Come on. I'm tired of arguing. I'm tired of fighting. You want to fight? Let's fight.' I'm not a submissive person. I came back and said, 'Let's do it. Put your dukes up. Let's fight,'" Teresa stated.

When asked if Stephen Barbee had ever threatened her, Teresa said that playing around, he had threatened to put her through a wood chipper.

"What's a chipper?" Bersano asked, attempting to clarify for the jury.

"It is a huge machine, where you take tree limbs and you put them in a box, and it grinds them up and it comes out like mulch on the other side," Teresa explained, adding that they owned one at the time.

"Was there ever a point in your marriage that you became concerned about the possibility of going through a chipper?" Bersano inquired.

"Once, July 3, 2003."

Teresa described a company party that was being held at their new house on that date. She stated that Stephen had gotten into a fight with a man and asked him to leave.

Teresa testified that others at the party had been telling her things Stephen was saying about her, including putting her through his wood chipper. She hit him and he left. He never moved back into the house after that.

"I couldn't take her telling me what to do all the time," Barbee had told his mother at the time. "When she hit me in the mouth, it bled, and I got out. She had become unbearable to live with, and I finally realized we would never have a child. We only had sex twice in the final year of our marriage."

Jackie Barbee stared at her former daughter-in-law in disbelief. As far as she knew, Stephen had always given Teresa everything she ever wanted. Even when Teresa wanted a pool and cabana, they had asked Jackie and Bill to loan them money for the construction. The senior Barbees withdrew a certificate of deposit (CD) from the bank to loan their son and daughter-in-law money for the pool. Jackie had blamed Teresa for the breakup of the marriage—her overspending, her degrading of Stephen in front of his workers, and her temper.

Jackie's attention returned to the testimony as Dixie Bersano asked Teresa, "What happened on your first anniversary?"

Teresa explained that she and Stephen were going out to dinner, driving down Loop 820 in Fort Worth, between Rufe Snow exit and Highway 377. She stated they saw a car approaching on the left side of their vehicle, on the shoulder.

The man driving the car then shot across in front of them and exited the highway.

Teresa stated Stephen exited as well, following the man to a dead end. She said Stephen was screaming at the man that he almost killed them, and she was screaming at Stephen to stop, the man could have a gun and shoot them. Teresa said she saw Stephen throw a punch at the guy through his window; then he returned to their car and they went on to dinner.

On questioning Teresa about her relationship to Ron Dodd, Teresa told Bersano that she first met Dodd when Stephen hired him to be a saw operator with Cowboy Cutters. She said Dodd left after five months because he wanted a raise, and he didn't get one. Dodd returned after Stephen offered him the position of supervisor. She claimed she didn't want Dodd back, because she didn't like him.

Then Teresa reported that she and Stephen divorced in December 2003, and that was when she got to know Dodd better. They eventually became "girlfriend and boyfriend." She admitted he began living with her in 2004 at the house she and Stephen had built in Haslet. Teresa also admitted Ron Dodd was in legal trouble, as it related to the Underwood case.

Bersano asked Teresa if she had been subpoenaed to testify, and she responded that she had been. Teresa stated she didn't want to be in court, but she had to be. She began to cry as she looked toward her former husband.

Bersano's direct examination of Teresa was complete.

Bill Ray handled the cross-examination for the defense, first asking Teresa about Stephen Barbee's siblings. Teresa told the court how Stephen had had an older sister and brother, both now deceased. She described the deaths of both Kathy and David for the court.

When asked about the ownership of both Four Seasons and Cowboy Cutters, Teresa acknowledged that at the time of the Barbees' divorce, they each owned 50 percent of each company.

"He doesn't own those businesses anymore, does he?" Ray asked.

"No, he does not. He told me to put the companies in my name," Teresa stated.

"Stephen had been in jail about three or four days, and you went to the jail and got him to sign over his rights to all these businesses, right?" Ray asked.

Teresa's chin tightened as she snapped back, "I didn't get him to do anything."

Stephen Barbee glared at his ex-wife. Shortly after he was first arrested, Teresa had brought papers to the jail and asked him to sign them. He had done it for her. Stephen Barbee, who knew he would always care for Teresa, acknowledged to his parents and Tina Church that he had signed the papers because Teresa claimed she'd lose all the businesses if he didn't sign them over to her.

Stephen Barbee had wanted to preserve them so when he was exonerated, he would have something to go back to. Now he knew Teresa had just wanted them for herself.

"Well, you took some papers over there and asked him to sign them, and he signed them, right?" Ray asked a second time.

"Yes."

"And, essentially, these papers gave you one hundred percent control of that business?" Ray prompted.

"Yes."

"Now, Ms. Trish Barbee, the lady seated right here in the

lavender shirt," Ray said, pointing at Trish, "she was Stephen's wife at the time, right?"

"Yes."

Ray asked Teresa if—theoretically—Trish would have been entitled to some income derived from the businesses while married to Stephen. "Yes and no," Teresa said ambiguously.

"Was he given any consideration for signing over the businesses? Did you give him a piece of land? Did you put some money on his book in jail? Did you give his parents any money? Did you give Trish any money?" Ray pressured Teresa.

"What do you mean by that?" Teresa asked defensively.

"Well, did you pay him anything for signing those two businesses over?" Ray explained.

"No."

Teresa claimed the businesses had no value, and that all assets were owned by the bank.

Ray pressured Teresa, asking if her lawyer hadn't sent a letter to the jail allowing her access to Stephen to get him to sign everything over to her.

"No," Teresa stated, irritation in her voice.

Ray turned his focus to the large house Teresa and Stephen had built in Haslet. The home, over four thousand square feet, was complete, with a media room and a pool in the backyard.

"Did Stephen's mother put up the cash collateral for the pool?" Ray asked.

"On a CD, yes," Teresa responded.

"Did Mrs. Barbee know that the businesses weren't making any money when she signed that note?" Ray asked.

"I have no clue," Teresa snapped.

Jackie Barbee frowned. *Teresa was only interested in*

getting her pool. A pool I paid for, since Teresa refused to pay me back, Jackie thought.

Ray left the subject of money and redirected Teresa to her statements to the prosecution that Stephen had threatened to throw her in a wood chipper. In particular, that before their party on July 4, 2003, she had believed Stephen was just joking, but she now claimed on that particular day she believed he was serious.

"Did you testify in front of the Tarrant County grand jury in regard to this case?" Ray asked.

"Yes."

"Were you asked, and did you say, 'No, it didn't bother me, because he said it all the time.' Did you say that back then?" Ray asked.

"I might have. I don't remember," Teresa said softly.

Ray approached Teresa, handing her a copy of the grand jury transcript, asking her to read the portion where she had indeed testified that she had not taken Stephen's threat seriously, because he said it all the time.

Teresa finally admitted she had, in fact, made the statement during the grand jury inquiry.

Stephen Barbee smiled slightly. Ray had damaged Teresa's credibility. The defendant was certain Teresa had deliberately attempted to make him look bad, to help the jury believe he was a physical threat, thus capable of capital murder.

"Let's go back to the week of February 14, 2005," Ray said, noting that was the week Lisa and Jayden Underwood had been killed. Ray asked Teresa what was going on with the businesses and with Stephen that week.

Teresa said she and Stephen had a big fight that week involving the operation of both businesses. She stated that her former husband was also upset because he had just learned that his father had cancer, and his frequent headaches had become more severe. Teresa acknowledged that Stephen's headaches had been caused by a five-hundred-pound pipe hitting him in the head while working on a job in Dallas County.

"Did he go to the hospital?" Ray asked.

"Yes. It broke his hard hat and glasses and hit his face into the ground where he was unconscious. They said they thought he was dead. He wouldn't move," Teresa stated.

"Was Stephen ever in the hospital any other time while you were married?" Ray asked.

"Stephen tried to commit suicide," Teresa said.

At Ray's urging, Teresa explained she had overheard Stephen talking on the phone to a woman she suspected he was seeing. She stormed into the room, told her husband she had heard what he said to the woman, and that she didn't want to be with him anymore. Teresa said she left the house and went to a girlfriend's shop in nearby Keller.

"He came there and wanted to talk to me," Teresa continued. "He was crying and upset. He said he was sorry, he loved me, he didn't want to hurt me. He said there were a lot of problems going on. He threw his wallet and keys at me and took off. He told me he was going to go be with his brother and sister."

"What did that mean to you?" Ray asked.

"That he was going to go hurt himself," Teresa said.

"Did he ultimately do that?" Ray asked.

"Yes," Teresa said, explaining she had driven around trying to find Stephen, when he called her. Stephen had told her again he loved her, he was sorry, and he didn't mean to hurt her. Teresa said Stephen told her he was saying good-bye, and he was saying good-bye to the dogs. She knew he was home, so she went back to the house.

Teresa had looked throughout the house for Stephen, and not finding him, she went outside, finding him by the pool.

"I saw him laying on the ground. It was really cold. He was halfway in the water, facedown," Teresa testified.

Teresa said she ran to Stephen, flipped him over, and screamed to a friend in the house to call 911.

"I tried to wake Stephen up. He was blue and really cold. I was slapping his face, telling him to wake up. The police and ambulance got there and took him to the hospital," Teresa said.

Stephen Barbee later told his mother he couldn't believe Teresa was telling the jury that he had attempted to kill himself. True, he was upset, had been drinking, and had gone out to the pool to sit and think. But his feet had been in the water, not his head. *"She was only trying to make me seem unstable,"* Stephen said.

Ray switched the questioning to the night Lisa and Jayden were killed, asking Teresa how Stephen was acting that night when she spoke to him.

"Stephen had a lot of headaches. He was lashing out at people because of the headaches. Me and Stephen [were] fighting. Him and Trish were fighting. He found out about his dad. We were having problems with the businesses. It was a lot of things that was going on," Teresa said.

"Had you ever met Lisa Underwood?" Ray inquired.

"I never actually met her, but I saw her one time. We called her the 'bagel girl,'" Teresa replied.

Sheila Underwood bristled at Lisa being referred to as the bagel girl. She asked herself if Teresa Barbee had any shred of empathy for her daughter.

Bill Ray's questioning was complete. As he took his seat, Dixie Bersano again approached her witness with questions on redirect.

"Teresa, on that Friday night, February eighteenth, was Ron home all night long?" Bersano asked.

"Yes and no," Teresa responded.

Teresa explained that after she and Ron returned home from eating dinner out, Ron left for about fifteen minutes with Stephen, then returned without him. She stated that no sooner had Ron arrived home, when Stephen called and asked Ron to pick him up. Although Ron was again back home in about fifteen minutes, he and Stephen had gone out to the metal building beside the house, and they stayed there for several hours.

Teresa testified that the phone rang again, about 3:00 A.M. She had answered the phone and awakened Ron, telling him Stephen wanted to talk to him. Teresa claimed to have overheard Stephen tell Ron he needed him to help him. A few minutes later, Ron left the house, and Teresa went to bed. She didn't see Ron again until Saturday afternoon.

"When was the next time you saw Stephen?" Bersano asked.

"Sunday."

"How was he acting?" Bersano asked.

"He was crying. He was really upset. He said his life was over with," Teresa said.

Teresa stated under oath that she asked Stephen who Lisa was, having been visited by two police officers the night before who had asked about Lisa and Stephen's Corvette. Teresa claimed her former husband said, "You know who she is. She is the girl who came to the metal building and was screaming at me, and the one you saw at the bagel shop."

Having heard the AMBER Alert on the news, and knowing Stephen's relationship with Lisa, Teresa said she asked him, "What have you done?"

But Stephen wouldn't tell her; he just asked her to help him. Teresa put it together. She begged Stephen to turn

himself in to the police so she wouldn't have to call them—
a call she never made.

Teresa told the jury that Sunday, following the murders,
was the first time Stephen told her to get the businesses out
of his name, saying he didn't want to hurt anyone else.

The next time Teresa spoke to Stephen was on Monday
night, following his arrest when he called her from Tyler.

"What was that conversation about?" Bersano asked.

"I asked him why. I said, 'I heard you confessed.' He said,
yes, he had to. I said, 'Why?' He said he didn't mean to. He
went over there to talk to her. He said he was going to talk to
her and do the right thing. They got into a fight, she hit him,
and they just got into it. Before he knew it, he had held her
down. I asked him, 'What about the boy?' He said he didn't
mean to. He was just trying to keep him quiet," Teresa stated,
sniffling.

"What else did he tell you, Teresa?" Bersano asked, urging
Teresa to go on.

"I said, 'Please tell me, I'm begging you. You know I'm
with Ron. Did Ron help you? Did he have anything to do
with this?' He said no. He said Ron's mistake was picking
him up," Teresa said.

Bersano asked Teresa when she next talked with Stephen.

Teresa said Stephen told his mom he needed to see her.
She went to the Mansfield Jail, where he was being held,
on Tuesday, after the murders. Stephen's parents, his niece,
his former brother-in-law, and Trish were also in the room
at the time. Stephen was behind a glass and they spoke
by phone.

"He said I had it all wrong, that he didn't do this. That it
was some mistake," Teresa said.

Teresa stated she visited Stephen in jail every week, continually asking him why his story had changed. She testified he told her he didn't do it, he cleaned up, but that was

it. Then, he once told her he and Ron were sitting in front of the house, and Ron said he would go in and do it. Teresa claimed she kept asking Stephen why he continually changed his story. He never answered her, only became angry because she wouldn't believe him.

Eventually, by the end of September, Teresa stopped going to visit Barbee in jail. She no longer felt Stephen was telling her the truth.

"What do you mean?" Bersano asked.

"Every week me and Stephen talked about our past, our relationship, things that had happened, things we could change. He said he wished he never divorced me. I love Stephen, and I'll love Stephen until the day I die. I may not like what he has done, but I love him as a person unconditionally. I was going to support him—no matter what—and that's why I continued to go see him," Teresa said with tear-filled eyes.

Sheila Underwood cringed, asking herself how anyone could possibly love a person who had murdered a pregnant woman and a seven-year-old child. She resented Teresa Barbee and her declaration of love for the person who had ruthlessly destroyed her family.

"Why did you stop?" Bersano inquired.

"Because of what he wanted me to do. He wanted me to say Ron did it. He wanted me to tell his attorneys and everyone else Ron slipped," Teresa said, bursting into tears.

Teresa claimed Stephen held up a piece of paper saying to call his attorney and his mother, and tell them that Ron had slipped. That Ron had a plan and had him set up.

"When he held up the piece of paper, what did you do?" Bersano asked.

"I started crying. I got up and walked out. Then I got a letter from him telling me he was taking me off his visitors' list," Teresa said, crying.

* * *

Bill Ray had few questions on cross-examination. He focused on the fact that Teresa and Stephen were youth leaders at their church for about two years, with Stephen putting on puppet shows for the youngsters. Teresa told the jury Stephen loved the kids, and they loved him.

Teresa Barbee's two-hour testimony had been emotionally draining for Stephen, Jackie, and Bill Barbee. The Barbees believed Teresa was lying, choosing to destroy Stephen, rather than lose Ron Dodd. They also thought Teresa knew much more about the events of February 18 than she was telling. There were telephone records indicating she and Ron had been in contact throughout the night.

The Barbees were convinced that Teresa had managed to maneuver Stephen's businesses away from him; now she was helping the prosecution take his life.

25

Marie Mendoza was a name Bill Ray and Tim Moore had read from the prosecution's witness list; however, they didn't know exactly what she would be testifying to, or how her presence would impact the jury. They watched the dark-haired woman carefully as she approached the witness stand.

After Kevin Rousseau asked the low-spoken Mendoza to move the microphone closer to her mouth, he asked her what she did for a living.

Mendoza, an attractive woman, explained she was a business owner who contracted with builders to make-ready new homes by cleaning the interiors. She had also worked for UPS for some twelve and a half years as a mail sorter.

It was at UPS in 1999 that Mendoza had met Stephen Barbee. At the time, five or six years prior to the trial, Barbee was working part-time, unloading trucks.

Mendoza stated that Barbee had approached her one day as they were leaving work. He said he understood that she owned a small business and explained he, too, was a business owner. From that day on, she and Barbee would frequently talk at work, and he would also call her at home.

Mendoza was quick to mention that they never dated, never met for drinks after work, and she never saw him outside business hours. They had become friends slowly, and although he had asked her out, she hadn't gone. Barbee had never been to her home either.

After Barbee told Mendoza about his tree-trimming business, she asked him if he would drop by, take a look at her trees, and give her an estimate for any work that needed to be done. To Mendoza's surprise, when she got home after work one day, he had already completed the labor.

"What did you think about that?" Rousseau asked his witness.

"I found it very surprising that he would take it upon himself to make a decision to do the work without approaching me with an estimate," Mendoza said.

Bill Ray stood, interrupting Rousseau's direct examination by asking the judge if he could approach the bench.

Standing before Judge Gill, Ray said, "I guess I'm presumptuous. I'm assuming there is some bad act coming along here somewhere."

"Yes," Rousseau interjected.

"This girl is on their witness list, but not about any act that he's done in 1999," Ray argued.

"It's under extramarital affairs," Rousseau pointed out. "It didn't actually turn into an affair, but she called it an 'attempted extramarital affair.'"

"Well, it's the notice he's given us, Judge," Ray complained.

ADA Rousseau handed Judge Gill a copy of the notice of witnesses, pointing out the amended portion pertaining to Ms. Mendoza's testimony.

"I don't mind telling you the rest of the conversation, what's left of it," Rousseau offered Ray.

"Yeah, go ahead. I don't see any problem with it," Judge Gill responded, handing the papers back to the assistant district attorney.

Having had Ray's objection overruled, Rousseau continued his questioning.

"When you would have telephone conversations with him, was there something odd about the conversations, something that caught your attention?" Rousseau asked.

"They were very short, brief, and a lot of times he would end the conversation by saying, 'I have to go, I'll call back later,' which was puzzling. This would happen numerous times, just about every time I was on the phone with him," Mendoza said.

"Was there a time when you heard someone else's voice in the background?" Rousseau asked.

"That was pretty much one of the last conversations, when I heard a female voice in the background. Of course, he went ahead with the same routine, 'Got to go,' and would hang up. I sat and thought about it for a while and figured this guy had lied to me, that he was indeed married," Mendoza said.

Mendoza testified that when Barbee called her the day before she heard the woman in the background, she complained to him that she hadn't been prepared for him to trim the trees. She had just wanted an estimate, had planned to get other quotes to compare prices, but he had gone ahead and completed the work.

Then, three days after she had heard the woman's voice, Barbee called again. Mendoza informed Barbee that she had made a decision that there would never be anything between them. She offered to pay for the work he had done.

"What was his response?" Rousseau asked.

"He had an outburst, a big outburst," Mendoza stated.

"What did he say? You can use exact language," Rousseau instructed the timid witness.

"Well, he started yelling and cursing. He said, 'You fucking bitch. I go out there and trim your trees, and this is what I get in return?' He said a lot of other mean, harsh things, where my mouth just about dropped to the floor, because I never heard someone speak like that to me. I had never been spoken to like that. Also, I didn't know him in that way. I expected respect. I wasn't getting that from him," Mendoza testified.

Mendoza stated she never talked to Barbee after that phone call. She never saw him again at work.

"Did you ever think of him again, until early last year?" Rousseau questioned.

"I just thought he was a very mean, cruel person, very cruel, and he had no respect for women. And if he didn't get things his way, he's going to throw a fit. That's basically what happened. That was my experience with him," Mendoza said, avoiding the stares of Stephen Barbee.

Mendoza admitted she had told Rousseau about Barbee's behavior when she called his office following Barbee's arrest for the murders of Lisa and Jayden Underwood. She had wanted the prosecution to know the Stephen Barbee that she had known.

Mendoza took a deep breath as Bill Ray approached to cross-examine her.

Ray asked the witness if Barbee had done a good job trimming her trees, and she acknowledged he had.

"Didn't cost you any money?" Ray asked.

"No. But I wasn't looking for a free job," Mendoza countered.

"Mr. Barbee was never violent with you?" Ray inquired.

"I think he could have been, if he were there in person," Mendoza said, referring to the fact they had spoken only by phone when he became angry with her.

"But in person he was never violent with you?" Ray asked.

"No, not in person," Mendoza admitted.

Ray concluded his questioning by having Mendoza reiterate she never heard from Barbee after the disturbing phone call.

Kevin Rousseau then stood and addressed the court. "Your Honor, the state rests."

People in the gallery muttered to themselves, questioning the state's decision to put on only two witnesses during the punishment phase of the trial. But they also knew Rousseau and Bersano had a second chance, after the defense, to add more testimony.

The two assistant district attorneys sat back in their chairs, next to one another, confident that the defense would not be able to counteract their efforts at getting the death penalty.

The defense's first witness, Nancy Kearly, squeezed Jackie Barbee's hand as Kearly stood to take the witness chair. She was a petite, well-groomed woman, with graying hair. She smiled at Stephen Barbee before answering Tim Moore's first question.

"Dr. Kearly, what do you do for a living?" Tim Moore asked.

"I'm administrator of Warren Robbins University International, and a pastor's wife," Kearly responded.

Kearly stated that she and her husband resided in Stephenville, Texas, where he was pastor of the Stephenville

Full Gospel Church. In 1988, Reverend Kearly was pastor at Gospel Outreach Church in Azle, where Bill and Jackie began attending in 1989. Stephen joined them in 1995, and Teresa later. In 2002, the Kearlys moved from the Azle area to the Stephenville Full Gospel Church.

Kearly told the jury that she and her husband had performed the wedding ceremony for Stephen and Teresa. Both Stephen and Teresa later became the children's church leaders.

"We had a small group of children, about ten, or twelve, or fifteen. Someone was doing it, Stephen and Teresa were helping them. Then we noticed how good they were with children and how much children loved them. As time went by, we approached them about doing children's church, which they agreed to," Kearly stated.

"How old were these children?" Moore asked.

"They ranged from seven to about twelve," Kearly said.

The Barbees led the children's church for about three years, and the group grew from ten or fifteen to more than seventy-five children attending each week. Those children would leave the regular service and go to another building for children's church, while their parents remained in the regular worship service. The Barbees had their own curriculum, which had been approved by church officials, and included puppet shows.

"You still visit Mr. Barbee?" Moore asked.

"Yes, I do, faithfully—every Saturday. I brought him a new Bible and Bible study books from our college," Kearly explained.

With the defense passing the witness to him, Kevin Rousseau began his cross-examination by asking Dr. Kearly about her college affiliation.

Kearly explained she was a doctor of ministry, and she obtained her degree from Warren Robbins University, the school she and her husband began in Stephenville, Texas, in 1995. The school had been named after Warren Robbins, a minister from Kentucky. Mr. Kearly served as chancellor, and Mrs. Kearly as administrator.

"What is your student body right now?" Rousseau asked, a smirk on his face.

"We are a correspondence college. We furnish curriculum for churches that want to have their own Bible college. We furnish their books and their courses. We have accredited people that write courses. I edit them. The Warren Robbins University got accredited about two years ago," Kearly stated.

"Accredited from whom?" Rousseau asked, knowing the answer, and using it in an attempt to discredit the witness.

"From St. Kitts, West Indies. We are accredited through them, because they are accredited in the United States. That's for someone who wants to get a doctorate or Ph.D.," Dr. Kearly responded.

After a recapping of the Barbees' participation in the children's ministry at church, Rousseau asked Kearly if some of the children Stephen Barbee taught were seven years old. When Kearly replied yes, Rousseau asked if she knew that the little boy Barbee killed was seven years old. She said, "Yes."

"You don't believe he killed either of those people, do you?" Rousseau asked.

"No," Kearly said with conviction.

"You sat through the trial, didn't you?" Rousseau asked snidely.

"Yes, I did," Kearly answered.

"You saw him admitting to his wife that he killed that woman, didn't you?" Rousseau asked.

"I saw what I saw," Kearly stated, not believing that Barbee actually admitted killing Lisa and Jayden on the videotape.

"And you don't believe it, do you?" Rousseau pressed on.

"No," Kearly said again.

With no further questions from either side, Nancy Kearly was excused.

Jackie Barbee and Nancy Kearly exchanged reserved smiles as Nancy returned to her seat next to her friend. Where Nancy was petite, Jackie was a woman of size, with the stress of the trial taking a toll on her health.

When a brief recess was called, Jackie made her way outside and stood in the hallway.

"We want to ask you something," Ray said as he and Moore approached Jackie.

The three made their way to a more private area just down the hall.

"Stephen doesn't want you to testify," Ray informed Jackie.

Jackie looked confused. She couldn't understand why her son would be opposed to her telling the court the truth about him.

"But I'd like to say I'm sorry to the [Underwood] family," Jackie argued. "What would you be asking me?"

Ray ignored her question and said, "Just answer the questions I ask."

Back in court Jackie raised her right hand and swore to tell the truth. The overhead lights bounced off the lenses of her glasses and made her gray-streaked hair glisten. She smiled at her son and glanced back at her husband as she straightened her jacket.

Bill Ray approached Jackie Barbee, smiling to set her

at ease. Jackie didn't return the lawyer's grin. She had no warm feelings for Ray. She believed Ray hadn't done his job during the trial. She'd prayed he would work harder to save Stephen's life.

Ray began his questioning by asking about the Barbee family. In addition to talking about the deaths of Kathy and David, Stephen's older siblings, and how their deaths affected their youngest son, Ray asked Jackie what she and Bill did for a living. Jackie told the jury she had been a teacher's aide in the Azle Independent School District for twenty-four years, and Bill had worked for Bell Helicopter for thirty-one years. Both Barbees were retired.

Ray picked up a stack of photos from the table where Tim Moore and Stephen Barbee sat, showed them to Kevin Rousseau, and approached Jackie on the witness stand.

The defense attorney showed Jackie a series of photos and asked if she recognized them. The first was a picture of Bill and Jackie Barbee dressed for an Easter Sunday service; the second depicted the entire Barbee family; the third showed Jackie with her three children.

Handing Jackie another stack of photos, Ray asked, "Do you recognize these?"

Holding a five-by-seven-inch photograph in her hands, Jackie wrinkled her brow as she strained to find the teacher in the class picture. If she could identify the teacher, she would be able to tell what grade Stephen had been in at the time.

"Tell me just the ones you recognize," Ray encouraged.

Jackie felt rushed. She needed to look at the faces in the photo, but Ray was hurrying her on to the next photo.

"I'm just asking you, do you recognize them?" Ray asked impatiently.

"Yes, second grade," Jackie said.

The defendant's mother continued to review photos

handed to her by Ray and acknowledged that she recognized each. But Jackie became flustered when given a class picture that didn't contain Stephen. He had been ill that day and had been absent when the picture was taken.

Jackie was disturbed. *Why did Ray give me a photo to identify that didn't even contain an image of my son?*

Before she could give her question much thought, Ray asked about Stephen's after-school job.

Jackie explained that Stephen and his brother decided to start a lawn-mowing business, but on their first day out, they came home empty-handed. When Jackie asked her sons why they didn't have any money, Stephen told her they mowed a little old lady's lawn for free, as they had for others in the neighborhood.

The jury learned that the defendant tried his hand at welding, had been a reserve officer on the Blue Mound police force, and began his own tree service.

"It started in my front yard," Jackie began. "A bolt of lightning hit our eighty-foot cottonwood tree. The tree people came by and wanted eight or nine hundred dollars to cut it off. Stephen said, 'Mom and Dad, I don't want you to have to do that.' He proceeded to go out and cut that tree. He cut it down and he went and planted a real pretty one. He had started working for a lawn care service and he liked that, and so he decided to redo my little yard and he had my grass the prettiest in the neighborhood. And that's how he got started."

Wrapping up his direct examination, Bill Ray asked Jackie if she understood that the jury had found Stephen guilty of capital murder.

"Yes, sir," Jackie responded, and, as she had feared, tears began to spill from her eyes.

She acknowledged that she and Stephen's father had been to the jail every week to see him, and that they would continue to support him when he went to the penitentiary.

Sheila Underwood shook her head a little. She wondered how anyone, even a mother, could support a killer. Then she realized Jackie Underwood must love her son as much as Sheila herself loved her daughter. Sheila knew a mother's love had no boundaries.

"Do you have anything that you would like to say to the Underwood family?" Ray asked.

"I have wanted to say something to the Underwood family from day one. Steve and Bill and I are so very sorry. We have been there." Tears began to fill Jackie Barbee's eyes. "I lost a daughter and she was pregnant. And I know your pain."

Sheila's body stiffened and anger filled her. *How dare she compare her loss to mine?* Sheila thought. *There is no comparison.*

"And I don't want you to feel bad. I want you to be forgiving and not bitter, because I've been there," Jackie continued. "And the only way you can do this is to have closure and forgiveness. I have prayed very deeply for that. I got over mine. I had a broken heart. I understand your pain. And just please try to forgive everything that has happened."

While Jackie's eyes were damp with tears, Sheila's eyes were filled with anger.

Bill Ray had no other questions.

Kevin Rousseau couldn't let the jury feel any sympathy for Stephen Barbee, or his family. His job was to get a death sentence, and he stood ready to neutralize any advantage the defense might have.

"Who killed your daughter, ma'am?" Rousseau fired.

"Who?" Jackie asked, confused.

"Yes."

"A virus," Jackie answered.

"Who did you have to forgive for that?" Rousseau asked sarcastically.

"The Devil," Jackie replied.

"I'll pass the witness, Your Honor," Rousseau said, a grin on his face.

With no further questions from the defense, Ray called Mary Hackworth to the stand.

Hackworth, Jackie Barbee's sister, slowly made her way to the witness stand, pushing her walker as she moved, a cast on her foot. Stephen Barbee had lived with Hackworth in her home in Goose Creek, South Carolina, for three months. Stephen worked for Hackworth's husband before he returned to Texas, completed his GED, and made plans to get on with his life.

Mary Hackworth's sole purpose in testifying was to let the jury know she loved her nephew and supported him.

Jennifer Cherry, Barbee's niece, followed Hackworth in the witness order. The young woman, in her twenties, was the daughter of the late Kathy Barbee Cherry. Unlike her mother, who was slim and blond, Jennifer was a large woman with beautiful, long red hair.

In direct testimony Jennifer described her relationship with Stephen as close—more like brother and sister, rather than uncle and niece. Like Mary Hackworth, Jennifer was in court to show her love and support for Stephen Barbee.

On cross Kevin Rousseau held nothing back. He quickly established Jennifer was a college graduate and employed as a magazine editor.

"What kind of magazine?" Rousseau asked.

"It's an adult magazine, like *Playboy,* very upscale. It doesn't show any kind of sexual content whatsoever," Jennifer stated proudly.

"What is the name of it?" Rousseau asked.

"*Bodacious* magazine," Jennifer replied.

Rousseau suppressed a sneer as he continued his questioning, asking Jennifer if she and Stephen Barbee were close, if she loved him, and if she supported him.

Jennifer, like Mary Kearly and Jackie Barbee before her, responded affirmatively to those questions.

"And when the time comes for him to go, if he ends up on death row, you will be there to give him a hug, if they let you do that, won't you?" Rousseau asked.

"If they let me."

"And you will say good-bye," Rousseau continued.

"Yes."

"And you will give him a kiss?"

"Yes."

Sheila Underwood took in a deep breath and asked herself how all of those people could love the killer of her family. A family she didn't get to hug good-bye or kiss before their deaths.

Ashley Vandever was thirteen at the time she first met Stephen Barbee at Gospel Outreach Church. Now, ten years later, she was called as a character witness in his trial.

"How well did you know him?" Bill Ray asked.

"He was a good friend. He would come over to our home, and him and my stepdad would work on trucks together and cars, and my little sister absolutely adored him. That's the whole reason she looked forward to going to church when she was younger, to go see Stephen," the witness responded.

Ashley stated that although she knew he had been convicted of capital murder, she still supported him.

On cross Dixie Bersano asked Ashley why she had gone to the jail every week since November 2005 to visit Stephen Barbee.

"Because I love him. I am there for him. And it was something I looked forward, every week, to do. He always made me feel better every time I would go in there. We'd laugh," Ashley stated.

"You knew the little boy Jayden was seven?" Bersano asked.

"Yes."

The courtroom fell silent following Ashley's response and as she stepped down from the witness chair.

Bill Ray then called Denise Morrison, who resided in Round Rock, Texas, just north of the state capital of Austin. Denise and Barbee had been good friends for five and a half years, after initially meeting at Six Flags Over Texas in Arlington.

The pair were casual friends, talking over the phone occasionally, but had become closer when Barbee confided that he and Teresa were having marital problems.

Denise was a pretty woman, resembling the actress Jennifer Aniston. Her sandy hair fell past her shoulders and her smile was pleasant. Denise, like Marie Mendoza, was soft-spoken.

"Were y'all ever involved romantically with each other?" Ray asked.

"After his divorce, for a while," Denise admitted.

"Did y'all ever contemplate getting married?"

"We did talk about it."

Denise explained that one of Stephen Barbee's main

wishes in life was to have a child. Denise was rearing a teenage daughter, and had no desire to start raising kids all over again. Additionally, Barbee lived in Fort Worth, she in Round Rock, some two hundred miles away. Neither she nor Barbee had a desire to relocate.

But regardless of the distance between them, Denise had driven to Fort Worth nearly every weekend to visit Barbee at the Tarrant County Jail. Denise testified she cared for Barbee very much, and she considered him one of her best friends.

"How do you feel about why we are here?" Ray asked.

"I don't agree with it," Denise stated.

"Do you feel sorry for the Underwood family?" Ray asked.

"Very much so," Denise said, her voice laced with sympathy.

Kevin Rousseau was ready to take on Denise Morrison and destroy her integrity.

"Describe your first meeting," Rousseau instructed.

"I was at Six Flags with my mother and my daughter and my sister, who is eleven months younger than my daughter. And he ran up behind me and tapped on my shoulder and gave me his name and phone number and said, 'I'm Stephen. Call me,'" Denise explained.

"So his wife is somewhere else and he runs up to you and hands you his phone number and says, 'Give me a call'?" Rousseau asked, sarcasm in his voice.

"Yes."

"Did you know he was married?" Rousseau asked judgmentally.

"Not at that time."

Denise explained that she was flattered by the gesture at

Six Flags, and she didn't discover Barbee was married until their first phone conversation. She continued to talk to him by phone, and he even visited her in Round Rock.

"And this was during his marriage, wasn't it?" Rousseau asked with a critical tone.

"It was during their breakup," Denise retorted.

"But it was *before* his divorce?"

"Correct."

Denise refused to give Rousseau the answer he was looking for when he asked if she was fine with the fact that Barbee was still living with his wife at the time the two became such good friends.

The prosecutor then asked Denise if she knew that she was the one he was talking to on the phone the night he attempted to hurt himself.

"No, sir, I didn't," she responded.

Rousseau asked Denise if she agreed with the jury's verdict of guilty; she stated she did not. However, she did acknowledge she wasn't there at the time the capital murder occurred, she didn't know the victims, and she only knew Stephen Barbee as a friend.

"Do you believe he did it?" Rousseau asked pointedly.

"No," Denise responded emphatically.

"Does it matter to you, or not?" Rousseau said, posing his final question.

"It does matter," Denise said.

It had been an emotional day for the Barbee family. Jackie was unhappy with the way Ray was conducting the defense, and angry at Rousseau for his attempt to belittle the witnesses. After long days in the courtroom, she was exhausted. She was thankful when Judge Gill recessed court for the day.

Jackie hoped to rest during the night, readying herself for another day of testimony, but it seemed as though sleep had been elusive for months. Between her son's trial and her husband's ever-failing health, Jackie Barbee didn't know how much longer she could remain strong for the sake of the family.

26

On the second day of the punishment phase of the Barbee trial, Stephen Barbee entered through one of the forward doors of the courtroom, just as he had done on each of the previous days. He was once again dressed in the khaki pants, brown loafers, and one of the two $3 short-sleeved shirts purchased for him at Goodwill by his defense team.

Barbee had lost the confident smile he displayed on the first day of the trial. He looked gaunt, weary, and defeated. The deep-tanned skin he had acquired through years of outside labor had disappeared, replaced by a jailhouse pallor.

The defendant was shaken by the guilty verdict, but his distress had been replaced by a frantic feeling of impending doom. Barbee's attorneys had limited time to convince the jury that he should live, rather than be put to death. He sat silently at the defense table, lost in thoughts of the enormity of his situation.

Jackie and Bill Barbee took their usual seats close to the rear of the courtroom. As customary, Nancy Kearly was beside Jackie, lending her moral support. Bill appeared weak, the trial and the cancer taking their toll. The lines in

Jackie Barbee's face and the redness of her eyes revealed a lack of sleep and the presence of extreme stress.

Sheila Underwood had yet to arrive, but the bench she always occupied was empty, waiting for her appearance. There was no way she would miss the remainder of the trial. Shortly before Bill Ray announced his first witness of the day, Sheila slipped in and took her seat.

Prior to performing home studies for the litigation of capital murder, Susan Perryman Evans had been a senior warden with the Institutional Division of the Texas Department of Criminal Justice. She was called by Ray as the first witness of the day.

As Evans was reciting her credentials, Ray interrupted her, asking her to focus her responses directly to the jury.

Following Ray's directions, Evans looked at the jury as she informed them there were currently 145,000 inmates incarcerated in 105 Texas prisons, with those facilities housing anywhere from 500 to 2,500 inmates each.

Bill Ray stopped the direct questioning to inform the court and the prosecution that Evans would be commenting on visual presentations she had prepared. A large screen was erected for the jury's viewing, and Evans first began to discuss the qualifications of TDCJ guards.

"This particular presentation comes directly from the TDCJ eligibility criteria," Evans began. "Employees must be a citizen of the United States or an alien authorized to work in the U.S. Must be at least eighteen years old. Must have a high-school diploma or a GED. Must not be on active duty in the military, unless on terminal leave. Must never have been convicted of a felony. Must never have been convicted of a drug-related offense. Must never have been convicted of an offense involving domestic violence. Cannot have had a class A or B misdemeanor conviction within the past five years. Cannot be on probation for any criminal offense. Cannot have any criminal charges pending or have an outstanding warrant."

In addition to those requirements, Evans stated, guards must also be able to perform the essential functions of a corrections officer (CO), with or without reasonable accommodation. That would include physical requirements such as being able to go up and down stairs, sit for long periods of time, climb a ladder, work at heights, squat, bend, and perform pat searches or strip searches. They would have to be able to restrain and secure inmates and to use force, even deadly force, such as chemical agents and firearms, if warranted.

A few heads could be seen shaking in the gallery. Obviously, those people would not be interested in a job as a prison guard.

Evans stated that if an applicant meets all the criteria, and he or she is hired, the individual must then attend a two-hundred-hour academy. She broke down the number of hours of each course required for completion, adding that the candidate must also spend one week a year retraining. Evans failed to say beginning corrections officers earned only about $2,000 a month.

After Evans's forty-five-minute presentation, there were questioning looks on some of the jurors' faces. What impact would the criteria for corrections officers have on their decision? They were to decide if Barbee would serve life or if he would die. He wasn't applying for a job at the prison.

Ray asked Evans to discuss her second presentation, the inmate classification system.

"What is the purpose of the classification system?" Ray asked.

"The purpose of the classification system is basically to group like offenders in like areas, to identify any deficiencies they may have with regard to education, security needs, medical needs, psychological needs, and have those addressed so they are assigned to the unit that's appropriate to them. They are placed in the custody level that is appropriate to that individual so that it is the safest and most efficient environment they can be in," Evans explained.

During her testimony Evans also noted that there is an educational school district within the prison system so, if an offender lacks a GED or high-school diploma, they can attend school while incarcerated.

"The purpose of classification is to evaluate and accurately group offenders on the basis of numerous characteristics, including age, type of offense, prior criminal record, institutional adjustment, medical and mental-health-care needs, education and vocational and work-related needs," Evans stated.

The former warden reviewed classification levels, beginning with G1, General Population Level 1, an outside trustee. Evans assured the jury that any person convicted of murder would never be considered for G1 status.

Heads turned toward Stephen Barbee to see if there was any reaction, but they found none.

Evans described the remaining general population levels, leading up to maximum security, including information that an inmate can be reassigned a classification if he commits any offense while incarcerated.

As she continued her presentation, it became obvious that Susan Evans had been called by the defense to show that if the jurors were to give Stephen Barbee life in prison, he would not be allowed outside the prison walls where he would be assigned. Evans added that anyone convicted of a violent crime would most likely be assigned a G5 status, the most restrictive.

Sheila Underwood's rigid expression left no question that she was unhappy with the discussion of prison life for

Stephen Barbee. She didn't believe he deserved to live after taking the lives of the two people she loved most in the world.

As if the defense had read Sheila Underwood's mind, the testimony turned from general population inmates to death row prisoners.

"As a general rule, they're in general population or on death row. Is that a fair statement?" Ray asked.

"Yes."

Evans referred to the PowerPoint presentation appearing on the large screen.

"Everybody on death row is in the same classification," Evans stated. "An admission summary is done on each inmate. They used to do a work-capable review, but the work-capable program is no longer in existence following the Gurule escape."

Martin Gurule was on death row at the Huntsville Ellis II Unit when he and six other inmates attempted to escape while they were outside for group recreation. Gurule was the only one who actually got out. He was shot in the shoulder when going over the high fence surrounding the unit, but he later drowned.

Gurule had covered himself with cardboard and magazines before scaling the razor-wire fence. He apparently stumbled into a creek on the outside perimeter of the prison, most likely in an attempt to avoid the dogs who were tracking him, and drowned when his paper armor became soaked and took him to the bottom of the creek.

Snickers could be heard from the gallery as viewers envisioned a man dressed in a prison uniform, covered in a paper and cardboard shell, thrashing about in the water like a turtle. Those persons, unsympathetic to any killer housed on death row, believed it ironic that Gurule was the only man ever to successfully scale the fence, only to die unexpectedly. His body was found two days after the breakout by surprised fishermen.

Gurule's getaway prompted the prison system to eliminate the death row work program, as well as group recreation.

"They are in their cells twenty-three hours a day, but one hour they are brought out for recreation," Evans explained.

Evans added that death row inmates have access to the prison library, they are allowed one noncontact visit per week for two hours in the visiting room, they eat in their cells, and they shower daily under supervision. Evans stated that at no time are death row inmates allowed to be unsupervised.

Ray produced a videotape provided by Evans that depicted a prison unit built exactly like that of the Polunsky Unit, which housed death row inmates. The video depicted a heavy chain-link fence, topped by razor wire that would wrap around a person and virtually cut away their flesh.

There were double doors that were controlled access, and a central interior control room. Inside the single cells were a metal bunk and tray, a small three-to-four-inch-thick mattress, a tiny slip of a window that did not open, and a metal toilet/sink combination. Each cell was approximately sixty square feet. In addition to their cell, the death row inmates were allowed in the dayroom, if they desired. But as with the outdoor area, they were in individual cages. They could talk to one another, and at times the noise level was extreme.

Evans made it clear that if an inmate must be transported from one section of the prison to another, he would always be accompanied by two guards, and he would be searched both before and after he left the cell area.

Jackie Barbee felt the warmth of tears in her eyes. She couldn't picture her son living in those conditions. He loved the outdoors, had chosen a vocation that would allow him to feel the sun on his face, the wind at his back. She believed Stephen could not exist in the extreme confinement of prison.

"If you have a person who is convicted of a violent crime, and he's serving a long sentence, are they always the worst inmates that you have?" Ray asked the former warden.

"No, sir, they are not, not necessarily. Generally, what happened that caused them to commit the crime in the free world was a situational incident and is not necessarily transposed into the prison system. In the prison they don't have access to the drugs as freely. They don't have access to alcohol or weapons. Of course, all those things can be attained, but we try to insure that doesn't happen, but occasionally it does. But they don't have free access to any of that.

"Generally, they are under a very controlled environment. You don't have all the stressors. They don't have to worry about paying bills, making ends meet, having a fight with their wife or anything. Their day is very structured and they are not as likely to have a problem. Generally, after a person has gotten some age on them, spent some time in prison, they tend to mellow. A person who's doing time when they are fifty or sixty is not the same person they were at seventeen, twenty, or even thirty. People mellow," Evans concluded.

Sheila Underwood looked intently at Stephen Barbee, who didn't look her way. Sheila believed Barbee was a selfish, self-centered man who would do anything, take any action that would get him what he wanted, or get him out of any situation he wanted out of. She didn't believe he would ever mellow to the point he wouldn't be a threat to anyone who challenged him.

Having completed his direct examination, Ray turned the witness over to Kevin Rousseau, who began questioning

Susan Perryman Evans on what he termed "survival training" for corrections officers.

"The whole idea behind this, the whole reason, is because you want people to go home at the end of the day, at least as well as they came in," Rousseau stated.

"Yes, sir," Evans replied.

"But the reason all this is done is because prison is an extraordinarily dangerous place," Rousseau said.

"It is a hazardous work environment," Evans agreed.

"And that is for civilians, including guards, as well as inmates, right?" Rousseau asked.

"Correct."

"You're housing the worst of the worst," Rousseau declared.

"Yes, sir," Evans acknowledged.

Evans stated that the techniques used by corrections officers had evolved over time. Whenever an incident occurred in any of the prisons, the program was modified to address that kind of situation.

"These felons go from minimally bad people, people who made a mistake, to people who have done the most heinous thing you can imagine," Rousseau stated.

"Correct."

"Such as brutally slaughtering innocent people in their homes," Rousseau said, reminding the jury of Barbee's victims.

"Uh-huh."

"And sometime people escape, right?" Rousseau asked.

"Yes, sir," Evans admitted.

Evans pointed out that Texas has a good record of catching escapees, stating that all but one had been apprehended. But in rebuttal Rousseau brought out that even if it took twenty years to catch an escapee, he would be considered one of the unsuccessful escapees.

The prosecution hoped this fact would have an impact on the jury, considering the infamous "Texas Seven," who had escaped and killed an Irving, Texas, police officer in 2000.

Rousseau pointed out that the Texas Seven were a mixture of classifications, four having been convicted of murder, two for rape, and one for injury to a child. They ranged from career criminals to first-time offenders, from college students to high-school dropouts.

"My point is that all of these people were walking around inside the same Texas prison that you just showed us on video, and all of them ended up on the street. They eluded capture for weeks. In the process they murdered Aubrey Hawkins, an Irving police officer. I'm not being critical of the Texas prison system, but there will be incidents of violence, right?" Rousseau asked.

"At some point in time, violence does happen in the prison," Evans admitted.

Rousseau pointed out that in 2005 there were 19,000 disciplinary convictions for staff assaults and offender assaults within Texas prisons. He also reminded the former Texas prison warden that in 1998, when Martin Gurule escaped and drowned, one of the men who attempted to escape with him was Howard Guidry. Guidry later took a nurse hostage on death row.

Also in 1998, a corrections officer was dragged into a cell and raped in a prison in Abilene. In December 1999, a corrections officer was stabbed to death in the McConnell Unit in Beeville. And in that same month, there was an uprising involving eighty inmates.

Rousseau wrapped up his time with Evans by reminding the jury that if Barbee were to be given life in prison, he could be sent anywhere within the Texas prison system's maximum-security facilities, including any of those that have already experienced significant incidents.

With that being said, Rousseau passed the witness back to Ray. Rousseau hoped the jury understood the point he'd attempted to make: Neither society nor the prison population would be safe if Stephen Barbee was sent to general population. That was why death row was being sought by the state.

Ray began by asking Evans if over the past twenty years, any incidents that had occurred prompted more restrictive custody for inmates as a whole.

"In the twenty years that I've been there, we have seen the loss of the furlough program. We have seen the loss of inmates who have committed murder being outside trustees," Evans stated.

Evans explained they had a system in place to avert problems.

"Whether an inmate is in administrative segregation, general population, minimum custody, the trustee camps, or on death row, the same corrections officers who have been through the same programs are going to handle them, day in and day out. What is going to happen or not happen is going to happen—no matter where an individual is placed. You have inmates who are trustees who have killed employees within the Texas prison system. Minnie Houston was an employee who was murdered by an outside trustee at a trustee camp kitchen.

"Bad things happen in all levels, but the prison system does the best we can to make sure it doesn't happen. We minimize things. We plug the holes where we find them," Evans stated defensively.

For Sheila Underwood, that wasn't good enough. She worried that the killer of her daughter and grandson could slip through one of those holes and kill again.

* * *

Dixie Bersano handled the second cross-examination of Evans.

"Without a doubt, the single-most secure place for any prisoner is death row," Bersano stated, again emphasizing the judgment the prosecution hoped for.

And that's where Barbee belongs, Shelia thought.

Evans didn't agree with Bersano's statement, saying death row wasn't much different than administrative segregation in other units.

"You said in prison another reason killers are less likely to be terribly dangerous is because they don't have access to drugs in prison, at least not as much," Bersano stated.

"Not as much," Evans replied.

"Drugs and alcohol do come into the prison, right?" Bersano asked.

"Yes, they do," Evans admitted.

"So drugs and alcohol are less of a temptation, and they don't have as much access to weapons, correct?" Bersano continued.

"Correct."

"None of that would apply to a person who didn't do drugs or alcohol, or who killed with his bare hands, would it?" Bersano asked, making reference to the defendant.

"I suppose not," Evans admitted.

That was the final statement jurors heard from Susan Perryman Evans.

Stephen Barbee sat quietly with tear-filled eyes. His mind was absorbing all that had been said about prison life. The year he had spent in the Tarrant County Jail had been hell. He couldn't fathom living in the conditions Evans had talked about. He dabbed tears from his cheeks and wiped them on his khaki pants.

Jackie Barbee's eyes also stung with salty tears. She truly believed Stephen was innocent and asked herself, how could he possibly be sent to live in a place like Evans described?

Kevin Rousseau and Dixie Bersano were pleased with the responses they got from Susan Perryman Evans. They could only hope the jury understood: Stephen Barbee deserved to be on death row.

But the defense wasn't finished; they had more witnesses to call. The next one to testify was Christy McKemson, a friend who had formerly dated Barbee's roommate and coworker. She told the jury she had seen Stephen Barbee often while dating his friend, and she was in court to show her support.

Jerry Jones had known Stephen Barbee most of his life. He dated Barbee's sister and played Pee Wee Baseball with his brother, David. "Anywhere we went, he was there," Jones said of the defendant.

Jones testified that he was also friends with Jackie and Bill Barbee, and kept in touch with them.

"Have you noticed Stephen's parents have been upset over this?" Ray asked.

"I believe it has tested their faith, yes. His father's health is not good. His mother's health is being affected by it," Jones said.

Stephen Barbee dropped his head and cried. He never intended to hurt his parents. They had always been his greatest supporters.

* * *

With no questions from the prosecution, Ray called David Derusha. Derusha, a bailiff in Judge Gill's court, was responsible for getting Barbee to the court's hold-over cells through the secure elevator and tunnels from the main jail across the street each day. Derusha stated he had no problems with Barbee and there had been no incidents while transporting him to court.

Bill Ray rested the defense.

Jackie Barbee was stunned. *What about all the information Amanda Maxwell had gathered for mitigation? Why didn't Ray mention Stephen's head injuries and all the stress he was under at the time?* Jackie shook her head. She didn't understand what was happening; it was all confusing to her.

She'd been on the phone often with Tina Church in Indiana, explaining the proceedings and asking questions, but nothing prepared her for the emotional trauma of sitting in court and hearing the testimony.

Amanda Maxwell sat quietly behind the defense table. She had worked hard gathering data for the defense to use in mitigation. She had discovered a number of issues, including developmental delay, hydrocodone abuse, and four closed-head injuries that could have been presented in Stephen Barbee's defense. The document she had prepared of the crime week stressors experienced by their client would have offered some explanation of his actions, but Ray had obviously chosen not to utilize her work. Amanda was confused and angry.

As expected, Kevin Rousseau and Dixie Bersano were prepared with rebuttal witnesses. They called Bruce Cummings, a private investigator who primarily worked for defense attorneys. In his spare time Cummings was a soccer coach and had had Jayden Underwood on his team.

Cummings described Jayden as just learning the game, and not one of the strongest players, but he gave all his effort. Jayden had been a year younger than his fellow team members.

The coach said each year the North Fort Worth Alliance Soccer Association held a tournament, and each year Boopa's Bagel Deli was a sponsor. He had gotten to know Lisa Underwood through her support of the team and the association.

Rousseau flashed a photo of Jayden's soccer team on a large screen in the courtroom. Jayden, dressed in his blue soccer uniform, his foot resting on the ball, stood in a line with his teammates, smiling and bright-eyed, full of fun, full of life.

As the jury looked at the photo, one could see sadness in many of their eyes. Jayden Underwood was a precious child who had barely begun to live his life. That was the image Rousseau and Bersano wanted to leave with the jury: the image of a cherished child who was senselessly murdered.

"We'll rest, Your Honor," Rousseau announced.

Judge Gill informed the jury that he had to prepare a charge for them, just as he had done in the first phase of the trial. He instructed them to return at nine the next morning to hear summations of the counsels, and to begin deliberations on the punishment issue.

Bill Ray stood and addressed the court.

"I need to put one thing on the record," he said.

Ray then asked Stephen Barbee if he wanted to testify on his own behalf. Barbee stated softly, "I don't want to testify," and court was adjourned.

Both Jackie Barbee and Sheila Underwood were surrounded by the press as they exited the courtroom. But, as usual, neither had any comment to make. They were both filled with anxiety for the following day's activity, and both knew there would be little sleep that night.

27

The tension in the 213th Judicial District Court of Judge Robert Gill was as obvious as an elephant in the living room. Sheila Underwood wrung her hands, while Jackie Barbee said a final prayer before Judge Gill called court to order.

Dixie Bersano would begin closing statements for the prosecution, with Kevin Rousseau having the final words. Both the defense and the state would have twenty minutes to persuade the jury—the defense wanting Barbee's life spared, the prosecution wanting death on the gurney.

Blond-haired Dixie Bersano stood and addressed the jury.

"You are dealing with two special issues here—Special Issue Number One, which is the future-danger issue, and Special Issue Number Two, which is the mitigation issue," Bersano began.

"When you are considering these special issues, you consider them separate. They're separate inquiries. You consider all of the evidence from the punishment phase and from the guilt/innocence phase.

"Ladies and gentlemen, on the future-[danger] question,

when you are deliberating, consider the circumstances of the offense, the murder of Lisa and her baby and Jayden as overwhelming evidence that this man will commit more criminal acts of violence.

"It was planned. It was cold. It was cruel. It was calculated. And why? So Trish would not find out. Trish, who had been married to him less than three months, would find out that he had been with Lisa seven and a half months earlier.

"A simple paternity test could have prevented all of this. He could have waited, but he didn't. Violence is how this man handles problems.

"Remember the testimony of the other witnesses. Remember Teresa Barbee, his ex-wife. She still loved him—even though he hit her, he punched her, he fought her. He left her on the floor, unconscious, while he ate ice cream. Wouldn't call 911. Won't go get medical help for her. She drove herself to the hospital after running off the road. He's cruel."

Teresa did all she could to send Stephen to death row. She lied, Jackie Barbee thought.

"Marie Mendoza. She confronted him on the phone about the tree estimate. He used obscenities, he called her names, and he told her, 'I trimmed your trees, and this is what I get in return?'

"She described him in two words. He's mean and he's cruel. That was years before Lisa, Jayden, and her baby were murdered," Bersano stated.

Judge Gill interrupted Bersano, telling her she had four minutes of her ten minutes remaining. Jackie Barbee was relieved that she only had four more minutes to listen to what she believed were lies the female prosecutor was telling the jury.

"After his arrest and after confessing, he strung Teresa

Barbee [along] again. She visited him every week in the Tarrant County Jail, and they talked about the good times. They talked about how much fun they had had, and he talked about, if he got out [of] jail, they would get back together and they would have a baby together.

"He strung her along until the end of September, when he held up a sign that said, 'Tell my mother and my defense attorney Ron did it.'

"You know, he slapped her upside the head again—without his fists this time—and she finally saw it. She turned around and walked out. But she still loves him.

"Ladies and gentlemen, without a doubt—without a doubt—there is a probability this man is a future danger, wherever he is," Bersano concluded.

As Dixie Bersano walked from the front, past the jury box, and back to her seat, she looked to Sheila Underwood. Sheila gave a slight nod and a small smile of approval.

Tim Moore began opening arguments for the defense, stating he would limit his discussion to the issue of future dangerousness.

"Steve Barbee, you have found, intentionally and knowingly killed these two people. He killed a pregnant woman and a precious seven-year-old child, a defenseless child. So your question may be 'You did that. Why shouldn't you deserve to die also?'

"And that's a legitimate question, and I will tell you why. Because it is a question the answer of which is based on pure revenge. And you have to be careful, folks, not to let the revenge creep into your deliberations. There is no place for revenge in our law," Moore said.

The defense attorney, who hadn't been heard from much during this part of the trial, reminded the jury that during their selection they had stated they wouldn't answer the question automatically, that they would want to hear all the evidence first.

"The state has the burden of proving this beyond a reasonable doubt, just as it did in the guilt/innocence stage. They've had a year to work on this case, knowing that if you found him guilty, you would be faced with this very question.

"Is there a probability that Steve Barbee is going to commit criminal acts of violence that would constitute a continuing threat to society? They have had a year to look high, low, and all over Tarrant County and elsewhere.

"What they did bring you was Teresa Barbee, a woman scorned, a jilted wife. What did she tell you? They were married seven years. They built a business together," Moore stated.

Moore then recapped Teresa's testimony, citing the four instances of domestic violence she had described to the jury. Moore reminded the panel that the incident mentioned by Bersano had been an unintentional act.

"I believe you could tell from Teresa she can take care of herself. In the other two instances over the seven-year period, no medical attention was needed. Police may have been called. If they were, Mr. Barbee wasn't arrested. He wasn't taken to jail. He has no criminal history whatsoever. I will guarantee you he doesn't—or they would have brought it to you if he did.

"And they brought you Ms. Mendoza. That's the best they could find. Teresa and Ms. Mendoza. There was no violence with Ms. Mendoza.

"So all you have got to go on—all you have to rely on—in deciding whether to execute Steve Barbee is the word of Teresa Barbee," Moore said.

Moore then addressed Teresa's statement that Barbee had

held up a sign to her at the jail saying, *Ron did it.* Moore reported to the jury that Teresa had never told the defense or the prosecution that story. She didn't make that claim until she was on the witness stand.

"I submit to you that if you are being asked to execute somebody, you ought to know that person. You ought to know a whole lot about them.

"Steve Barbee was thirty-seven years old when this happened. For three hours he was not a very nice human being. But there were thirty-six years before that where he was not a violent person," Moore stated.

Moore told the jury that the defense had called Jackie Barbee to the stand to let them know he was raised in a good family, that he was emotionally affected by the loss of his siblings, and that he had started a successful business.

"That's the kind of person he is. He wasn't some juvenile delinquent. He wasn't getting in trouble all the time. He was a contributing member of society," Moore stressed.

Moore emphasized how the other witnesses the defense called knew Barbee well. They listened to all the evidence during the first phase of the trial, including Detective Carroll's testimony and the video confession, and they continued to love and support him.

The defense attorney explained that Steve Barbee was almost thirty-nine years old now. If given a life sentence, he would spend at least forty years in prison, day for day, no matter how good he was. Barbee would be eighty years old before he would even be eligible for release, if he lived that long.

Barbee hung his head, tears spilling on the table in front of him. He knew—regardless if given life in prison or death—his life was over.

"I submit to you, based on the evidence, not on revenge,

the state has not proved that he's going to be a continuing threat to commit criminal acts of violence in the penitentiary.

"We're not asking you to excuse his conduct. We're not asking you not to punish him. We are saying give him a life sentence," Moore concluded.

With nine minutes left for the defense's closing arguments, Bill Ray replaced Tim Moore in front of the jury. Ray told the panel that because Stephen Barbee took the police to the burial spot of Lisa and Jayden Underwood, thus allowing their family to give them a proper burial, that act reduced Barbee's moral failings.

Ray pled with each juror to make their decision independently and not to change their mind as a result of pressure to join the other members of the jury panel.

"If you do, you will feel awful about it for the rest of your life," Ray stated.

As Moore had done, Ray reminded the jury that Teresa Barbee had testified she thought Barbee's comment about the wood chipper was a joke, but now she believed it was serious. He also repeated the fact that Teresa had changed her story after testifying before the grand jury.

"There is nothing wrong with a life sentence. Make sure you feel good about your answers because you can't change them tomorrow," Ray finished.

The defense's time was up. Moore and Ray had done all they could to convince the jury to spare their client's life and grant him a life sentence. They would hear Kevin Rousseau's final argument; then the jury would retire to deliberate.

Jackie Barbee was shaken with fear for her son.

Bill Barbee sat throughout the closing arguments with his head bowed in prayer. He never looked up. He never stopped praying.

* * *

Kevin Rousseau walked to the jury box, his expression somber.

"Ladies and gentlemen, I told you, you were going to hear and see some very unpleasant things. I believe you have probably been changed now, and you will probably never go about the little things in life the same.

"For the rest of your lives, or for a very long time, when you throw that bolt at night on that front door, you are going to see that bloodstain. And when you put your children to bed and you tell them, 'Good night, sleep tight, don't let the bedbugs bite,' you are going to see Jayden, and you are going to think of what that man did," Rousseau said, looking toward Barbee, whose head was down.

Rousseau talked about keeping children safe, and keeping the nameless, faceless fear outside.

"But that fear has a face. It is his face," Rousseau said, pointing to Barbee. "And its name is Stephen Dale Barbee. And you fear him because he's dangerous."

The assistant district attorney told jurors that Tim Moore was wrong; there was room in the case for revenge. Rousseau told them the opposite of mitigating evidence is aggravating evidence. Things that would make their blood boil. He wanted them to consider those things during deliberations.

"His entire life had led up to this point. The pattern was clear—just no one could see it yet. No one wants to see something that horrible. No one, despite sitting through a week of trial, wants to believe that anybody is capable of what that man has done, especially the ones who love him.

"It was building and he was showing his character all along the way. His marriage to Teresa Barbee lasted six or seven years. Throughout that marriage he lied to her, he

cheated on her, he beat her, and he threatened her. He
threatened to kill her.

"The pattern was there, the warning was there. Unfortu-
nately, Lisa Underwood never had the benefit of that warning. She never had a chance.

"It never occurred to him to do the right thing. If it did,
he rejected it, because he has no heart, no spine, and no
character. He couldn't do the one thing that made any sense
in this case, which is just tell his wife. Tell her, 'By the way,
months before we were married, when we were dating, I
was seeing another woman. She's pregnant and it might be
my child, and I will do whatever I have to do. Okay? And if
it's mine, we'll deal with it. If it's not, we don't have to deal
with it.'

"He couldn't confess—even that minor sin—because he
was afraid. He was afraid he would lose his wife. Because
he has no character. He weighed his personal potential loss
against the value of Lisa's life, and it went like this—Lisa's
life meant nothing."

I've been raised to tell the truth, and believe the truth will
set you free. If God be with you, who would be against you?
But Kevin Rousseau is underhanded, hateful, and uncaring,
Jackie thought as she listened to Rousseau's closing.

Rousseau reminded the jurors that Barbee went to Lisa's
house not once, but twice. The first time he was unable to
make her mad enough to fight. Rousseau contended the
second time Barbee arrived at Lisa's, he must have known
Jayden was in the next room.

"What is mitigating in the light of this? What makes
this somehow less bad? The fact that he mows his mom's
yard? The fact that the owner of a diploma mill will get up
here and say he was a Sunday school teacher and did a nice
job? The fact that his mistress takes the stand and says he's
a good boy? Or maybe the editor of a skin magazine who

says she still loves him despite it all? Is that mitigating?" Rousseau asked.

The hairs on the back of Nancy Kearly's neck bristled. How dare he call her college "a diploma mill"?

Jackie Barbee cried, not for herself but for her granddaughter, whom Kevin Rousseau had just insulted in open court. *Hasn't this family faced enough ridicule?* Jackie pondered.

"Less than forty-eight hours after he slaughtered this family and buried them in that little grave, he was yukking it up at the police department, and he kept right on yukking it up until he knew that he was caught. That's when he went into the 'I'm sorry' mode."

As Rousseau gave his fiery summation, he held up a photograph of the makeshift grave, reminding jurors Lisa was seven-and-a-half months pregnant, and Jayden was only seven years old.

Rousseau reviewed the murders of Lisa and Jayden Underwood with all the emotion, passion, and drama he could find in his soul. He directed much of his attention to the young woman on the jury who he was still uncertain could bring back a death sentence. Rousseau wanted this death sentence more than he had ever wanted one. He believed Lisa, Jayden, and Lisa's unborn child deserved it.

He reminded the jury that Stephen Barbee had gone to Lisa's house, her sanctuary, in the middle of the night. He looked her in the eye, drew back his fist, and hit her in the nose. He hit her, again and again. A pool of blood saturated the floor. Barbee climbed on her back, and with enough force to leave bruises with his fingers, he ground her face into the carpet. She'd wiggled. She'd squirmed. She'd tried to keep an airway open, but she couldn't. He'd kept her down long enough for her to die.

"Then Jayden ran into the room to help his mother. He

couldn't even see without his glasses. Then Barbee slapped Jayden upside the head, enough to leave a bruise, and then held him down until he died.

"I dare you to say there is a reason to spare his life. You are the voice of Tarrant County and you need to speak with one voice, and your message needs to be clear and unmistakable. You need to tell him with your message, with your verdict, that Stephen Dale Barbee, for the crimes you have committed, for the lives you have taken, your life will be forfeited.

"Dixie and I and Lisa Underwood and Jayden Underwood and Marleigh will await your answer. Thank you," Rousseau concluded.

Sheila Underwood's eyes glistened. The mother and the grandmother inside her struggled to hold herself together.

There were few dry eyes in the courtroom. The emotional closing by Rousseau had touched the hearts of many. Throughout the four-day trial, the jury and the gallery had come to know Lisa and Jayden, had come to care about them through Kevin Rousseau and Dixie Bersano. They had done the job Deputy Chief Assistant District Attorney Greg Miller had known they were capable of doing.

Both the state and defense had done all they could. Prosecutors had portrayed Stephen Barbee as a lying womanizer who was prone to violence and extramarital affairs. The defense presented their client as a churchgoing man who loved children, but who was deeply troubled by the untimely deaths of his brother and sister when he was a teenager.

It was now up to the jury. The men and women had the option of sending Stephen Barbee to prison for the rest of his life, or have him face death on the gurney.

Sheila Underwood sat with her hands folded in her lap; sadness clouded her eyes. It had been difficult to hear Kevin's summation.

Now the waiting began. Sheila retreated outside to calm her nerves, just as Bill and Jackie Barbee chose to do. They all continued to avoid the press, emotions running too high.

But shortly after the recess was called, Jodi Fratta, a woman who had married death row inmate Bobby Fratta, addressed the media on behalf of the Barbee family. Fratta attended the trial as a show of support for the Barbees, and as an active supporter of the anti–death penalty coalition.

Fratta informed the press that the Barbee family blamed the guilty verdict on the unwillingness of Barbee's attorneys to listen to their ideas.

"The state of Texas didn't convict Stephen Barbee of capital murder, his own attorneys did," Fratta said.

As the spectators and the media mingled in the courtroom, awaiting the verdict, the buzzer from the jury room sounded, signaling that a decision had been reached.

Just three hours after the jury retired to deliberate, Sheila Underwood and the Barbees reentered Judge Gill's courtroom for the final verdict. Neither Teresa Barbee nor Trish Barbee had attended the day's proceedings. They were not present to see their former husband sentenced.

Kevin Rousseau and Dixie Bersano were feeling confident. Three hours was a quick verdict. They, along with Tim Moore and Bill Ray, stood and watched as each of the jurors filed in, hoping to get any indication of their decision. But their expressionless faces gave no indication of whether Stephen Barbee would live or die.

Judge Gill addressed the jury.

"Special Issue Number One—do you find from the evidence beyond a reasonable doubt that there is a probability that the defendant would commit criminal acts of violence that would constitute a continuing threat to society?"

"Yes," the foreman responded.

"Special Issue Number Two—whether taking into consideration all of the evidence, including the circumstance of the offense, the defendant's character and background, and the personal moral culpability of the defendant, there is a sufficient mitigating circumstance or circumstances to warrant that a sentence of life imprisonment rather than a death penalty be imposed."

"No," the foreman said.

Kevin and Dixie smiled broadly. Bill Ray asked that the jury be polled, to make certain each of them agreed with the verdict. All seven women and five men of the jury panel answered in the affirmative, and the verdict was accepted by the court.

"The jury, having answered Special Issue Number One yes, and Special Issue Number Two no, it is mandatory that the punishment in this case be set at death," Judge Gill announced.

Although he presented a stoic demeanor, Stephen Barbee was shocked. He had expected the guilty verdict, Detective Carroll's testimony had been damning. But he believed because he had never been in trouble before, and he had served as a reserve police officer in Blue Mound, the jury would have mercy and sentence him to life.

Jackie Barbee showed none of the emotion she had displayed throughout the trial. She was in shock. Sheila Underwood looked upward toward Heaven and nodded, as if affirming to Lisa and Jayden that justice had been done, while friends and family around her cried.

"It is the order, judgment, and decree of the court that—determined by this court upon a Mandate of Affirmance, issued by the Court of Criminal Appeals of the State of Texas—at the state penitentiary at Huntsville, you shall be caused to die by intravenous injection of a substance or substances in a lethal quantity to cause your death, and until you are dead," Judge Gill declared.

Within minutes Sheila Underwood was standing in front of the man who was determined to have murdered her family. Her eyes sparked with anger; her small frame trembled with rage.

"Do you know who I am?" Sheila asked Barbee. "Look at me when I speak to you," she demanded. "Do you know who I am?" Sheila repeated.

"No, ma'am, I don't," Barbee said softly.

What the hell? What is that about? Sheila thought. *You haven't figured out who was who in the courtroom?*

"I'm fifty-three years old and I don't have anything left. You put me in Hell, but I'm not alone. You put your parents in Hell too," Sheila said angrily.

Sheila was disappointed that Barbee showed no sign of remorse. He simply sat mute. He had nothing to say to Sheila Underwood or any of the other Underwood family members who addressed him in court.

Gidgett Reynolds, Lisa's cousin, told Barbee he should be glad that he was not headed to the prison system's general population.

"Every man hates baby killers," Reynolds said. "You're lucky you got the death penalty."

Then Reynolds turned to look at Barbee's family and

friends. "I hope that whatever God that you pray to, you realize he (Barbee) did this, and you pray for him," Reynolds said.

Marla Hess, Lisa's aunt and the person whom she named her unborn child for, struck out at Jackie Barbee personally by saying, "Jackie Barbee, how dare you compare your loss to my sister's? She has nothing."

Jackie Barbee lowered her head. *I also have nothing,* she thought. *I lost Kathy, David, and now I've lost Stephen.*

Judge Gill thanked the jury for their service, dismissed them, and adjourned court.

Kevin Rousseau and Dixie Bersano stood, congratulated one another, and celebrated their victory with laughter. Kevin Rousseau hugged Sheila, and she thanked him for all he had done to bring her family's killer to justice.

Jackie Barbee remained in her seat in the back of the courtroom, where she watched the celebratory activities of the prosecution. It made her sick. *This is not my country. This is not justice,* Jackie thought. *When is the trial going to begin? They did nothing to save my son.*

Then she was stunned to see Bill Ray's wife go to Sheila Underwood and give her a hug. Was everyone against Stephen?

Nancy Kearly left her seat, walked up to Detective Mike Carroll, and asked, "Are you a Christian?" Carroll smiled and acknowledged that he was.

"Did you know lying is a sin?" Kearly asked.

Mike Carroll laughed and left Kearly without an answer.

Sheila Underwood received word that one of the jurors wished to speak to her. Confused, she met him in the jury room.

"I wanted you to know, during the trial I just wanted to jump over the jury box rail and beat him," the man said.

Sheila smiled, thanked him for his verdict, and left the

room. She sneaked past the media and slipped into the bathroom, where Bill Ray's wife was standing by the sinks.

"I just want you to know my husband and I want to give you our condolences," Mrs. Ray said.

Sheila was stunned momentarily; then she looked Mrs. Ray in the eyes and said, "I want to see that motherfucker die."

After the courtroom was cleared, Stephen Barbee returned to court dressed in a jail-issued blue jumpsuit. Jackie Barbee and Stephen, their faces red from crying, were given a few minutes to hug and say their good-byes. Bill Barbee also had a short time with his son.

Outside, Jackie and Bill Barbee were bombarded by the press. A microphone jammed in her face, Jackie made her first comments to the media.

"I think you tried and convicted my son on the first day," Jackie said angrily, "but I forgive you." Jackie also forgave the Underwoods for their negative comments about her testimony.

Within hours Stephen Barbee was on his way to Huntsville for processing by the prison system. It would only take one day to complete their evaluation.

Two days after the jury returned their decision that he should die, Barbee sat in a white prison van, heavy mesh wiring on the windows, on his way to the Polunsky Unit and death row.

Even though she had seen her family's killer sentenced to death, the ordeal for Sheila Underwood wasn't over. She had vowed to be at Ron Dodd's trial—to face him, just as she had faced Stephen Barbee.

28

Ron Dodd had enjoyed the freedom of being out of jail on bond, but on October 9, 2006, police were dispatched to the home of Teresa Barbee on a call of domestic violence.

Tarrant County deputies arrived at Teresa's Haslet home, about 9:00 P.M. Teresa Barbee had evidence of minor injuries that didn't require hospitalization or an ambulance.

Teresa reported she didn't want to press charges. But, after so many allegations of domestic violence had been dropped by scared victims, Texas law had been changed. The state now took over the filing of charges that could no longer be dismissed by those harmed during episodes of domestic violence. Ron Dodd was taken off to jail, leaving Teresa Barbee at home alone, crying.

Dodd had served nearly half of an eight-year prison sentence for a 1997 aggravated assault conviction in Dallas County. He was scheduled to be on parole through December 6, 2006, but when the Texas Department of Criminal Justice learned of the new assault charge filed against Dodd, they revoked bail and issued an arrest warrant for a parole violation.

Dodd was transferred to the Denton County Jail, where

he would face a jury in November for two counts of tampering with physical evidence in connection with the Underwood murders. Whatever sentence was imposed on Dodd, he was headed back to the Institutional Division of the Texas Department of Criminal Justice (TDCJ), where he would complete his original sentence for aggravated assault. It was anybody's guess what punishment a Denton County jury would assess Dodd for helping to bury the bodies of Lisa and Jayden Underwood. Denton juries were known for tough sentences, and Dodd could be given as much as twenty years for his part in disposing of the Underwood bodies.

Dodd's attorney, John Haring, of the Dallas firm of Lyon, Gorsky, Haring & Gilbert, didn't want to take the chance on a Denton jury. He approached Tony Paul, a Denton County assistant district attorney in charge of the Dodd case, to see if a plea agreement could be made to keep Dodd from spending twenty years behind bars.

At the time of the plea negotiations, the Denton County District Attorney's Office was in the midst of controversy. In a postelection move, the newly elected district attorney, Paul Johnson, fired twenty-five staff members, including a number of highly competent assistant district attorneys.

Tony Paul was thought of by some in the legal system of Denton County as the "fair-haired" boy, not due to his blond hair, but for being a favored tough prosecutor. Paul was well respected by fellow prosecutors, as well as criminal defense attorneys. If Dodd went to trial against Paul, he could very well receive the maximum sentence. Dodd's sentencing guidelines had been enhanced due to his prior conviction for assault—meaning he could receive more prison time than if he hadn't had a prior conviction.

Sitting in his windowless office on the third floor of the Denton County Courthouse, Paul met with Haring concerning the possibility of a Dodd plea. Haring presented his case for not taking his client to trial, pointing out that Dodd would have to serve the remainder of his initial prison sentence, in addition to any new term a jury might impose.

Paul was quite familiar with Dodd's position in the justice system. He also knew that although he was certain he would win a conviction, a trial would cost the taxpayers money, and Dodd might still only get the minimum sentence of ten years, rather than the maximum of twenty.

Before Paul agreed to plea Dodd to a ten-year sentence in the Institutional Division of the Texas Department of Criminal Justice, he discussed the plea with Lee Ann Breading, first assistant DA. Breading, knowing full well that Sheila Underwood wanted Dodd to face a jury, took the position that although the DA's office took the victims' wishes into consideration, it was a judgment call their office had to make for the best resolution to the case.

On November 2, 2006, thirty-five-year-old Ron Dodd stood before Judge Lee Gabriel in the 367th Judicial District Court. The blond female judge looked more like a soccer mom than the stern, no-nonsense judge she was known to be. Judge Gabriel was respected throughout Denton County for her tough sentences.

Ron Dodd stood silently before the bench. A Texas flag hung opposite the American flag at the back of the judge, and a large amber bowl-style lamp hung from the ceiling. Spectators could see squiggly shapes inside the lamp bowl and looked inquisitively as they silently tried to identify them. In fact, they were rubber bands, shot into the light fixture by bored attorneys waiting for the return of juries with their verdicts.

Judge Gabriel announced the acceptance of the plea

agreement made between the state and the defendant. Dodd was assessed no fine, but he was ordered to pay $228 in court costs. The ten-year prison sentence was imposed and commenced the same day.

Sheila Underwood sat in the gallery and watched the procedures. Anger rose from deep within her and fueled her determination to address the man who had helped to bury her child and grandchild. Sheila was disgusted with Ron Dodd and displeased with the plea agreement. Dodd had admitted offering to hire a hit man to kill Lisa for Stephen Barbee, and he had provided the shovel used to bury her.

Driven by heartache and resentment, Sheila made her way through the low swinging doors that allowed officers of the court and witnesses to enter the heart of the courtroom. Dressed in a well-tailored business suit, Sheila stood with her head high, and her small body rigid with defiance, as she stared at Dodd through narrowed eyes behind wire-rimmed glasses. Standing less than two feet from Dodd, Sheila Underwood spoke with bitterness in her heart, and venom in her words.

"You only got a ten-year sentence," Sheila began indignantly. "I have been given a life sentence without my only child and grandchild."

"I'm sorry," Dodd replied softly, staring back at Sheila through red eyes.

Sheila looked at Dodd questioningly. He was visibly trembling, and she thought he was on the verge of tears. Sheila thought it may have unnerved Dodd that she was standing so close to him. It was a bizarre sensation for the brokenhearted mother and grandmother. To Sheila, it was as if they were the only two people in the room.

The petite Underwood verbally hammered Dodd for

offering to hire a hit man to kill Lisa. She also told him that despite what others said, she believed he had a major role in the deaths of her family.

"How could you have done this?" Sheila demanded to know.

"He was my boss," Dodd replied nervously. "What else was I supposed to do?"

"You're a thirty-five-year-old man. She was a pregnant girl, and he was just a little boy. Why didn't you stop it?" Sheila quivered slightly—not from fear of Dodd, but from a year of suppressed anger.

"I wish I could have," Dodd said, slowly lowering his head.

"I wish you could have too!" Sheila said loudly.

Judging from his expression and demeanor, Sheila believed Dodd truly wished the murders had never happened, but, nonetheless, she still considered him to be a bad person.

Sheila assured Ron Dodd she would be at every parole hearing to insure he would spend each day of his ten-year sentence in a Texas prison.

She also promised, "I'll do all I can to make your life in prison Hell. Because I'm in Hell," Sheila spat. "Now I have to figure out what to do with the rest of my life."

Epilogue

STEPHEN BARBEE

Stephen Barbee is an inmate confined to death row at the Polunsky Unit in Livingston, Texas. Since arriving on death row, Barbee's health has deteriorated significantly. His headaches are more frequent and he has developed muscular degeneration that has confined him to a walker and/or wheelchair. Barbee suffers from pain twenty-four/seven and takes over-the-counter painkillers daily. Doctors believe Barbee suffers from the effects of his numerous head injuries, and possibly from untreated Lyme disease.

It has been determined that Barbee has one untreated herniated disk and two bulging disks in his back. Barbee is also in need of a hip replacement, denied him due to his status as a death row inmate.

In November 2008, Barbee's direct appeal to the trial judge was denied, but it has been appealed to the supreme court. A state appeal to the Texas Court of Criminal Appeals was filed in March 2009. It was affirmed by the court of criminal appeals, and the appeal denied. A federal appeal will be filed on Stephen Barbee's behalf once the state supreme court has ruled on the direct appeal.

RONALD DODD

Ron Dodd is incarcerated at the Coffield Unit of the Institutional Division of the Texas Department of Criminal Justice in Tennessee Colony, Texas. Dodd was eligible for parole January 16, 2009, but his bid for parole was denied. If Dodd serves his entire sentence, he will be released on August 3, 2016. Sheila Underwood has vowed to be at every parole hearing in an attempt to block Dodd's early release, and to insure he serves every day of his ten-year sentence.

SHEILA UNDERWOOD

In April 2007, Sheila Underwood attended a tree planting held at Tarrant County College's South Campus to honor crime victims. Sheila talked about how victims' service organizations helped her through difficult times after the loss of Lisa, Jayden, and Marleigh.

Sheila continues to work in the administration area at a south Fort Worth hospital. She has remained friends with Detective Mike Carroll. Although surrounded by friends and family, she often ops to vacation out of state during holidays, rather than celebrate without Lisa and Jayden. The pain of their loss remains always present.

On February 16, 2007, three days short of the two-year anniversary of the deaths of her daughter and grandson, Sheila Underwood filed a $5 million wrongful-death lawsuit against Stephen Barbee. Also named in the lawsuit were Ron Dodd, Teresa Barbee, and Trish Barbee. The lawsuit also seeks to determine if Mr. Barbee transferred assets to his first and second wives to shield money and property from lawsuits. Although the suit asks for monetary damages, Sheila is far more interested in making those who, she believes, helped Barbee after the deaths of her loved ones pay for their involvement.

Both Teresa Barbee and Trish Barbee claim their former husband left them only with debts.

BILL BARBEE

Bill Barbee continued to believe in his son's innocence until the cancer he so ardently fought took his life on December 18, 2008. Bill had wanted to live long enough to see his son exonerated of the murders of Lisa and Jayden Underwood.

Only weeks before his death, Bill had tried once more to visit his son on death row in Livingston, Texas. Jackie Barbee had packed the car with everything Bill would need to make the 250-mile trip as comfortable as possible. But when Jackie attempted to load Bill in the car, she was unable to raise his frail body onto the seat. After much struggle and effort, Jackie gave up, took Bill back into their modest Azle house, and unpacked the car. Bill knew he would never again see his son.

JACKIE BARBEE

Jackie Barbee remains alone in the house where she and Bill raised their three children. She goes to see Stephen whenever she can, often taking a friend with her. Dr. Nancy Kearly accompanied Jackie to Livingston the day she had to tell him his father had died. The mother and son shared tears, but they were unable to comfort one another with any physical contact.

Jackie, like Bill, continues to believe Stephen is innocent of the horrific murders of Lisa and Jayden Underwood. She also contributed $20,000 to New Mexico attorney Don Vernay for Stephen's state appeal.

HOLLY PILS

Inside Boopa's Bagel Deli, Holly Pils continues to serve up food with the same warm spirit she did with her business partner, Lisa Underwood. Holly will not let the memories of Lisa and Jayden fade. On one wall is a painting of Lisa and Jayden, titled *Boopa and Mom*. Jayden's blue Cub Scout uniform hangs above a table devoted to keeping his memory alive. On the tables are pictures of the smiling mother and son.

Holly Pils misses her best friend and the child she loved as though her own. She also acknowledges Marleigh, Lisa's unborn daughter, as part of the Boopa's family.

TERESA BARBEE

Teresa Barbee continues to live in the house she and Stephen Barbee built in Haslet, Texas. She closed both Cowboy Cutters and Four Seasons, claiming both businesses were in debt.

Since Ron Dodd's incarceration, Teresa has found another man with whom to share her life.

TRISH BARBEE

Trish Barbee still resides in Fort Worth with her children. Like Teresa, Trish claims Stephen Barbee left her little, except for a bed, a big-screen television, and a personal watercraft, as well as big monthly payments on a time-share and a trailer. She contends Barbee's Corvette was repossessed and his truck was owned by Cowboy Cutters. Although Barbee made good money, it appears he owned nothing outright. Trish has not remarried.

KEVIN ROUSSEAU AND DIXIE BERSANO

Both of the assistant district attorneys continue their work with the Tarrant County District Attorney's Office.

DETECTIVE MIKE CARROLL

The detective remains with the homicide division of the Fort Worth Police Department. He has been praised for his work on the Stephen Barbee case.

MORE SHOCKING TRUE CRIME
FROM PINNACLE

Lethal Embrace   0-7860-1785-6 $6.99/$9.99
Robert Mladinich and Michael Benson

Love Me or I'll Kill You   0-7860-1778-3 $6.99/$9.99
Lee Butcher

Precious Blood   0-7860-1849-6 $6.99/$9.99
Sam Adams

Baby-Faced Butchers   0-7860-1803-8 $6.99/$9.99
Stella Sands

Hooked Up for Murder   0-7860-1865-8 $6.99/$9.99
Robert Mladinich and Michael Benson

Available Wherever Books Are Sold!

Visit our website at **www.kensingtonbooks.com**

au

800 266
2278

800 266
2278